THE RISE OF BUILD TO RENT IN THE UK

THE RISE OF BUILD TO RENT IN THE UK

BRENDAN KILPATRICK

Designed cover image: cover photo by Quintain/Chris Winter, cover design by Ross O'Brien.

First published 2024

by Routledge

605 Third Avenue, New York, NY 10158

and by Routledge

4 Park Square, Milton Park, Abingdon, Oxon, OX14 4RN

Routledge is an imprint of the Taylor & Francis Group, an informa business

© 2024 Brendan Kilpatrick

The right of Brendan Kilpatrick to be identified as author of this work has been asserted in accordance with sections 77 and 78 of the Copyright, Designs and Patents Act 1988.

All rights reserved. No part of this book may be reprinted or reproduced or utilised in any form or by any electronic, mechanical, or other means, now known or hereafter invented, including photocopying and recording, or in any information storage or retrieval system, without permission in writing from the publishers.

Trademark notice: Product or corporate names may be trademarks or registered trademarks, and are used only for identification and explanation without intent to infringe.

Library of Congress Cataloging-in-Publication Data

A catalog record for this title has been requested

ISBN: 9781032556932 (hbk)

ISBN: 9781032556949 (pbk)

ISBN: 9781003431824 (ebk)

DOI: 10.4324/9781003431824

Typeset in New Frank and Heebo

by Ross O'Brien, Lukasz Mlynarczyk and Alan Blacker

Publisher's Note: This book has been prepared from camera-ready copy provided by the author.

Contents

vi
Foreword

2
Preface

3
Introduction

5
CHAPTER ONE
Foundations of the Rise

23
CHAPTER TWO
Pioneers

31
CHAPTER THREE
Consolidation

43
CHAPTER FOUR
Economic, Social and Sustainable Stewardship

73
CHAPTER FIVE
The Climate Challenges Facing the Sector

87
CHAPTER SIX
The Key Design Ingredients for Success

101
CHAPTER SEVEN
Digital Autonomy

113
CHAPTER EIGHT – CASE STUDIES
1 Moda, The Lexington
2 The Mercian
3 Coppermaker Square
4 Lewisham Gateway II
5 Wembley Park

183
CHAPTER NINE
Conclusions

188
ACKNOWLEDGEMENTS
189
BIOGRAPHY
189
IMAGE CREDITS
190
REFERENCES
194
INDEX

Foreword
Ian Fletcher

When Brendan asked me to write this foreword, I was genuinely excited. Here was somebody writing thoughtfully about what is a rare housing success story of the past decade. A success though that neither Left or Right of the political spectrum necessarily wants to trumpet, because it is neither adding to the Right's totem of homeownership, nor directly to the Left's desire for more social rented homes.

For many readers of this book, it will represent a personal, as well as collective journey. Much blood, sweat and tears, but also passion, creativity and learning by the "pioneers", as Brendan refers to them, have gone into building the sector we know today. I think those pioneers can reflect on a job that is thus far well done, which is also captured in the case studies at the back of this book.

Build To Rent was born out of the global financial crisis, with housing delivery at its lowest figure (outside periods of war) since the 1920s. A strong motivation for Government support was the diversification of housing supply and finding new forms of delivery. However, the Government of the time was also facing significant pressure to improve standards of private rented accommodation and Build To Rent and therefore also had an objective to raise sector quality.

Build To Rent has lived up to both objectives. The sector's supply has seen steady growth and is now pretty much nationwide. I also know personally from numerous visits to Build To Rent buildings, how much pride the sector's staff take in the design of their buildings and the quality of their service provision, ultimately enhancing the experience of their customers. As an architect, Brendan explores this with passion and expert knowledge.

It is a happy coincidence that the sector has run side-by-side with innovation and advances in Proptech. That has made management of Build To Rent buildings more efficient and improved the range and responsiveness of customer services. The book explores this too.

Another huge change during Build To Rent's relatively short existence has been the far greater emphasis on Environmental, Sustainable and Governance (ESG) outcomes across the property sector at large. I have found nothing but good intentions to support ESG outcomes in the Build To Rent sector, but what are good outcomes and how are those measured? The book devotes an appropriate two chapters to these questions.

Current challenging economic circumstances also seem like a good time to pause and take stock. Can the sector weather current conditions and underline its counter-cyclical credentials by delivering growth in a wider housing market downturn? Only time will tell.

Overall, in a relatively short time, I believe the Build To Rent sector has been a force for good. It has provided additionality and drawn new capital into housing provision. It is setting the bar for customer experience. It is a market that is deepening, with a broadening range of offers at different price points for the sector's customers and widening variety of opportunities for investors. The sector is dynamic and willing to innovate. It exerts significant economic and social impact. And most importantly in a housing crisis, it diverts private capital into delivering much needed, quality homes. This includes new homes for workers and their families who cannot access social housing or home ownership, as well as homes for an increasing part of the population who are choosing to rent and enjoy greater flexibility to support other lifestyle choices.

I therefore strongly believe the sector's best days are ahead of it, even more so if Build To Rent practitioners take what we have collectively learned over the past decade and apply it to the future. Brendan's chronicle of the sector's course is therefore both welcome and essential. Enjoy the read and the vivid journey he describes.

Ian Fletcher is Director of Policy at the British Property Federation

Preface

In February 2016, a group of partners from a London-based firm of architects embarked on a trip to New York to investigate a new form of tenure in housing. This tenure is known as Build To Rent (BTR) in the UK and "multi-family housing" in the United States. PRP's architectural practice is known for its residential expertise but in 2016 had only marginal experience of this form of housing. The group visited five residential complexes in Manhattan and Brooklyn under the expert guidance of two representatives from one of PRP's principal client organisations, and early pioneers of BTR in the UK, Quintain.

The residential buildings in New York were part of the North American multi-family boom where people rented their homes from professional, bespoke organisations rather than renting in the unregulated market or purchasing and owning outright. Quintain's team representatives had previously worked on a number of multi-family developments in America and their funders were passionate about its suitability for exporting to Europe. The visit formed the groundwork for a number of large BTR developments designed by PRP which are now complete or are approaching completion – an indication of the incredible energy surrounding this form of housing and its potential impact on supply and choice in the UK housing market.

2016 would become the breakthrough year for BTR in the UK.

Introduction

Build To Rent (BTR) is a form of residential tenure which is relatively new to the UK. It sits within the Private Rented Sector (PRS), that is the wider, largely unregulated market in the UK which is dominated by small landlords. BTR first emerged in the United States where it is known as multi-family housing and where it is a mature investment and management asset. Its concept is one of social living by a community of renters sharing facilities with access to top-up additional services and spaces within or around the building. The degree of facilities offered by rental operators varies greatly, with rental levels following suit. Whilst it has been a mature asset class in the United States for over a decade it is only now becoming so in the UK and Ireland.

This book sets the scene for the initiation of this new form of housing and its emphatic emergence in the UK in the breakthrough year of 2016. It casts a glance backwards to the pioneers of the movement and it examines the key ingredients of success – social, economic and political – given the historically widespread coverage of the rental sector and the more recent move to traditional home-owning within UK society from which this new sector has emerged. The architectural practice, PRP, has been at the forefront of housing design, research and discourse within the UK for 60 years and this experience helps form a base for the themes explored. The book provides detailed illustrations of some of the largest BTR projects in the country, three of which the practice has designed and delivered and a fourth and fifth in Liverpool and Birmingham which are setting the standard for rental living in the UK. The book points to the reasons for the success of these projects. Finally, the book examines the way ahead and how this type of housing can play a key role in leading the entire residential sector in streamlining design and construction activity in a forward-facing manner, one which embraces climate change resilience and digital methods for delivery and management within the circular economy.

CHAPTER ONE
Foundations of the Rise

The rise of BTR in the UK is recent but it is dynamic by any measure. It is not unique to the UK and similar enterprise, albeit proportionally smaller, is following suit in Ireland. It exists as a credible commercial product in a number of northern European countries with relatively large rental markets such as Holland, Germany, Sweden and Denmark. The rise is part of a monetary inflow which sees the UK placed as one of the top two countries in Europe in attracting foreign direct investment.

The birth of BTR stems principally from north American expertise in this sector and the successful models that operate there which have been introduced here in relatively recent times. It is in the United States that housing for rent has assumed the characteristics of a genuine financial asset class. However, the UK housing market differs markedly from the US in its make-up, principally owing to the effects of two world wars and the massive societal change that followed each conflagration. Such social upheaval and the resultant social housing programmes that followed simply didn't occur in the United States, isolated as it was from many of the first-hand horrors of war by the breadth of the Atlantic and Pacific Oceans and by an economy that became turbo-charged by political and industrial reaction to the Second World War.

The development of housing over the past century has laid a unique and stable foundation for the BTR movement in this country. Continuing population growth through immigration is boosting the appeal.

In the early 1920s, almost 80% of the UK population lived in rented homes. Living conditions varied greatly in large towns and cities within overcrowded 19th century terraces and tenements with minimal services and sanitation. The government of the time was compelled to act. This action came in the form of the first large council estates built after the First World War as part of the Homes for Heroes programme and initiated by the 1919 Housing and Town Planning Act, also known as The Addison Act. This was the first housing act passed in the UK and provided state subsidy to local councils requiring them to make plans to procure housing for the working-class. The initial estates were constructed on "Garden City" principles, attempting to create environments which offered living conditions that were a physical, geographical and visual escape from the Victorian-era slums of the UK's large urban centres. When Becontree Estate in Dagenham was completed in the mid-1930s it was the largest municipal estate in the world, accommodating over 100,000 people in 27,000 rented homes.

FACING PAGE Moda, The Lexington, Liverpool.

1930s houses on the Becontree Estate, Dagenham, London.

Large scale housing programmes continued after the Second World War.

> *The majority of housing estates in the UK appeared in the late 1950s, 60s and 70s as the UK finally emerged from the privations of post-war austerity and the Government began to address a new emergent housing crisis. This was made possible by the political direction of the post-war Labour government with housing placed centrally as an instrument of welfare reform and with Aneurin Bevan, the Minister of Health, at the helm of change. The 1946 Land Act gave councils enhanced compulsory purchase powers and then, in 1947, legislation came into being which formed the basis of our current planning system, The Town and Country Planning Act. German bombs and an incomplete inter-war slum clearance programme had left an estimated shortfall of 750,000 homes. The gap between the end of World War Two and the building programmes of the late 50s and 60s was filled with the production of Pre-cast Reinforced Concrete Homes (PRCs) to combat a post-war shortage of materials. Around 1.5 million homes were built utilising new or largely untried construction systems in the decade after the war but they would prove problematic for residents in relation to thermal performance and water ingress.[1]*

The construction of these estates across the nation, as well as a number of new towns that were created such as Harlow, left a physical, environmental and social legacy (some would use the word stigma) on the UK's town and cityscapes which remains to this day. It belied the utopian ideals of their conception, marvellously exemplified by the writer Jason Cowley.

> *To grow up in Harlow was to be on the front line of the English Revolution. More than this, you were a cog in a grand social and political experiment. I understand this now but back then I was just living. My friends and I were children of the welfare state. The social transformations and central planning of the immediate post-war period, as the new Labour Government set about building what Attlee called a "New Jerusalem" had created thrilling*

possibilities for us. The National Health Service was established; the National Insurance Act abolished the hated means test for welfare provision; essential industries such as the railways and mining were nationalised; the Town and Country Planning Act was passed, opening the way for mass housebuilding and the redevelopment of huge tracts of land; Britain's independent nuclear deterrent was commissioned; the gap between rich and poor narrowed.[2]

The utopian dream gradually faded, mirroring the slow ebbing away of central and local government funding for social housing. Rebranding and renaming of a decaying estate were often required to alter perceptions. Their existence, and the politics surrounding their maintenance and renewal, perhaps points to the relatively late arrival of a Build To Rent form of housing which targets the opposite end of the social and political spectrum from where the estates were conceived. These estates constituted a significant part of an essentially binary housing supply model, the other component being provided by housebuilders and developers of homes for sale where market conditions prevailed. By the 2010s, the model had co-existed for decades, overlapping with each other occasionally as the 21st century commenced, principally on estate regeneration schemes where funds from the sale of private homes were needed to help finance new social housing provision replacing what previously existed on an estate. This was the point at which private developers and contractors would become engaged for the first time in estate regeneration. Typical regeneration schemes would see most of the existing buildings on these estates demolished to make way for new blocks of housing and apartments. Private rent formed no part of the finance models for these regeneration projects at this time.

Writing in his essay entitled "Regeneration", Brendan Sarsfield, in his position as Chief Executive of Peabody, a housing association, summarised the difficulty of achieving successful regeneration and it is as true for estate regeneration programmes as it is for new BTR initiatives.

Maiden Lane Estate, Camden , London.

> *Rebranding has its place, but it is not going to change things on the ground. The hearts and minds of people living and working in a place will determine the success of a regeneration programme. I think there are two keys to this. The first is improving the lived experience of people, getting the basics right in terms of neighbourhood services and maintenance of public spaces. The second is developing programmes and resources based on what local people want and need.[3]*

In relation to the needs of locality, the economist Liam Halligan writes of the era when the enhanced value created by municipally funded infrastructure which enables land to be developed in the first place was captured by Government and not by private developers. This land value capture (LVC), or planning gain by another name, helped fund the government's post World War II building boom as it depressed demand for land by speculative developers, keeping the cost of developable plots reasonable. However, the era was not to last.

> *During the 1950s, through successive Conservative governments led by Churchill and then Macmillan pandered to big landowners and developers, passing a series of laws stymying the use of LVC. Ultimately, the Tories passed the Land Compensation Act, ensuring that landowners and land-holding developers were entitled to the full land valuation upside when planning permission was granted, including the "hope value" of any conceivable future development. This legislation has since fuelled rampant speculative investment in land and remains in place to this day. The 1961 Act, more than anything else, explains why the price of land for residential building – and, in turn, the cost of housing – has spiralled over the past half-century, resulting in our current affordability crisis and chronic lack of social housing.[4]*

Mr Halligan argues convincingly for a reversal of the Land Compensation Act so that planning gain achieved when planning permission is granted can be shared fifty-fifty between landowners and local authorities to help break down barriers to entry of a restricted market and to provide councils with a badly needed new funding stream for new affordable housing. The potential gains are staggering. If you could somehow translate a few acres of agricultural land in the south-east of England into a plot with a residential planning consent, the factor increase in value could be 50 to 60, depending on location.

Within this UK housing context, the emerging BTR market may well be compared to the great housing programmes of the 20th century, not least because its developments will often sit cheek-by-jowl with some of them or form part of the regeneration of others. It is likely to have its success measured for good or for bad against a gradually declining social housing sector and the affordability and inclusiveness that the movement heralded.

Prior to 2016, the private rented sector within the UK was centred around the amateur, unregulated and largely dysfunctional market for renting homes of various sizes and condition. There existed a niche, premium market for rent in London, with concierge services and supporting leisure amenities, but this was an inconsequential proportion of the overall market. The sector frequently came under government scrutiny because of its poor service reputation, operating at the bottom of the market. It also attracted periodic political sabre-rattling from national or local government during property booms with the threat of rent controls to attempt to cap spiralling rent levels. Various forms of legislation were introduced to protect tenants' interests but the reputation of the sector remained poor. This is principally because the number

New Lodge, New Earswick, Yorkshire.

of large, commercially stable companies with a consistent service record providing good accommodation were very few in number. Instead, the market was dominated by small, amateur companies or single individuals, each with a handful of properties operating on a very amateur basis.

Few organisations have analysed the private rented sector as much as The Joseph Rowntree Foundation (JRF). This is a social policy and research-focused charity and an agent for social change. it is also a developing housing association which gives the organisation the rare opportunity to practice what it preaches. It is ambitious in its aspirations for delivering quality in design and construction, as evidenced by projects for later living such as New Lodge, in New Earswick near York, designed by PRP and completed in 2022.

As far back as 2008, the foundation produced a report for the University of York which reads a little like a prospectus for a BTR movement that didn't yet exist in the UK. The paper recognised the private rented sector as being a vibrant market for the young professionals but examined if it had a role to play in achieving wider policy objectives such as sustainable mixed communities that could help address the needs of socially disadvantaged groups such as homeless households.[5] The Trust urged government to direct policy to form a smaller, higher quality private rented sector while at the same time creating alternative, more affordable ways of getting onto the property ladder and eliminating the gap between rental and the intermediate ownership market. It also recommended the creation of policy to level the playing field of low-income renters through reforming the benefits system and improving the life opportunities for this group.

Current Government statistics state that over a fifth of the 4.4 million households that rent privately endure poor conditions and lack security and control over the homes they pay to live in.[6] This part of the rental market has come under increasing financial pressure in recent times with the removal of certain tax reliefs. It will face increasing regulatory pressure with the requirement to upgrade homes to higher energy performance certification by 2030 with the forthcoming introduction of the Decent Homes Standard, a set of minimum criteria focussing on the health and wellbeing of people within their homes. The equivalent of these standards has been a requirement within the social rented sector since 2001. An already identifiable side-effect of these regulations is a sell-off of properties which have been rented out for decades – thus negatively impacting on the supply of rental properties.

More recently in a 2022 discussion paper, JRF has recognised that the potential reduction in the size of the sector is an opportunity to implement policies which see homes change hands from landlords to tenants in an alternative way of addressing the housing crisis. These policies would encourage the lending market to favour first-time buyers in a move away from blanket support for the built to rent sector. This would help would-be homeowners previously unable to access the market to find affordable, secure homes and give them the chance to build wealth and achieve economic security.

> *...twelve years on from the Global Financial Crisis in 2008 the private rented sector had grown by around 1.4 million homes, a 39% increase – spurred on by a demand for homes, due to barriers to accessing homeownership and social housing, and macro-economic, fiscal, and regulatory conditions which incentivised individuals to become landlords given the potential capital gains and rental yields. Were this growth to be reversed overnight, the proportion of homeowners could increase by 9%, offsetting its recent decline, or the proportion living in the social rented sector could increase by a third (33%).*[7]

The foundation's research is based on the premise that an understanding of prevailing market conditions is a prerequisite of forming future policy decisions, including determining who owns and lives in the country's 25 million homes. It remains to be seen if the Government will pick up on JRF's alternative approach. Without such interventions, any reduction in numbers of historic rental properties is likely to be offset by the rise of BTR as we will see in the following chapters. With the recent ending of the Help to Buy initiative, a scheme to encourage less well-off first-time buyers to buy a newly built home with an equity loan, there is now no government direct assistance funding programme for first-time buyers following a decade of such support. The scheme was initiated in 2013 and helped 350,000 people to buy their first home.

The sector has attracted occasional political attention with concern being expressed for tenants' rights being abused by unscrupulous landlords. In general, however, a lack of scrutiny has prevailed and is a direct consequence of the UK's historic obsession, fuelled by successive Conservative governments from Margaret Thatcher onwards, with individual home ownership. This political dogma rested on the premise that home-owners were much more likely to vote for the Conservative Party than the Labour Party in local and general elections. The more home-owners that exist, the longer the Conservatives stay in power. The approach is most evident in the policy instrument known as Right to Buy, introduced during the Thatcher era and which allowed Council tenants (who would conventionally vote Labour) to buy their own homes and thus disrupt a layer of traditionally socialist or working-class support. Right to Buy made significant inroads into the social rented sector as local councils were compelled to sell off their properties to any of their soon-to-be former tenants who wished to stop paying rent to their social landlords and who would become homeowners for the first time.

Clarion's estate regeneration at High Path in Merton, London.

This policy has had significant impact on the nature of estate regeneration and renewal to this day, including the decimation of the quantum of social hosing. The dwellings sold very often sub-let to other parties, harming the social fabric of the community. The pepper-potting of tenure complicates and makes much more expensive any plans for renewal or regeneration of the estate. In all, 2.8 million homes have been sold, 40% of which are in the hands of private landlords.[8] These homes have not been replaced. It is predicted that 100,000 more socially rented homes will be sold by 2030 but that only 43,000 will be replaced, contributing to the malaise on existing estates and exacerbating the chronic shortage of socially rented homes.[9]

Despite the disruption of Right to Buy, the social rented sector within the UK survived and remains large. Councils are today generally trying to retain their rented stock rather than sell it off and some are building their own housing at scale for the first time in a generation. Certain housing associations have grown into huge national enterprises following periods of growth and mergers with other housing providers. Clarion, a housing association, is one of the largest housing companies in Europe, with over 120,000 homes under management across the country. These mega-associations have diversified their tenure with a number of intermediate forms including shared ownership, a form of tenure which provides for part-rent and part mortgage payment allowing tenants to embark on the first step of home ownership and to "staircase" upwards their proportion of ownership thereafter. Many housing associations have acted as developers in their own right in order to create cross-subsidy finance from the outright sale of homes in order to build more affordable homes for rent. However, the cross-subsidy model doesn't work for all, particularly outside London.

Occasionally, a combination of funding from the Greater London Authority (GLA), the devolved regional governance body of Greater London, and Homes England, a non-departmental government body that funds new affordable housing in England, can ensure the delivery of developments which are 100% affordable. Owing to increased financial constraints and heightened perceived risks, procurement of large housing developments has become more protracted. Many housing associations have come to prefer forming joint ventures (JV) with private developers to deliver collaborative development projects. This could be viewed as a growing aversion to risk as housing associations traditionally led the delivery of their developments alone. Alternatively, it could be regarded as a method of precluding contagion from development failure impacting on the management responsibilities of the organisation. In recent times the need has grown for housing associations to prioritise the care of their existing customers, given their responsibility to maintain aging estates whilst managing revenues which have been progressively eroded by successive governments over the last two decades.

It is interesting to consider that housing associations, with their vast experience in managing large tracts of rental properties for extended periods of time, should be easily able to retrofit a BTR capability onto their current business and management models. The philosophy of Build To Rent requires a different approach to tenant management including a "customer is king" mantra and a swiftness of service operation and customer care that few housing associations possess. Some have considered active development in Build To Rent but this remains politically or managerially out of reach to many housing associations. It is widely thought that housing associations need to develop to survive but housing management remains their core activity. This is at the heart of their social purpose and it must be remembered that housing association tenants are often from a disadvantaged section of the community, often bereft of the life chances enjoyed by the BTR operators' target audience for their shiny new developments. The management function that is required within the social sector operates within a very different sphere. The scale is also different from the nascent BTR sector. A single housing association, Clarion, with a huge portfolio of 120,000 homes is approximately 30,000 more than the entire UK BTR sector in mid 2023.

Most housing association personnel that I have spoken to welcome the new BTR operators because they recognise their role in providing part of the solution to the housing crisis. This might seem surprising given the alternate ends of the housing provision spectrum within which each operates. Guy Slocombe is the Chief Investment Officer at the Hyde Group, a housing association. He is one of a number of relatively recent arrivals at the housing provider from a financial or City of London background, an unusual source of talent for social housing providers. Hyde is amongst the forerunners, an agent for change, in helping transform the commercial outlook of the sector. But Hyde's hunting ground for talent makes complete sense when you consider that the association has 50,000 dwellings under management and a portfolio worth £10 billion, equivalent in financial heft to British Land, one of the biggest private property development and investment companies in the UK. According to Guy, the culture of social rent is slowly but surely changing. He believes that the traditional financial model of a housing association is unsustainable and needs to adapt to ensure better customer outcomes and more effective business management. Guy embraces the potential to work alongside BTR providers on large multi-tenure development, either within a joint venture or in an off-balance sheet partnership, to share risk and to get more homes built overall. Hyde's change of direction has attracted the interest of other associations. It has been supported by a cognisant board which seems determined to keep Hyde's social purpose to the fore, backed by astute commercial business planning.

It is useful to examine further the contemporary conditions in the UK that have made BTR such a compelling prospect to potential investors.

By 2016, there were approximately 9 million renters living in the UK. True to the Thatcherite agenda, the Conservative government remained focused on home ownership and the economy had recovered from the shocks of the financial crash of 2008. However, as demand for new homes to buy is largely fuelled by personal debt, the Bank of England was becoming concerned about the implications for the economy of such a specific political aim.

The perennial demand for housing in the UK, particularly in London and the South-East, was now beginning to attract institutional investors and the emergence of a new residential asset class. Manchester was also becoming a hot-spot at this time. The average age of a first-time buyer in London was pushing close to 40, an indication of the scale of pent-up demand for housing buoyed by a sea of would-be purchasers who had little choice but to rent from a largely sub-standard rental sector. House prices at this time were more than five times the average earnings of a first time buyer and in London this figure was closer to ten times average salary. These figures are two to three times the equivalent figures that prevailed in the 1980s and 1990s.[10] At the same time, the classic developer model of high-rise development, typified by expensive apartment blocks in London's docklands and close to the River Thames around Vauxhall, offered little in relation to variation of apartment type, or to external amenity or other interactive life experiences. Whole swathes of these developments were purchased by overseas investors, who often left the new homes empty, anticipating future financial gain through appreciation without renting. Pockets of these development would typically remain lifeless throughout the day's cycle, blighting whole zones of the new neighbourhood.

The issue of a lack of an accessible housing supply is therefore clear. This is the result of a myriad of factors interacting. I have identified five of these factors, over and above the politics around social housing described above and which are, as an ensemble, fuelling the seemingly intractable and perennial housing crisis that is all but endemic across the country.

The first factor relates to the shortage of land being released to build new homes which is exacerbated by policy to protect the Green Belt around large conurbations. Whilst this policy shields the countryside from development and largely prevents urban sprawl, not all of the Green Belt is what many would consider green or worth protecting and it creates value in property only for those who live within it. It approximates 13% of the land mass of the United Kingdom and surrounds most of the major cities. The notion of releasing even a small proportion of the Green Belt is as politically toxic as legalising cannabis, even though England has 434 dwellings per 1000 people while France has 35% more at 590.[11]

> *The Green Belts do their jobs well, pushing development into the rural areas between them. Indeed, most parts of the planning system work as intended. Councillors retain democratic control over the planning system. Environmental watchdogs enforce their mandates fiercely. Stringent rules protect bats, squirrels and rare fungi. Courts ensure that procedures are followed to the letter. But the system as a whole is a failure. Britain cannot build.[12]*

The second factor is the cost of developing the brownfield land that is available to develop. All of the low hanging fruit of brownfield land has already been developed, generally leaving the more contaminated, topographically disadvantaged or

Housing on the Edge of Green Belt at Ninewells, Cambridge.

environmentally challenged tracts of land left over. There are only a handful of developers of sufficient size to contemplate such developments as greater up-front investment and attendant risk is required.

Competition in developing at scale is therefore limited, which is a third factor. Even on smaller sites, the number of small housebuilder/developers who built so much in the 20th century have largely disappeared, culled by decades of boom and bust in an ultra-competitive market. Their near-extinction exacerbates the supply conundrum. Those few that do exist face almost insurmountable challenges in demonstrating a credible track record in delivery and regulatory compliance in order to win the few tender opportunities that are available to firms their size. Foreign firms seeking a foothold within what appears to be a lucrative sector face stern challenges from a tight market dominated by relatively few domestic corporations. A contributary fourth factor is that the cyclical nature of the housing market is a risk to long term development which land-banking (the deliberate holding of land without developing it) is, to a certain extent, used to defray. Conversely, this is not a barrier to long-term rental investors, who are largely insulated from the punishing highs and lows of conventional housebuilder speculation because of their long-term vision for investing in their assets.

The fifth and perhaps most significant factor is the UK planning system, which contributes significantly to the restriction in the supply of new housing, directly impacting on the cost of housing and the on-going crisis of affordability. There has been an agglomeration of planning policy requirements introduced over the last two decades which has massively increased the time and the cost of preparing a planning application. These policies may be viewed as inevitable in an increasingly regulated society, but their impact is huge. They have been introduced to amplify municipal control over development in multiple areas of policy, including the need to respect the wishes of local communities, to ensure that health and safety measures are considered, to protect the environment and local ecology of the development location, to seek to address climate change and to attempt to enshrine design quality within prospective planning applications. The effect of what I call the 'regulation curse' is examined further in Chapter Four.

This increased complexity is exacerbated by a limited pool of planning officers available to municipal planning authorities, a pool which is also variable in quality and subject to perpetual churn contributing to a resourcing crisis within councils. The private sector has traditionally attracted the more talented individuals within the planning profession by offering higher remuneration packages than local authorities can afford. The Royal Town Planning Institution, in a statement accompanying analysis published in mid-2023, have drawn attention to the widespread abuse and mistreatment of local authority planning officers to the detriment of their mental health and working conditions as a result of the on-going housing crisis. A quarter of their number have left the public sector between 2012 and 2020.[13]

The drain on planning resources also affects a Council's ability to write or renew their local plans, localised policy instruments which form the basis of the UK planning system. Their absence is exacerbated by recent changes in direction on planning reform from the UK Government and often leads to planning appeals to arrive at planning decisions, lengthening timeframes for realising development.

Planning application processing times for large projects have effectively doubled since the early 2000s. Linked to this is the suspicion which many local authorities have for large UK developers and housebuilders, who are often viewed as robber barons by Labour administrations within local authorities or convenient cash-cows by the Conservatives. Both political dispositions serve to lengthen the process by which large scale panning consents can be achieved. Party political bickering amongst planning committees also often delays or prevents decisions from being made on planning applications. Negotiations around viability analysis to justify reduced Section 106 contributions and the Community Infrastructure Levy – financial contributions which developers are expected to pay for social or transport infrastructure, affordable housing or other needs of the development – can add several more months to the planning programme even after the point where a resolution to grant planning permission has been achieved and a consent notice is formally issued allowing development to proceed.

Once you achieve a detailed planning consent, the arduous administrative process is not over. Every detailed planning consent is accompanied by a schedule of planning conditions, the number of which has been growing inexorably over recent years depending on the complexity of the project. One of the case studies in this book, Coppermaker Square, has 55 of them. 13 of these conditions are "pre-commencement" conditions, which must be discharged before works can commence on site. Some planning jurisdictions treat the discharge of these pre-commencement conditions as mini applications in their own right, with formal registration and decision timeframes of up to eight weeks, even for alterations to a single dwelling house as I have recently found to my cost.

A further barrier to progress of planning applications is the ability of certain external organisations to delay, disrupt or stop the process.

> *Natural England was created in 2006 with the aim of protecting flora and fauna. After a European Court of Justice ruling in 2018, it was tasked with ensuring "nutrient neutrality", meaning any development could not increase*

nitrate or phosphate pollution in rivers. Natural England came up with a blunt solution: building could not go ahead unless developers could prove it would not lead to an increase in nutrient levels, a stipulation that few could provide.[14]

Nutrient neutrality stipulations have posed a major barrier to development, particularly for regional developers in the south-east of England. Nature, or the drive to preserve it, presents other barriers. Newts are a protected species in the UK and their presence can add months to a development programme or halt it altogether if the invertebrates cannot be safely migrated to an alternative site. Bats enjoy the same protection.

The inertia of the planning system tends to cause appreciation in the value of the limited supply of developable land. Whist the topic of land-banking has been much debated in recent years and largely repudiated, this tendency to appreciate land value causes its own inertia amongst developers. This is because there is little or no concern that land value will ever fall, particularly in the South-East of the country, such is the restriction in supply. The lack of concern has been underscored by an unprecedented period of low interest rates, which has amplified the attractiveness of property as a sound investment. This comfort blanket even withstood the rapid rise in interest rates which the Bank of England used to combat run-away inflation in late 2022 and early 2023.

It would take significant government action to address the failings of the planning system, including significant additional funding for planning departments across the country. It is very difficult to see that happening within the current administration. Added to the difficulty is the UK parliamentary cycle, which is too short to build critical momentum for change. This is overlain with the prevailing political mood of the country where differences between the main political parties have closed to the extent that addressing the issue head-on is politically problematic for them all. The malaise, of course, does not simply cover housing but extends to crucial national industry and energy infrastructure. A headline in *City AM*, a free business-focused newspaper distributed in and around London, in 2023 perhaps sums up both the irony and the scale of the issue – "***If we can plan for nuclear reactors on the moon, we can relax planning here in Britain."*** [15] Embers of hope are flaring, with the Labour Party beginning to distance itself from the Tories entrenched position on planning with a hint of significant reform in the run-in to the next general election. As we have seen, there are many barriers on this path of change.

So if restricted conventional housing supply is helping set up the need for an alternative, it isn't the only factor germinating the BTR seedbed. An article in *The Economist*, a weekly newspaper with a global circulation, points to two further factors.[16] The first of these is the endurance of the housing sector. After all, the UK housing market managed to shrug off the greatest economic collapse in 300 years caused by the onset of the Covid-19 pandemic. Ironically, this resilience was created to a large extent by the last recession the aftermath of which produced some protection against the pandemic downturn. It may even endure the inflation crisis of late 2022 and 2023. A direct consequence of the Great Recession of 2008 is that it has become harder for people to secure mortgages in both America and in the British Isles. Those that have taken out mortgages since then have better average credit scores – they are essentially better off than before the financial crash with more stable income and are far less likely to lose their homes because of unpaid mortgage debt. People with mortgages are also far less vulnerable to increases in lending rates, which remained, until recent times, historically low for far longer than anyone would

Lower density housing development on the Olympic Park at Chobham Manor.

have predicted. This condition underscores the strength and, by recent historical standards, the relative stability of the sales sector. This in turn is boosted by the UK's demographic, with more and more Baby Boomers each year retiring within under-occupied, larger sized homes which they own outright but which are not contributing to a fluid housing supply. Perhaps the current wave of investors in UK BTR recognises that the next generation of older people will be less insulated than the current one, protected as they are by accrued property, and that "generation rent" is therefore set to expand inexorably. This senior sector of the market is examined in more detail in Chapter Four.

The second reason is a direct result of the pandemic and the flight to suburbia to find more space in the home, space to work from home, better private and accessible public amenity or to take early retirement from cramped urban living and working conditions. Houses rather than flats became much sought after, thus pressurising the mid-to-upper end of the market and keeping pressure on supply. Manisha Patel, a Senior Partner at PRP and an influencer in multi-generational living, in her essay on the future of estate generation which was written during a Covid-19 lockdown predicted how we would need to address the conditions that some were forced to endure.

> *The current requirements for private external amenity are arguably inadequate and outside London they are non-existent. The pandemic has taught us that these spaces are at a premium. Marginally larger balconies than current requirements in London dictate can be constructed as winter-gardens – providing an invaluable outdoor room to those in isolation or living in cramped conditions. The principle can be extended to terraces and roof gardens, widening the choice and variety available to the individual. Health and wellbeing are also enhanced and the dependency on the National Health Service can be greatly reduced by incorporating both social and technological features that facilitate health-conscious communities, contributing to physical and mental wellness with homes and vibrant landscaped amenity areas designed to promote healthy lifestyles. Future developments will see a lot more people working from home, with pressure on local amenities and open space throughout the week and weekends.[17]*

The UK government policy of Help to Buy was an artificial stimulant to the market, introduced in 2013 and set to run for ten years. However, the policy had little impact in the areas of greatest need such as London, where housing is eye-wateringly expensive.

Each of these factors (with the arguable exception of the Help to Buy initiative) combine to reduce further the choice available to first time buyers or serve to increase the age at which one can purchase a home for the first time, therefore encouraging the propensity to join "generation rent".

So, despite the Government's push to increase home ownership, or more likely because of it, the market remains broken. The doctrine also has a direct effect on the rental market because the greater the tilt towards home ownership, the less new housing for rent becomes available within a sector which habitually fails to meet targets for new homes. The inevitable consequence of this is a pushing up of rents. In the final quarter of 2022, with the UK skirting around economic downturn, it was impossible to find rental accommodation in certain UK locations because new listings were being snapped up as soon as they were posted. In Bradford, Hull and Newcastle the number of responses to rental ads has increased by a factor of six in the three years since September 2019. The fight amongst a growing group of would-be renters to find a home within a dwindling supply of rental property is at its worst in these three cities but Manchester, Cardiff and Glasgow are not far behind.[18] The number of homes available to rent has seen a staggering decline over the last two years, with over 50% of the market in mid-2022 having disappeared, coinciding with the largest rise in rent in over a decade over the same two-year period. The increase is the monetary equivalent for renters of losing a room in relation to their buying power.[19] In London, there are a quarter fewer new properties available to rent at the end of 2022 compared to one year before[20], contributing to an annual increase in rental levels of 15%. The on-line real estate property portal Rightmove have declared a staggering average price of £3,000 per month for inner London in the Spring of 2023 and £2,480 for the outer London area. This has had the Mayor of London calling once again for rent controls in the capital but rent controls create their own difficulties through reductions in supply and increased waiting times to access a property.

The government has contributed to the lack of supply with a tax regime which continues to favour investment in short-term holiday lets at the expense of conventional buy to rent properties.

The situation in Dublin is arguably worse than anywhere in the UK as the Irish Government faces increasing criticism for its failure to boost housing supply in the country's capital city. Approximately 30,000 new homes are being constructed a year in the Republic of Ireland but the estimated need is double this figure.[21] The upward pressure on rent levels is in direct response to unprecedented demand as the country's population expands and economic activity increases. However, the crisis is creating a barrier to international investment as multi-national corporations require a stable and well-housed local population from which to build their employment and skills base. High metropolitan rent levels can also lead to a drain on a city's critical workers, exacerbating the skills shortage. Even Dublin's rock bands are raising a hue and cry on the subject. The venom in the words of "Death to the Landlord" by a band named Meryl Streek and released in 2022 should give Ireland's politicians, and perhaps would-be landlords, pause for thought.

> *Say no to wanker landlords running the country,*
>
> *Say no to paying someone else's mortgage your whole life,*
>
> *Say no to living in a tent and being happy with it,*
>
> *Say no to having to pay yourself into debt to keep on top of your mental health and stability,*
>
> *Just say no.*

This spike in rental demand is counterweighted by concerns from organisations such as Shelter, a homelessness charity, who claimed that almost one million renters faced eviction because of soaring rents as 2022 drew to a close. The charity called for the Government to address the issue by unfreezing housing benefit rates to protect both landlords and tenants.[22]

Dr Desiree Fields, a psychologist, is an Associate Professor in the Department of Geography, University of California at Berkeley and has drawn attention to aggressive behaviour against multi-family renters in America including rapid evictions and intimidation. Her focus is on the large rental corporations which sprung up in the wake of the economic wreckage of the 2008 financial crash. They have grown on the back of targeted acquisitions of large swathes of foreclosed properties, principally in the southern sunbelt states. Their interventions have had the effect of pricing out local first-time buyers as the market has been artificially altered in the corporations' favour. The acquired properties were quickly flipped to multi-family rental homes. Rent levels began to increase and rental agreements were appended which were loaded with additional fees and charges. Rent levels in these locations subsequently increased dramatically during the pandemic. Worse, the effect on local markets and corporate profits becomes self-perpetuating to the benefit of the big corporations because, as the number of properties for sale are scooped up and changed to rental products, the price of properties goes up because there are less of them for sale. With attendant mortgage costs increasing, local young people and first-time buyers are forced to rent and the surge in demand for rent pushes rent levels upwards. Rental investors in the United States bought 24% of all single-family homes in 2021, up from a typical figure of 15% year-on-year going back to 2012.[23] This loss to the sales sector is not being replaced by new construction of homes so the effect on the rental market is an inevitable surge upwards in rent levels.

Dr Fields has testified on this subject at a US Senate hearing, where she spoke of the "far-reaching social consequences of institutional landlords enjoying outsize powers", for there seem to be few or no state or federal checks or balances to the commercial activities of these large corporations who appear to be clearly and cleverly operating within the law of the land.[24] We will analyse another aspect of these particular landlords' behaviour in Chapter Four.

So far, there is little evidence in the UK that the new BTR developments or other multi-family ventures are having such negative effects on local markets.

An understated factor influencing the market is the increasing apathy that young adults have in the UK to the idea of owning their own property.

> **Ben Page, the boss of Ipsos, a global research firm, points to what he terms the "loss of the future", common across the West but acute in Britain. In 2008, as the financial crisis struck, only 12% of Britons thought youngsters would have a worse quality of life than their parents, Mr Page notes. Now that figure is 41%.[25]**

Canada Gardens, Wembley Park, London.

This apathy is borne partly from the knowledge of how difficult it is financially but also partly due to a new mindset amongst the young which is more to do with living for the experience of the day rather than stockpiling for some future dream. It is not necessarily that young people's income has gone down over the years, but the stability of that income has shifted with the rise of the gig economy, with increased movement between jobs and more short-term contracts. House price inflation is, of course, a huge factor. UK house prices have risen by more than 400% since the early 1970s compared to 180% in Germany and 40% in France, taking its toll on home ownership, which has fallen from 70% in the 1990s to 40% today for those aged 25–34.[26]

Some young people are also appalled at a state that makes so little available for them and yet dishes out seemingly limitless funds to the elderly through guaranteed pensions or National Health Service funding. British people in their 90s receive health and social care that costs the country about £15,000 a year, which is about half Britain's GDP per person, and the budgets rise year on year.[27] The number crunchers at *The Economist* have worked out that, on average, someone born in 1956 will pay approximately £940,000 in tax throughout their life but they will receive about £1.2m in state benefits. Someone born in 1996 will enjoy less than half of that figure, such is the erosion of the welfare state.[28]

One might regard apathetic attitudes as potentially dangerous for a future society, coupled with its inevitable dependence on a state that will increasingly struggle to support the populace in their later years. Alternatively, it might be lauded as a more northern European mindset, where a much greater proportion of people are happy to rent, where it is not the dominant expenditure item coming out of a monthly salary, where the urge to own real estate exists but is not the raison d'être of the workforce and where the non-creative service industry that pushes and supports society to own their own homes are free to concentrate on other areas of life and the chances that this offers. The issue of financial and care support in the years of "Later Living" nonetheless remains in this European type of model, and it is particularly relevant to the UK – especially in the "affordable" part of the market. Later Living, however, is also a further area of interest to the rising BTR sector, which we examine further in Chapter Four.

Another helpful factor for the BTR operators is the method by which development projects are procured in the UK. As well as the political challenges of the planning system that conventional residential developers have to face, an increasing amount of their development is delivered through joint ventures with housing associations or local authorities to ensure that a significant proportion of affordable housing is delivered within a shared risk procurement vehicle. These joint arrangements typically add a year to a development programme, as strangers get to know one another and the minutiae of contractual collaboration are resolved. Whilst BTR developers are not free from affordable housing commitments, they are not usually dependent on a registered provider to ensure delivery and further, the proportion of the affordable element expected to be delivered is much less, typically 20% compared to 35% of total dwelling numbers and as much as 50% in London. The benefits of avoidance of these procurement programme milestones are significant in relation to productivity and to commercial outcomes for BTR operators.

A sweet spot for rental organisations is the group of upwardly mobile people in their mid-30s to early 40s, ageing millennials who have relative fluidity of movement and will seek areas with good schools and social services and if they need to rent because of a shortage of homes for sale then so be it, because "kids come first". The children of baby boomers and baby boomers themselves represent a sizeable cohort in both America and the UK and it is attracting the BTR specialists. However, both economic advisors and long-term investors need to ask themselves what happens when the last of the baby boomers turns the key for the final time in their oversized abode because their demise will change significantly the financial support mechanisms that fuel the market but which are currently taken for granted.

Before closing this chapter on the foundations of the UK housing sector, it is important to recognise the increasing factor that devolution of municipal power to the UK regions is playing on the market. It is perhaps too early to say how BTR will be affected but there are sure to be regional differences which emerge and which impact demand. For instance, there is a huge variance in commitments to social housing. In the past five years, only 12% of the affordable homes built in England were available at social rent level, compared with 68% in Scotland and 79% in Wales.[29] This might suggest that England presents a happier hunting ground for rental investors, not just because of chronic under-investment in social rent, but because of the huge population sink that England contains, given that the combined populations of Northern Ireland, Scotland and Wales make up less than a fifth of England's. The likelihood that these stark differences are going to produce relatively more homeless families in England rather than feed a growing pool of renters should not be lost on the reader. Another regional difference is the introduction of rent controls imposed by the devolved authority in Scotland in 2022, which has virtually stopped new BTR developments coming forward.

Turning back to 2016, the conditions therefore seemed good by this time for the BTR ship to venture further afield with its early voyages. Challenges would arise for sure, particularly around the vagaries of the Government's monetary and taxation policies, not to mention a global pandemic. As we will see in the following chapters, certain events presented early protagonists with some potentially strong headwinds.

CHAPTER TWO
Pioneers

The United States is responsible for many of the leisure, cultural and technological imports that guide our lives and which feed and entertain us. We in the UK and Ireland are relatively relaxed about this foreign influence compared to many European countries. Solutions to how we live within our homes however have not been a tangible part of this importation of ideas to the UK, with the clear exception of big fridges and other kitchen accessories.

Manhattan, where the US sit-com *Friends* is set, is home to much of the innovative thinking in BTR. Residents there, like the characters in the long-running comedy, are entirely content living within a rental environment within new or converted buildings close to where they work. Lower Manhattan leads the world in converting former office buildings to rental properties. It was here that conversions to residential use helped keep the city vibrant after the stock market crash of 1987, which emptied a third of office buildings in New York City. This was only possible with the introduction of tax incentives by the City authorities. There are 83,000 people living in Lower Manhattan, compared to a mere 700 in 1970, within a vibrant multi-generational enclave, creating a model of change for struggling inner urban zones across the planet.[1]

The latest crisis following the pandemic has resulted in new desertions from the city, more in Manhattan than in many other world centres, leading to soaring office vacancies. Rental solutions are once again saving the city. A huge single building at 25 Water Street, formerly 4 New York Plaza, accommodating 1.1 million square feet of office space has been converted into 1,300 rental apartments with a full complement of amenities including swimming pools and a basketball court. It follows an even larger conversion of an art-deco icon to apartments for sale at One Wall Street, formerly known as the Irving Trust Company Bank, dating from 1929. This building is at the centre of the New York financial district. Perhaps the grandees of the Corporation of London should pay a visit to the Big Apple to see an example that could breathe new life into the financial district of the Square Mile, which is a ghost town at weekends and relatively lifeless on Fridays.

UK housing solutions have traditionally been home-grown, the status quo having been handed down from one builder generation to the next with minor variations. Most British people want to live in houses that are made of bricks so this is what they get from the national housebuilders. Modern methods of construction or

FACING PAGE Canada Gardens, Wembley Park, London.

Detached housing at Broadbridge Heath, West Sussex.

factory assembled components have had an uphill battle in weaving their way into our construction industry, particularly within the housing sector. Traditional values, systems, techniques and traditional external appearances tend to hold sway.

The BTR pioneers may be instrumental in changing this.

The majority of the rental accommodation in the United States is not inhabited by *Friends* type groups of renters but instead consists of low-density family housing. It is from this base that more dense rental developments emerged. Single-family housing as it is known is widespread across the country, with the higher density developments concentrated in the large cities of the eastern and western seaboards, with New York leading the line in terms of dwelling numbers and dwelling density. The sector includes the corporations that Dr Fields has been lampooning, which we encountered in Chapter One.

The low-density accommodation generally consists of detached family homes in suburban locations. It has taken off in the US ever since Blackstone, a huge private equity corporation, entered the sector after the recession of 2007–09. Today, the sector is booming and is outperforming annual returns from office space, retail malls, homes for older people and even general needs apartments. The value of homes owned by large institutions has doubled since the financial crash of 2007–09 to $4.7trn, totally outstripping the value of American offices at $1.9trn.[2]

This is not to say that Britain didn't have early pre-cursors to BTR and rental pioneers of its own. Throughout the 19th century, wealthy and socially-conscious industrialists started building stewarded rental communities for their workers. Places such as Saltaire, Bourneville and Port Sunlight were constructed not just to provide the workers with high quality rental accommodation, but also to cater for their physical, social and spiritual needs (see Chapter Four for more on this).

Until recent times, the low-rise type of development was the only kind of contemporary corporately controlled Build To Rent housing within the UK.

Sigma Capital, an Edinburgh-based developer of homes for rent, were one of the first companies in the UK to deliver this low residential density model at scale. Before 2014, Sigma acted as a regeneration specialist for community infrastructure, liaising with local authorities in the North-West. Since then, the organisation has been developing and managing family homes for rent in low density communities, principally in the North of England and Scotland. They have been assisted in their growth with funding streams from Homes England and latterly, the Scottish Government. In 2017 Sigma set up a real estate investment trust to develop family homes for the rental market, one of the first of its kind in the UK. After initial unsuccessful forays into the London market, including at Barking Riverside, Sigma set up a JV with EQT Real Estate in 2020 capable of delivering 3,000 homes in the capital and look set to be engaged on the first phase of the Clapham Park masterplan, the largest detailed planning consent for housing ever achieved in the UK, totalling 2,500 dwellings.

Around the time that Sigma were transforming into development, an off-shoot from a London-based housing association (Thames Valley Housing Association as the social landlord was then known) called Fizzy Living started to develop Build To Rent properties at reasonable scale with assistance from a sovereign wealth fund. Fizzy Living initially acquired existing planning consents for private sale homes and made minor adjustments to these consents to adapt them for a rental model, typically around 75 dwellings per project, such as Lewisham Gateway in South London. These design amendments were chiefly around entrances and reception areas but few changes were incorporated. Part of its success was centred around its branding and marketing coming from a fresh and innovative landlord directing its appeal to a new and younger generation of renters. An added attraction was the tenancy comfort offered to renters, something that was decidedly lacking within the private landlord market. Assured Shorthold Tenancies (ASTs) are the most common form of tenancy in the institutionalised sector, with a further success note for Fizzy Living being its use of longer rental agreements with a minimum fixed-term of six months. They

Clapham Park, Lambeth, London.

Lewisham Gateway Phase 1, Lewisham, London.

were one of the first to offer three-year tenancies with tenant-only break clauses. The organisation has since expanded their offer to renters to include more communal amenities in their developments. The wider Lewisham Gateway development is featured as a case study within this book.

Grainger, a property management company based in London, has existed as an organisation for over 100 years and grew in the 1970s and 80s by acquiring swathes of tenanted properties from various sources including the former nationalised industries such as British Coal. The company launched its first purpose-built BTR scheme at London Road, Barking in 2015. This was a significant move for a developer with a huge asset base across London. With almost 10,000 homes they are one of the largest private rental organisations in the UK.

Essential Living, a London-based property developer, might justifiably claim to be the UK's first bespoke BTR operator as the company was established in 2012 to design, build and manage rental properties across London and the South-East.

The rental market received an injection of energy in 2016 when Legal & General, a UK-based multi-national financial services and asset management company with little track record in development, announced that it was setting up a factory to deliver a pipeline of 4,000 homes, ostensibly for the rental market. This was an indication of the potential for rapid construction for a sector which did not need to be restricted in their build-rate of new homes by the likely sales rate of completed dwellings. In due course, Legal & General failed to deliver on their off-site manufacture aspirations but other players began to take interest in factory assembled production. We return to this subject in Chapter Six to gauge the general response of the sector and to examine how the sector is pioneering digital asset management techniques. Volumetric systems aside, Legal & General were pressing ahead with development and commenced their first BTR development at Slate Yard in Manchester. The project included a range of amenities for renters and launched in mid-2017.

The established rental market received a jolt when in 2016, the Mayor of London, Sadiq Khan, in his manifesto to be re-elected targeted the rental sector, albeit the shadier end of it. Mr Khan proposed a landlord licencing scheme as well as a name-and-shame policy to un-earth rogue landlords. He also planned to set up a cross-London not-for-profit letting agency for *"good landlords and responsible tenants"*. Mr Khan was re-elected but didn't pursue rental reform. The failure to deliver on his manifesto promises perhaps says more about the transformation of the sector by new investor/developers than the need for regulation of an under-strata of London rental scene. It would be another six years before meaningful rental reform would be placed before parliament (see Chapter Three).

A further political jolt came with the result of the 2016 Brexit referendum. The BTR sector was one of the few areas of the UK construction industry that saw a silver lining in the dark clouds of the UK vote to leave the European Union. This was a confident view of potentially stable long-term investment returns in the sector which would supersede the forthcoming ruptures of de-coupling from the UK's greatest trading partner and its most important supplier of building materials and of human resources. Seven years after the vote, there is no reason to challenge this optimistic outlook even if the after-shocks of Brexit have still to be fully assessed and properly acknowledged by the UK Government.

One of the first of the overseas operators to make a serious impression within the emerging sector was Greystar, an international real estate developer and manager founded in the United States. Greystar have an asset base in excess of $30 billion and over 140,000 homes under management in the United States, where they are the largest portfolio holder. In 2016 Greystar announced plans for one of the largest UK BTR projects at Greenford in West London with a proposed expenditure of £600 million. 2016 also saw the announcement by Legal & General that they had formed a £600 million joint venture with a Dutch not-for-profit pension fund called PGGM to deliver over 650 BTR homes.

BTR development at scale in the UK by Greystar has been equalled by Quintain, a property developer and regeneration specialist. They were backed by the American private equity firm, Lone Star, to develop Build To Rent at scale at their flagship site at Wembley Park. Here was an example of a number of new delivery models being created, in this instance an international funder drawing on a developer's local market knowledge.

Momentum was building in the sector. Not even the scrapping of plans to exempt large developers from an additional 3% of stamp duty by the then Chancellor of the Exchequer in early 2016 could tame the nascent market. This tax was set to apply equally to purchasers of second homes by individuals as well as corporate investors. Many at the time believed that the Chancellor's about-turn would reduce liquidity in the commercial property sector and that George Osborne had shot the Government in the foot in sealing off a channel of investment with clear potential to ease the housing crisis. Regardless of this apparent set-back, within a week of the Budget announcement, Watkins Jones, a Welsh developer and contractor with a focus on student housing, had floated on the stock exchange, raising £131m from investors, providing a platform for its expansion into the BTR environment from its traditional student housing staple. At the same time St Modwen, a Birmingham-based developer, announced a switch to BTR on a number of sites within their existing portfolio, including at St Andrew's Park in Uxbridge.

Housing by St Modwen at St. Andrew's Park, Uxbridge.

Get Living London, a bespoke BTR developer and one of the first to remove the need for a security deposit from renters, secured one of the largest early BTR projects in London. The Athletes Village in Stratford was constructed as part of the London Olympics in 2012 to accommodate the participants in the games and the Paralympic Games that followed. I recall visiting the locality in 2011 shortly after completion of the village complex. Set within an industrial hinterland which was undergoing massive pre-Olympic construction, the white/grey repetitive rational architecture stood out in the urban landscape. It was as if a pristine residential section of East Berlin had been transported into East London. The response to context was zero and the word "village" was pushing the use of language to my mind. It appeared as transitory as its short-term function decreed. However, if you make a visit to the village today, with the legacy of the Olympic Park secured, the local landscape features have matured and the recently completed medium density streetscapes of Chobham Manor on its eastern flank effectively anchor the project with a London vernacular of its very own. There is a calm confidence to the neighbourhood. The use of the word "village" no longer seems so outrageous even if the scale of the buildings is significant. The local landmark is the Olympic Velodrome, arguably the finest of all the architectural buildings created for the Games. The village has become an integral part of a truly cosmopolitan and multi-tenure housing offer in this part of East London.

The residential blocks were designed to be quickly retrofitted after the athletes had left to leave them suitable for general needs rental accommodation. This part of their portfolio would grow to 1900 dwellings with post-Olympics plot developments by Get Living London, including the introduction of student housing and the incorporation of more variety in architectural styles between buildings. The neighbourhood became known as East Village. This is one of the first recognisable BTR schemes with management structures, amenities, structured tenant feedback and monitoring and a long-term tenancy agreement with tenant-only breaks.

These early pioneers must be given the credit for breaking new ground within a moribund residential market. In 2012, the UK was still recovering from the financial downturn of 2008. The country had amassed debts which were higher than any major country bar Japan, exacerbated by a programme of quantitative easing. Almost a quarter of people with mortgages were struggling with their mortgage debt and,

East Village, previously the London 2012 Athletes' Village, Queen Elizabeth Olympic Park, Stratford, London.

then, as now, we were not building enough new homes. The economist and journalist Ambrose Evans-Pritchard painted the picture of the time.

> *Britain's home market is sui generis. We don't build houses because of planning law. Construction was 3.5pc of GDP during the boom, compared to 6pc in Germany, 12pc in Spain, or 13pc in China today. Given the chronic property shortage, prices cannot fall much. But that does not in itself shield Britons from brutal retrenchment, since many stretched mortgages to the limit thinking prices must rise. Some have lost their jobs. Monthly debt figures are a third higher as a share of incomes than in the US.*[3]

Perhaps the UK was ready for a change.

The pioneer UK city for BTR might correctly be Manchester, which initially seemed to be eclipsing the capital in both the size and number of individual developments. LaSalle Investment Management became one of the larger players and in 2016 initiated what was arguably the largest UK institutional investment to date in the UK. This was the purchase of almost 500 apartments at Greengate from a conventional private developer. LaSalle had correctly tapped into a market suffering from chronic under-supply in a city which was growing in prosperity and with a negligible housing offer within the city centre. A comparatively frenetic few years of activity in the residential sector involving both private for sale and BTR would have a knock-on effect beyond the city-centre, where most of the development was taking place. Andy Burnham, who has served as Mayor of Manchester since 2017, describes this effect.

> *Rents have risen in Manchester, but Stockport has come in with a solution, offering city-centre style living in apartments but at a much lower cost, and people can get into Manchester city-centre in ten minutes.*[4]

Burnham goes on to suggest that Stockport is becoming the Brooklyn to Manchester's Manhattan, with potential for further regeneration.

As 2016 drew to a close, the Government announced direct financial support or financial guarantees for BTR projects in regional cities, recognising the ability of the sector in helping to plug the perennial gap in UK housing supply. UK banks appeared to be more willing to lend to BTR operators compared to conventional housing developers, presumably because they viewed the risk-adjusted returns as being better for the BTR sector.

CHAPTER THREE
Consolidation

The Housing White Paper of 2017 confirmed the UK Government's interest in and support for the Build To Rent sector. This policy document encouraged local authorities to proactively plan for more BTR homes as well as making provision for affordable rents to be offered by private developers and promoting a greater choice for tenants generally.

It was one year earlier, in 2016, that the client for one of the case studies in this book, Quintain, announced their commitment to deliver 5,000 BTR dwellings across their wide-area Wembley Park masterplan adjoining Wembley Stadium. This number has since increased to a commitment to deliver over 6,000. Situated close to Wembley Park underground station and other public transport nodes, this is an ideal location for quick access to central London.

Quintain was a regeneration-focused private developer with an eye to higher end product when they were acquired by Lone Star, an American private equity firm, in 2015. This heralded a major change in development strategy for Quintain, who had been developing housing for sale plots at Wembley for almost a decade. Their strategy was set to address the lack of choice available to those who could not afford the deposit to buy flats in London and to build these homes more rapidly compared with their own traditional housebuilding programme, being unconstrained by sales rates and market absorption.

This commitment to rapid delivery was indeed delivered. Quintain handed over three phases of development, which were constructed concurrently by two different contractors, by the end of 2021 in a truly remarkable build programme. These elements of the overall scheme, situated around Union Park to the northeast of Wembley Stadium, total over 1,800 dwellings and even more impressively include huge infrastructure installations to support the wider development and the stadium itself. The development incorporates a 168-coach parking garage for major event days within a massive concrete structure and an energy centre serving not only the three-phases of BTR development but also some of the recently completed residential blocks, plus the remainder of the homes yet to be completed within this sector of the masterplan. The design approach is strongly influenced by the contemporary American model and has set the benchmark for Build To Rent quality currently available in London.

FACING PAGE Lewsiham Gateway II, Lewisham, London.

Beyond London, cities which had seen little or no residential development in the preceding years suddenly became active, with BTR schemes commencing in Sheffield, Bristol, Derby and Newcastle. Leeds was already active, whilst Birmingham and Manchester were holding their position on rental yield.

There were further entrants into the sector around 2017. Lendlease, a multi-national construction and property company, commenced developing a phased scheme at Timberyard in Deptford, with another in York. Delph, a residential investment company, received planning consent for a small BTR scheme as part of a major mixed-use town centre regeneration project in Redhill, Surrey.

Meanwhile, Grainger was effectively leading the charge in the consolidation of the sector, extending their operations beyond London including to Milton Keynes and by mid-2018 had built up an investment pipeline. By the end of 2018, this pipeline exceeded £1 billion, with a hugely increased stake in a REIT fund they were already managing, named GRIP, on a quarter share of the fund. Legal & General effectively doubled their BTR portfolio in Manchester with the acquisition of a 44 storey, 350 apartment scheme in Manchester's Deansgate. Liverpool too saw further investment as Barings Real Estate, a global investment manager, opened their account with a 240-dwelling acquisition on the banks of the Mersey. The regions of the UK overtook London at this time in the number of completed or planned BTR properties signalling the strength of the sector across the country. There was significant investment in the Irish market also, with investment funds being formed and JVs set up and consolidated.

By the end of 2018, roughly £3.1 billion of investment deals had been completed in the UK, a third more than had been achieved in 2017. The Ministry of Housing, Communities and Local Government released figures illustrating that the number of private rental homes in the UK had increased to 4.5 million compared to 3.6 million in 2011.

Marketfield Way, Redhill, Surrey.

Coppermaker Square, Stratford, London.

The first significant event of 2019 was at Westfield, the giant retail facility at Stratford in East London. Westfield's new owners, Unibail-Rodamco-Westfield (the European operation of Westfield having recently been bought out by a huge French/Dutch retail conglomerate) had commenced design work on a 1,220 dwelling single-phase BTR complex above their retail complex. It was an early sign of retail developers making the most of their asset in an increasingly distressed shopping environment with on-line retail growing inexorably. It was also the largest single-phase residential development within the UK, even eclipsing the massive, but phased Battersea Park. This was a bold move for the retail company. Whilst it had some limited residential development experience centred around their retail outlet at White City in West London, it had no previous BTR experience. The organisation countered this by assembling a consultant team with the requisite knowledge and proceeded at a startling pace. This project is the second of the case studies contained within this book.

Another significant 2019 event was the completion of the first block on Greystar's BTR masterplan at Greenford Quay, comprising 379 dwellings. This is the redevelopment of the old GlaxoSmithKline site on Grand Union Canal in West London, a site that had lain derelict for decades. The block was one of the first to be completed in London based on the North American model, with a full range of resident amenities, including a residents' lounge, gym, dining room, bar, games room cinema and bespoke external amenities.

2019 was set to be a bumper year for the UK construction industry and this continued into early 2020 – until the onset of the Covid-19 pandemic.

By the end of March 2020, the country was going into its first government-imposed lockdown. Office workers were sent home to work remotely and many building sites were shut. The majority of residential developers and housebuilders took advantage of the Government's Coronavirus Job Retention Scheme by placing droves of their staff on furlough. However, within a matter of weeks, many building sites were operational again with infection control protocols in place. Progress at the largest BTR construction site in London on Quintain's masterplan adjacent to Wembley Stadium was virtually unaffected. The initial release of rental dwellings within the Eastern Lands, to the general public occurred during lockdown and, once again, results confounded expectations. Whilst the build-to-sell sector was impacted by the pandemic, with the flight to the suburbs and the search for better private and communal amenity, the BTR sector emerged largely unscathed.

Perhaps it was the nature of the rental offer at Wembley Park which was key to such resilience, with a strong emphasis on the importance of external communal amenity, including its variety of activity, its anticipation of working from home, its visual attractiveness and the quality of its construction and finish. If we have learned anything from the pandemic it is the value we now place on accessibility to open space, both private and communal. This is in sublime abundance within Quintain's Wembley Park development.

The pandemic no doubt boosted the potential for investors in the sector who were now looking for areas other than commercial or work-space opportunities as the debate continued on how empty our city-centre office buildings would remain. The pandemic also dramatically reduced the life-expectancy, already on the decline in the face of the online assault, of big urban centre retail facilities. Of course, the silver lining for many large central retail complexes would come in the form of new Build To Rent possibilities either built in the air space above these complexes or displacing them entirely.

One of the pioneers of BTR, Get Living, were also moving forward positively on the second phase of Lewisham Gateway with the acquisition of 649 apartments from Muse/London Borough of Lewisham, within a masterplan designed by PRP, Arup and the Dutch practice UN Studio. At the same time, Get Living London were developing at scale within Elephant Park, the large masterplan by Elephant and Castle, in the adjacent London borough of Southwark. Not all London boroughs were as enthusiastic about BTR as Lewisham when these masterplans were commencing. Get Living also started concentrating on development beyond London in towns such as Maidenhead and Leatherhead, towns with good transport links and a dearth of high-quality rental properties.

Boris Johnson was re-elected as Prime Minister in 2019 with an eighty-seat majority in the UK Parliament on the back of a so-called "Levelling Up" agenda – spreading the wealth and opportunity that existed within certain pockets of the UK more evenly across the country. He need not have had any concerns about the BTR sector. Whilst London staged the largest new BTR developments, the regions were not being left behind. Birmingham for instance had established itself as the second most attractive market behind Central London by 2021, with demand falling behind supply. Moda Living, a bespoke BTR developer, announced plans for a £200 million plus BTR Development in Glasgow under a joint venture arrangement at the end of 2021. Plans were under way for a similar scheme in Edinburgh. Moda Living were also

Lewisham Gateway II, Lewisham, London.

part of a joint venture with the American private equity firm KKR which around this time saw the completion of a 325 dwelling high-end tower adjacent to Pier Head in Liverpool. This project features as the fourth of our case studies in this book.

One sure sign that the BTR market was in rude health was the entry into the sector of the giant banks, which also occurred during the pandemic. Lloyds Banking Group set up a BTR business called Citra Living in mid-2021, with plans to quickly establish 800 homes for rent and a lofty target of 50,000 properties under management by 2030. Shortly afterwards, the strategic developer Urban & Civic entered into a three-year framework agreement which would allow for the construction of up to 700 homes for Goldman Sachs Asset Management, with an initial development in Rugby. Urban & Civic had been bought out by the Wellcome Trust prior to this transaction. Even UK retail majors were getting in on the action. The John Lewis Partnership, a premium UK department store retailer, entered the BTR sector in early 2022 with proposals for over-shop development in two locations in London and a potential pipeline of 10,000 dwellings within ten years. By the end of 2022 it had formed a joint venture with Abrdn plc, an Edinburgh-based global insurance and investment company formerly known as Standard Life Aberdeen plc, to deliver the first tranches of development.

The UK Government has played an important part in the growth of the sector. It first began to take notice of the potential of BTR in 2010 when the Coalition Government signalled the need to increase institutional investment into the Private Rented Sector to fund large, professionally-managed developments. In mid-2012, a document which examined barriers to institutional investment in private rented homes was published called the Montague Review. The timing of this report happened to coincide with benign economic conditions at the time, with low inflation and low interest rates creating a virtuous backdrop for nascent BTR investment. However, the importance of Montague cannot be overstated, skilfully set up and managed by the then civil

Criterion Capital's Delta Point building, Croydon, London.

servant Bob Kerslake (who was later to be knighted). The government adopted a number of the recommendations of this review and later that year published the Build To Rent Prospectus, accompanied by a £200 million Build To Rent Fund announced in the Autumn Statement and part of its Housing Stimulus Package. This fund was massively oversubscribed and was increased to £1 billion in the 2013 Budget, ostensibly to support the delivery of 10,000 homes. In the same year, the Government set up a seven-person strong Private Rented Sector Task Force to drive policy forward, also a recommendation of the Montague Review. This review is regarded by some as a transitional moment in the rise of the sector in assisting the un-locking of long-term institutional investment. More than a decade after its publication many of its core aims have been achieved.

Ironically, another Government policy had the effect of tilting the rental market back towards unregulated misery. This was the relaxation of rules governing the conversion of commercial property into flats introduced in 2013 to help boost housing numbers and help tackle the housing crisis. These "Permitted Development Rights" (PDR) allowed developers to by-pass the usual design standards that apply to new-build planning applications, including balcony and private amenity provision. Precise numbers are hard to find but as many as 90,000 homes were provided between 2014 and 2019 against a growing chorus of political objection regarding the quality of living standards coming onto the market. A large proportion of the numbers provided were in the form of studio apartments, or bedsits, to use a more befitting term. Most of the accommodation being delivered was for the rental sector. Some architects, including PRP, refused to work on such schemes.

Fortunately, after a period of frenetic development between 2015 and 2016, interest in PDR receded as the relatively simple to convert buildings were gobbled up by developers. The fading interest was also helped in part by the rise of the BTR sector, with its focus on delivering quality within well connected town centre locations, making regeneration rather than conversion the focus. This has had beneficial consequences for our urban environment, with BTR's focus on placemaking and provision of lively ground floor activity, a position which compares favourably with the limited quality offer of many of the projects developed under Permitted Development.

A challenge for BTR operators, however, which will be discussed in Chapter Four, is how to open up their facilities to the wider public, to create true ground floor activation and social integration.

PDR refuses to go away however. In early 2024, the Home Secretary, Michael Gove, announced plans to belatedly address the Government's appalling record on housing delivery including the return of office to residential conversion. This and other aspects of his plans were widely criticised.

On a more enlightened track, Argent, one of the most successful and far-sighted regeneration specialists in London joined forces with the US giant Related, a multi-tenure development specialist with a high-end portfolio. Related Argent commenced work at Kings Cross with a 218 dwelling BTR scheme, a dry run for the huge Brent Cross Town development, which will bring 6,700 new homes to the North London borough along with 3 million square feet of offices and other facilities. Related Argent formed a JV with Invesco Real Estate, a global real estate investment manager to procure the first phase of the masterplan, comprising 800 private sale and BTR properties.

In an indirect boost to the BTR sector, the 2015 Budget initiated a series of measures which acted against small private landlords, including reduction in mortgage tax relief, increased requirement for Energy Performance Certificates and a 3% stamp duty surcharge on investment properties. It can prove very difficult to boost the energy performance of existing residential buildings, particularly when occupied by renters, compared to new-build BTR developments, which are constructed to current Building Regulations on energy and thermal efficiency. The effects of these measures were most keenly felt in London but they can be viewed as a front to professionalise the rental sector, particularly as homes owned within a corporate entity were excluded from the reduction in mortgage tax relief.

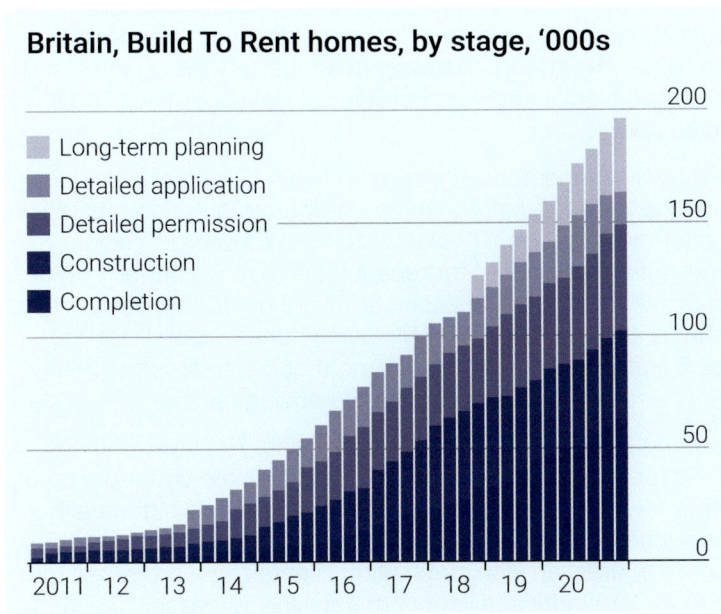

SOURCE Savills Research, British Property Federation, Molior.

Nine Elms, Wandsworth, London.

By the middle of 2021, a market which was barely 1,000 homes strong in 2011 had increased to 62,000, with a further 133,000 homes under construction.[1] The table below represents a snapshot of the period and is a graphic representation of the rise of the sector.

It is worth taking a look at this point at Nine Elms, a huge development masterplan south-west of Waterloo Station and close to the River Thames. Once a semi-derelict hinterland, within the space of ten years it has become one of the largest regeneration zones in London and, apart from a relatively lonely incursion by Greystar, most of the development is for private sale, which is aimed at the higher end of the market. Greystar's project has been developed in conjunction with Henderson Park, a private equity real estate investment manager headquartered in London, and comprises 894 dwellings in two blocks and incorporates multiple amenities and a roof-top open-air swimming pool.

The success of the area may be connected with the significant benefit of an extension of the Northern Line from Kennington to two new underground stations at Nine Elms and Battersea Power Station. The new American Embassy is also located here. The area was initially promoted for regeneration by the London Mayor Ken Livingstone and subsequently by his successor, Boris Johnson, who envisaged provision of 20,000 dwellings, a big increase over Mr Livingstone's vision for 3,000.[2] This number of dwellings requires residential development at super-density, which has attracted the interest of large Chinese developers of housing for sale.

We may be able to learn something from the Chinese approach. The layer of the market that they are aiming for requires an approach to quality in the construction of building and landscape that few UK developers are able to match. The high-quality application to materials selection, the quality of design and construction of the public realm and internal finishes is to draw an elite purchasing clientele to a protected community which bears many similarities to, and perhaps even surpasses, the best BTR schemes in London.

On 1 April 2021, Michael Gove introduced the Residential Property Developer Tax (RPDT). This was effectively a windfall tax on residential developers. The tax applied a 4% levy to any of their annual profits which were in excess of £25m and its function was to cover past and on-going expenditure in replacing dangerous cladding on tall buildings in the post-Grenfell environment. Plans were mooted to extend this to 10% of their profits. Once again, BTR operators were excluded, it being recognised that these investors were operating a model which secured their projected returns over a long period of time and any windfall tax would damage the credibility of the sector. The exemption, it should be noted, did not extend to the contractors building these tall buildings, nor the developers buying land to form a development agreement to forward fund the delivery of a BTR scheme to a BTR operator.

Michael Gove was sacked by Boris Johnson in early July 2022 (he would return to his position under a different leadership three months later). The Prime Minister announced a new leadership contest shortly afterwards, catalysing the lengthy replacement protocols within the Conservative Party. The political sideshow to find a new Prime Minister formed the backdrop to an increasingly concerning cost of living and energy crisis, with inflation rising at a rate not seen for 30 years and with interest rates rising in response. The BTR sector initially appeared unperturbed by the economic headwinds coming to bear on the UK. It is established that demand for rental properties increased during periods of economic turbulence. Bob Faith is the chief executive of Greystar, the largest multi-family homes operator in the US and now one of the largest BTR developers in Britain. He signed off one of the biggest property deals in the UK since the onset of the coronavirus pandemic.

> **Bob Faith has predicted the company will expand further in the UK after last week's £3.3bn deal to buy student housing business Student Roost with Singaporean sovereign wealth fund GIC.**[3]

Before Michael Gove was forced from Government, he introduced the Renters Reform Bill as part of the Government's Levelling Up agenda. This was the signal policy which helped secure a huge majority for the Conservatives at the last General Election, promising a re-distribution of income, services and industry to benefit those beyond London and the South-east. The Bill made its way through the statute book in the tumultuous months of late 2022. It represented a *volte face* on decades of effective *laissez-faire* on the private rented sector and envisaged the introduction of a series of measures to improve the long-term security of renters in their homes, to tackle discrimination and to improve the management practices of landlords and letting agents.

On the face of it, the proposals would be likely to further reduce the number of properties within the "unregulated" rental sector and to enhance the market position of the specialists. There was also potential concern amongst investors about the law of unintended consequences of the legislation producing an army of ambulance-chasing lawyers queuing up to represent tenants in spurious actions against landlords, even those in the BTR sector. The protections for renters were finally set out in the King's Speech (the speech that the King reads out in the Lords Chamber on the occasion of the State Opening of UK Parliament, setting out the Government's plans for the year ahead) in early November 2023, alongside an overhaul of leasehold laws. The measures included the scrapping of "no fault" evictions and the prevention of landlords from refusing to rent properties to those who receive welfare benefits or who have children. However, doubt remained about whether there was time to pass new laws as a General Election loomed, potentially within 12 months of the King's Speech.

Mr Gove made a fortuitous return to Government in October 2022 following the demise of Liz Truss' ill-fated spell of leadership. He is one of few Government ministers with a reputation for getting things done quickly. In his previous Cabinet position, he threatened major housebuilders in England with a nationwide ban if they failed to sign a building safety contract. His initial tirade was directed against the builders of tall residential towers who seemed to dodge responsibility for their role in constructing dangerous cladding and insulation on these buildings. Despite its draconian nature, the move was widely received as sensible, even by some of the targeted constructors, as it aimed to ease the plight of leaseholders caught in tall buildings and who were facing gigantic remediation bills. Most of the developers signed up.

However, Mr Gove was just getting started. Shortly afterwards, he accused the nation's biggest housebuilders of operating a cartel. A year later, in his new role as Levelling Up Secretary, and despite most builders continuing to follow his tune, he launched an investigation into their commercial activity even after an independent review of build out rates of private developers produced by Sir Oliver Letwin in 2018 found little, if anything, wrong with the sector.

Not content with demonising the private sector, Mr Gove then turned his ire to the social housing sector. This shift followed the tragic death of two-year old Awaab Ishak in a socially rented dwelling in Rochdale. The Government tabled an amendment to the Social Housing Regulation Bill relating to hazards in social homes, compelling Registered Providers, as housing associations and local authorities who provide housing are termed, to ensure that the homes they rent to families are safe. While no-one would argue against this direction, it is unfortunate that such a measure was required at all. Last December, Mr Gove singled out Clarion, one of the UK's largest housing associations, for what he called a string of failures and went on to name and shame three other registered housing providers for basic failings on their watch.

So far, the BTR sector has avoided the brickbats of the Right Honourable gentleman, Mr Gove.

Despite a series of interest rate increases in 2022, annual rental growth in October of that year was 12.3% across the UK and 17.8% in London. The stock of homes for rent was 46% below the five-year average, with demand sitting at 42% above the five-year average.[4]

The effects of the war in Ukraine on global economics have been stark. By the end of September 2022, it was estimated that Russia had lost more troops than America did during the entire Vietnam War. In that same month, OPEC, which controls 40% of the world's oil supply acted to keep the oil price high and Europe was suddenly bracing itself for a winter with severely constricted gas supplies, Russian sources having been all but extinguished. The cost of building materials ballooned within a highly inflationary environment and European economies were jostling to avoid economic recession.

Overall, however, investor interest in BTR remained undiminished. The British Property Federation, a not-for-profit membership organisation that works with Government and regulatory bodies, estimated that the sector would be worth £170bn by 2032, with BTR dwellings in the UK rising from 76,800 in late 2022 to 380,000.[5] This optimistic outlook is challenged by two significant factors. The first was a downturn in investor interest on rental opportunities in the capital in early 2023 as London land prices remained sticky despite the gradual increase in UK interest rates. The second is the on-going docility of the UK economy and its bottom-of-the-class record on productivity. By 2024, real living standards are projected to fall by the greatest amount over a two-year period since records began and are forecast to remain below their pre-pandemic levels until 2028. Eight years of under-achievement and sliding relative wealth is a headwind affecting the entire residential sector as well as the wider wellbeing of the population.[6]

Ultimately, rental growth is dependent on economic growth and the BTR developers were not immune to the market conditions of 2023. Some made significant staff cut-backs, but they did not stop. Quintain temporarily scaled back their operation at Wembley, and others such as Moda Living and Greystar looked to diversify part of their investment into student housing. In a case of reverse-engineering, the student housing operator, Unite Students, entered the BTR market in late 2022 with an acquisition in East London to facilitate an extension of its offer to young professionals as they emerge from studenthood. Sigma Capital's investment trust, PRS REIT, posted strong financial results in mid-2022, showing the resilience of the multi-family part of the sector. The listed company added 800 homes in the year to its circa 5,000 home portfolio and anticipated strong on-going rental demand in the regions.

One of the regions where there has been little BTR activity is Northern Ireland. This is about to change, with the announcement in mid-2023 of a deal between Watkins Jones and Lacuna Developments, one of Northern Ireland's leading development and investment companies, and Legal & General Investment management in what may be the largest ever private sector residential investment in the province.[7] The project, in Belfast's Titanic Quarter, will provide 627 BTR apartments and 151 affordable homes managed by Clanmill Housing Association. This development will be a huge boost to the on-going regeneration of the York Street area and finally puts Belfast on the BTR map.

In the difficult trading conditions of 2023, a different form of BTR emerged with some prominence and its financial model was outcompeting both conventional residential development as well as BTR, particularly in London. It is called Co-living. In essence, Co-living has been developed to bridge the gap between bespoke student accommodation and BTR, predominantly catering for people in their early adulthood, or to provide for those who require short-term lets. It includes the provision of a large amount of communal space with small studio apartments that are enhanced versions of student rooms. Co-living has a strong focus on this communal experience, centred around cooking and dining, which appears to appeal to those with a more nomadic and lifestyle-centric existence. It is a small sub-set of the BTR sector, but many are watching its potential with interest.

The last word on consolidation in this chapter must go to the British Property Federation, a not-for-profit membership organisation that works with Government and regulatory bodies. The organisation has quietly supported the growth of the movement since 2011, lobbying housing ministers, leading educational visits and influencing policy through the National Planning Policy Framework. Their Director of Policy, Ian Fletcher, is a staunch supporter of the sector, has helped guide important outcomes as a panel member of the Montague Review and continues to promote the sector across the political divide.

CHAPTER FOUR
Economic, Social and Sustainable Stewardship

The social and economic environment of the United Kingdom has transformed more within the last six years than in the previous two decades. The twin forces of Brexit and the Coronavirus pandemic have significantly affected all areas of commerce, not least the construction sector. But prior to these two upheavals, the industry was reeling from the aftermath of the Grenfell tragedy, the aftershocks of which are still dissipating. In the background is the ever-increasing hum around planning policy and regulatory confusion, principally related to fire safety, which adds further to the kaleidoscope of change. The financing and housing of an ageing demographic in the UK, affecting the Western world in general, is not being properly considered and will be more challenging as the years go by. Then, in early 2022 came the invasion of Ukraine by Russia, heralding an economic shock to the West akin to a stone being cast into a millpond. The war that ensued had ground to a stalemate by the end of 2022 but its baleful effect on Europe's economy remained, particularly in the cost of constructing new homes and then providing energy to both new and existing homes.

Despite all of this turbulence, there is little doubt that the greatest challenge of all, climate change, has yet to be seriously addressed in the design and servicing of homes we live in. Indeed, the years since 2016 have been so tumultuous that the rise of a radical form of rental housing tenure, by UK standards, has gone largely unnoticed, shielded as it has been by these significant "events". That it is a form of housing which may allow us to deal more readily with the effects of these events is examined in this chapter.

Before getting into the grain of this chapter however, a mea culpa and an exhortation that it is all of us involved in property, including the design professions, that must do more.

> *Architectural culture's apparent disregard of the causes of climate breakdown can be explained through its self-absorbed obsessions which are first established in the founding tenets of architectural magazines*[1]

Most contemporary UK architects probably feel content in their own skins that they are doing what they can within their professional existence to save the planet. The words above, which are from a 2023 edition of the *Architectural Review*, are honest and are accompanied by a recognition, shared by this writer, that a gap has opened between what an editorial position demands and what is delivered by architects. The comfort blanket of doing just enough was badly ruffled by the profession's involvement in designing and constructing most of the temporary-use football stadia in Qatar for the 2022 FIFA World Cup, stemming from the nature of the country's ruling regime and the inherent unsustainability of placing these huge, heavily-serviced structures in the middle of a desert.

The criticism that was directed against those involved came principally from within the architectural profession and had little impact. Architects are often described as the canaries in the coal-mine, the initial harbingers of doom as economic trouble approaches, given their early position on projects at their initiation. It is true to say that the profession is detecting the noxious fumes of the climate emergency perhaps more quickly than other professions and trade bodies. There is therefore no excuse for continuing to do just enough.

THE CHOICE OF SUSTAINABLE LONGEVITY

> *It is clear that what we are doing is unaffordable, socially divisive and physically defective. It is clear what we should do to improve this state of affairs. Which government or political party has the courage to show the necessary leadership?* [2]

These words are not part of a critique of current UK municipal governance. They were written in 2005 in an article penned by a prominent Canadian architect, Jack Diamond, which he directed at the Government of Canada. We are not alone in the challenges we face, nor in dealing with timelines which drift with seemingly little action. But occasionally, the means of making significant change reveal themselves.

The emergence at scale in the country of BTR, multi-family and single-family developments, offers a unique opportunity for the built environment to re-address the way we think about design, procurement of buildings and the way we live whilst embracing the ultimate importance of sustainability in all of its aspects – economic, social and environmental. The traditional private rented sector continues to form a significant part of the rental offer in UK towns and cities. The legacy of mis-managed rented homes within the public sector remains, a legacy which today's housing associations and progressive local authorities are attempting to redress.

People are seeking something different. They are choosing to live sustainably, choosing life on demand, choosing to work from home and choosing a home that is a place where they are content and proud to live. They are seeking a place that works for them, which reflects and enhances its context and acts as an expression of their life chances. They are seeking life-enriching experiences. The BTR operators know that customer retention, the average length of stay for an individual or a family, is their chief measure of success. Furthermore, the operators have the technological means to collect the data that will help improve the service offer and enhance retention statistics. The subjects of the data collection, the renters, know this too. They have free access to residential review websites and can compare living experiences with renters in other developments and obtain critiques on service offers.

Across London and in the regional cities, the housing sector has continued to deliver dense private housing schemes of mostly private tenure, almost unaffected by the pandemic. The perception of the existing housing stock, on the other hand, has been affected by the pandemic. Those that have been able to have moved away from cramped accommodation with no form of individual private amenity in search of something better. How many people living within these existing developments have a sense of belonging and how many of them feel happy at home? From one massive residential sink to the next, the offer is generally the same. Only prime central London, completely unaffordable to the vast majority, has in the past offered something above the norm. A private sector market existed where apartment living or renting had become a last choice for those on average income rather than a first choice. For many, the only option is to remain in place. The advent of BTR represents an exciting opportunity for some to hope for something better.

The case studies detailed in this book are large-scale developments which were completed within rapid construction timeframes. The size of the projects brings economies of scale either on a single, large project or on multiple, distinct development sites by a single BTR developer through enhanced buying power and certainty of forward build programmes. Scale also ameliorates development start-up costs and is attractive to investors wanting to deploy large amounts of capital quickly, something which is difficult to achieve with the for-sale housebuilder model.

This advantage of scale and the compact, high-density nature of the majority of new BTR developments is inherently more sustainable than suburban or edge-of-town development. This is because, firstly, these developments optimise the infrastructure required to support it. Secondly, the developments are well constructed and meet or exceed current Building Regulations in relation to thermal performance, energy use and provision of renewable technology. A third factor is that these developments are effectively car-free and are typically situated close to public transport nodes, local services and leisure amenities. However, there is still massive room for improvement in the UK. More than a third of Londoners commute to work by car compared to only 7% in Hong Kong.[3]

Let's examine further that notion of choice. We touched on the effects of Margaret Thatcher's housing policies in Chapter One. In 1975, she declared her vision to the annual Conservative Party Conference that the UK should be a "property-owning democracy". Since then, our overall outlook towards home ownership has shifted. Increasing house prices feed societal difference between those who have equity and those who do not, a difference which has become even more acute when measured across different generations. But look closely at what is available to purchase within new-build housing for sale across the country and you will see that choice has actually been eroded. In his foreword to the publication "Distinctively Local", a call for a return to contextual variety in new homes to reflect the different geographical characteristics of the UK, Lord Taylor of Goss Moor made an important observation.

> *If the great majority of what we build is poor quality "anywhere estates" (and I believe it is) we simply reinforce opposition to new homes being built at all. Yet every village, town and city we love, every neighbourhood and community village we aspire to live in, was built for people by people. Why have we lost faith in our ability to do so as well?* [4]

The Build To Rent "revolution" has, as we have seen, been quietly creating ripples within the UK's housing market that are beginning to provide an alternative vision to home ownership and can perhaps lead us away from the "anywhere estates" for living in to which Lord Taylor refers.

Becoming a homeowner in Britain today is a significant individual endeavour. For new apartment buildings, the residents who manage to purchase a flat are often left in the clutches of a faceless leasehold management corporation with untoward charges and questionable servicing. The developer quickly departs to the next project following building completion, a new word, "fleecehold", has emerged to help categorise the injustice in certain quarters.

The travails of leaseholders have increased starkly since the Grenfell tragedy, especially for those living in high-rise apartment blocks, where fire safety concerns have shone a spotlight not only on the costs of removing dangerous cladding but on the general costs of repairing and maintaining buildings of height. Service charges will rise further with the requirements introduced in 2023 for additional stair-cores, including lifts, on buildings taller than 30 metres in height. A study released in early 2023 concludes that the rights and obligations of leasehold purchasers are not well understood. It points out that developers are under no obligation to design with future maintenance in mind nor to provide long-term cost scenarios for future repair and maintenance which falls back on leaseholders.[5] The study also highlights a missing link between current planning policy where tall buildings are involved and the amount of private and localised amenity and open space that should be provided to support sudden massive increases in residential population. The authors make a series of recommendations for addressing these leaseholder concerns, including mandatory future maintenance cost plans from developers at point of sale and projected service charges to be made available from freeholders or their management agents.

Most of these worries are absent in a BTR environment, where there are no leaseholders and a different approach is taken. When you move into an established BTR development, you are welcomed into a pre-existing community structure that is carefully managed to appeal to its residents. There is none of the ambiguity about costs that leaseholders face. Facilities that support the tenants' lifestyles are often provided within the building, such as gyms, lounges, cycle repair, library and cinema spaces and occasionally, swimming pools and dog-care provision. Social events are curated, health and wellbeing is encouraged and entertainment is laid on. Continual monitoring of use and flexibility of offer means emerging trends are accommodated and variety provided.

However, even before we look at the successful and recently completed BTR developments set out as case studies in this book, there are hugely successful historic precedents that set the tone for success.

CAPITALISM MEETS SOCIAL RESPONSIBILITY

> *It would not do you much good if you send it down your throats in the form of bottles of whisky, bags of sweets, or fat geese at Christmas. On the other hand, if you leave the money with me, I shall use it to provide for you everything that makes life pleasant – nice houses, comfortable homes, and healthy recreation.*[6]

We could be forgiven for thinking that the leading BTR developers have looked at the past, particularly the select grouping of industrialists with a philanthropic leaning from the late 18th and the 19th centuries in the UK, and that they have learned some valuable lessons about how best to house people and to keep them happy. Places such as Lanark, Saltaire, Bournville and Port Sunlight were created by wealthy industrialists who were concerned about the wider wellbeing of their work forces. The words above are attributed to William Hesketh Lever, perhaps the greatest of the English industrialist philanthropists.

They built great new communities from scratch with high quality rental accommodation and wider facilities, catering for their tenants' physical, emotional and spiritual wellbeing. Art galleries, schools, hospitals, pools, allotments, concert halls and recreation facilities were all present, often within a nostalgic recreation of bucolic worker tradition juxtaposed with an increasingly industrialised and urbanised environment. It was "brave new world" thinking with a clear emphasis on "sense of

Port Sunlight, Merseyside.

place", with dedicated outside space to promote healthy living and enjoyment during non-working hours. Some may wonder how truly beatific their social consciences were. After all, William Lever had established plantations in the Solomon Islands and the Belgian Congo at the end of the 18th century, formerly important nodes on the transatlantic slave trade route.

Lever's concept was one of "prosperity-sharing". This meant that the success of his business enterprise enabled him to provide decent homes for his workforce, with amenities and welfare provision which were almost unheard of in this era. Port Sunlight, with its aesthetic roots in the Arts and Crafts movement, placed a clear emphasis on the importance of good design to the sense of wellbeing of a community. Lever also wished to embed a sense of loyalty within his workforce – an important consideration today in relation to tenant retention rates within BTR developments.

Lever established Port Sunlight in 1900, a model village of 900 buildings, now Grade II listed, on the Wirral in Merseyside. The village was named after the most famous soap manufactured by his company. An organisation which started off making simple bars of soap would grow to become a giant global conglomerate under the name Unilever.

Bournville Village Trust, an initial estate of 313 homes, was established by George Cadbury in 1900 to the south-west of Birmingham. Cadbury was a true BTR pioneer. The initial phase of development was a homes-for-sale project which extended beyond the workforce of his chocolate factory. However, because of the enlightened setting of the new neighbourhood and the attractive environment of a model village, this wider-area casting for purchasers resulted in homes being re-sold at inflated rates and brought a cohort of transient residents. This directed Cadbury to start building homes for rent and these were controlled to provide for specific families on low incomes. Cadbury's vision of affordability has survived to this day and his concerns for the health and fitness of his workforce ring louder today than ever.

CHAPTER FOUR – ECONOMIC, SOCIAL AND SUSTAINABLE STEWARDSHIP

Arts and crafts style houses, Port Sunlight, Merseyside.

> *By their example of making civilized places and civilized communities the foundations were laid for conscious city planning: here were models for efficient industry and for healthy and cultured living for ordinary families. Here also were living examples of the benefits of single ownership of land and of masterplanning, which highlighted the merits of having a vision for a place, of single-minded implementation, and of self-governance and long-term management.*[7]

The world's first model village was established by the philanthropist Robert Owen at New Lanark in Scotland, following his purchase of a cotton mill there in 1799. He proceeded to transform the working and living conditions of his workers, with commercially uplifting results. He introduced nurseries for children, established an eight-hour day and set up education programmes for his workforce. His philosophy of utopian socialism attracted the Government, which sought his advice on how to assist parts of the population suffering the privations of the Napoleonic Wars. Based on his experience at New Lanark, Owen believed that communities of 1200 people should be assigned 400–600 hectares of land, living in one building, with families allocated their own apartments and dining communally.

Not all such model villages endured as well as Saltaire and Port Sunlight. Worsley, once a small village, is currently a picturesque town in Salford to the west of Manchester, famous for its historical mock-Tudor buildings and its coal-mining heritage. At the end of the 1700s it became the location for 30 workers' cottages, supplementing the existing fabric of the village. They were built by the third Duke of Bridgewater, one of the great pioneer canal builders of the Industrial Revolution, to further the enterprise of transporting coal from his estates into Manchester. After the death of the Duke in 1803 however, things began to unravel and the village turned into *"a god-forgotten place, its inhabitants were much addicted to drink and rude sports, their morals being deplorably low. The whole district was in a state of religious and educational destitution; there was no one to see to the spiritual wants of the people, and teaching was all but nullity itself."* [8] Today, fortunately, there is little sign of such depravity in this part of Salford.

The parallels between these great estates and the emerging new BTR developments are striking. But not all that was deemed to be relevant in the 19th century is relevant now. Good quality homes, with wider facilities and a focus on community, are a given for those who can afford to buy or rent within new residential developments. In the age of the online ecosystem and an increasingly competitive environment for attracting renters, perhaps the larger BTR operators will embrace the digital *zeitgeist* and move the ethos of well-meaning industrialists of a by-gone era firmly into the 21st century. Such enterprises could use their buying power to offer their customers wider packages beyond the obligatory gym membership. Music, live-streaming, online content and media subscriptions, electric car, cycle and travel contracts and tickets, barista coffee subscriptions and delivery deals, discounts on fine wines or on-line meal kits, food growing areas, mental health and wellbeing programmes, charity and carbon offset contributions, savings, pensions and other portable financial products – all made available from one rental payment, tailored to each tenant through a dedicated app.

The entrepreneurial spirit of the rising companies and the market will determine the nature and extent of the roll-out of these intangible top-up services, but it is already clear that BTR stewardship has the potential to go way beyond the physical volume of a home and that it can offer a wider, more enriched lifestyle package. The question of whether the big BTR corporations can go further, building on their already positive impact in the UK, to actively strive to address the lack of inclusivity and equality that was so starkly exposed across the country during both the Brexit debacle and the pandemic crisis, remains untested.

Food growing garden at Canada Gardens, Wembley Park.

The former Somalian refugee, Hashi Mohamed, is now a broadcaster and writer when he is not doing his day-job as a planning barrister. He has particular views on equality within the housing sector.

> *A more equal society is one that can give its citizens space to find their own definition of success: instead of a narrow winner-takes-all mentality we could find something that rewards – and sees as a genuine end in itself – jobs that support others, strengthen our society from within, where compassion and generosity are as valuable qualifications as intelligence and drive. For some happiness will always be linked with material possessions: flashy cars, higher salaries and exotic holidays. For some, it will be about power and status. But for others, it will be about a happy family, love, belonging; or about making a difference, creating change. We could build a society that values all of these outcomes equally – but we will need to use our imaginations.*[9]

Hashi would be a fan of Japanese governance in this area. The socio-economic inequality that limits large parts of UK society is greatly reduced in Japan when compared to both Britain and America and this is to do with the education system, levelling the playing field of life chances for most of society.

> *Social status in Japan depends more on education than on heredity and family connection: again, the reverse of U.S. trends. In short, instead of investing in just a fraction of its citizens, Japan invests in all of them...*[10]

His Majesty's Government take note. Japan's global economic output is twice that of the UK with a population of 120 million compared to the UK's approximate 76.5 million.[11]

CLIMATE CHANGE AND GEOPOLITICAL RESILIENCE

The American political scientist Francis Fukuyama called time on history in 1992 with the end of the Cold War and the ascendancy of Western liberal democracy. He believed a permanent plateau of equilibrium had been reached.[12] Mr Fukuyama might have paid more attention to one of the more famous sayings of an American professional baseball player from the 1940s to the 1960s, Lawrence Peter "Yogi" Berra, who advised *"The future ain't what it used to be."* [13]

Fukuyama was writing 18 years after the oil shock of 1974 and the effect that actions of the oil-producing cartel, OPEC, had on economies across the world. Despite the economic chaos of this period, people generally remained ignorant to the potential effects on one's personal wellbeing of distant geopolitical actions. The financial crash of 2008 changed everything and the ignorance dissipated. With the advent of digitally-transmitted news, fake, politicised or real, and the relentless surge of social media, we are now more aware than ever before that a dispute over an island on the far side of the world has at least the effect of changing the value of the pound in our pocket, if not a great deal more.

Much of the Western world is currently experiencing a series of unsettling events. The plateau of equilibrium which lasted for a generation was an illusion. Brexit, Covid-19 and the ongoing war in Ukraine all contributed to economic uncertainty and an ensuing energy crisis, which in turn created a spike in inflation that continues to affect all sectors of society. Much of the commercial pain of high inflation was borne by the UK construction sector. Build costs rose at the fastest rate for decades at the beginning of 2022, exacerbated by labour and material shortages arising from Brexit. Compounding this further, viability models were squeezed by emerging regulations, many of which relate to post-Grenfell regulatory reform. Project costs remained under pressure across the industry well into 2023. Predictably, these market conditions led developers to drive out "unnecessary" costs in a search for efficiencies.

The recent changes in the UK Building Regulations are aligned with the UK Government's objectives in reducing carbon emissions. They push us along the right path but we must do more as a collective and set examples for others to follow, both within UK borders and beyond. The more energy we save the better, the more materials we can recycle or re-use the better, the more alternatives to car usage we can provide the better. The more effort we put into reducing our impact now the less impact our activities will have on future generations.

The unique aspect of BTR over open market sale homes is the stewardship of the investor and the long-term hold of the building. Long-term efficiency can be more important than short-term capital gain. That means a more holistic view of specification can be brought to bear focusing on robustness, reduced labour and materials within future maintenance programmes, reduced overheads and enhanced environmental credentials. This aspect of the management of maintenance and repair is expanded upon in Chapter Six.

Reduction of energy and water usage over the long term is a positive for the environment as we strive to reduce the impact of our footprint on nature. Greater thermal efficiency, a passive and positive approach to designing out overheating of our homes, good detailing to increase air tightness, grey and black water recycling, low energy fixtures and fittings are some of the measures which help reduce our footprint of degradation. As well as reducing the relative impact on the environment, it is also beneficial for investors' balance sheets, as more and more Environmental, Social and Governance (ESG) protocols are adopted by corporations. Lower overheads allow for lower rents and lower rents enhance customer uptake or allow expansion of the wider offer to residents.

Increasing the lifecycle of building elements and facilities reduces waste and carbon usage, while extending maintenance and replacement cycles and the casual acceptance of build lifespans of a mere 60 years should be challenged. What is wrong with 100 years, or longer? Components and plant become redundant over time and need to be replaced but structure and certain elements of fabric should avoid built-in obsolescence. Using materials that can be recycled and re-used supports the circular economy and makes good fiscal sense. Operational and replacement costs matter in the same way that reducing energy bills and reducing carbon footprints do.

In relation to operational costs, the capital expenditure on a building programme is a small proportion of its operational expenditure over the life of the building and can be four or five times as much as the initial contract sum required to construct and fit out the building. This should reinforce the case for doing more than the minimum in thermal performance, energy efficiency, water saving and in installing robust materials and systems. The very people who BTR most appeals to are those most likely to select a home, in part, because of its environmental credentials. This will become a more important consideration as the evident effects of climate change worsen. Doing more therefore, not less, for the sustainability of BTR buildings now makes good business sense for the future and will protect the long-term attractiveness of BTR developments. A recent survey of UK renters in both the BTR and PRS parts of the sector by JLL, a global property consultant, suggests that 63% of tenants would pay a premium for more energy-efficient homes. Furthermore, 90%

Clapham Park, Lambeth where PRP and the consultancy, Mace, carried out dynamic cost modelling to assess both capital and operational costs across the masterplan.

of tenants in this survey would make energy efficiency a consideration when moving to their next home. 71% of these renters living outside London don't own a car and this rises to 81% within London.[14]

While such statistics are encouraging, unfortunately they cannot be taken for granted. The big new BTR developments across the country once included energy bills within a holistic rental bill covering rent, local tax and services. Energy bills have now been decoupled by the operators because the previous arrangement offered no incentive to renters to switch lights off or turn the heating down, even when their home was vacant. Energy bills became unsustainable. This behaviour is sadly reflective of wider society, as the economist Paul Ormerod describes.

> *In surveys, people often express support for policies which are designed to meet climate change targets. Economists are more sceptical about the result of such surveys. In the jargon, they show stated preferences. People are merely asked what their response might be in hypothetical situations. Yet in real life situations, when energy prices rose in a way which would have drastically reduced consumption and facilitated the achievement of climate targets, they were wildly unpopular. Governments scrambled to offset the impacts as fast as they could. There is a clear implication. Policies to meet climate change targets are broadly acceptable if they impose few costs on electorates. As soon as they do, there is a huge adverse reaction.*[15]

There is mounting evidence pointing to a substantial gap between the theoretical performance of buildings as measured at the design stage and their actual performance when built. The calculation that feeds into buildings has little relationship to real-world build quality and performance. Innovate UK, a UK governmental innovation agency, ran a programme of studies on 76 homes and concluded that carbon emissions from new homes are two-to-three times higher than design estimates. This is even before allowing for energy use from cooking and appliances.[16] This should be addressed and covered in building standards as early as possible to manage the performance gap. Including design standards metrics such as Energy Use Intensity (EUI) in the Building Regulations could be a much easier way to compare the projects' design and actual built performance. Also, it is crucial to consider that the adopted metrics are simple enough to make users understand and use them as a benchmark to inform their behavioural decisions. Having grown up in the 1970s, I remember well the oil shock of that period and the energy black-outs that ensued. To this day, I cannot exit a room without turning off the light switch, much to the annoyance of my family. It seems that a lot more education is required to influence user behaviour, from Cabinet member to tenant, as not enough of us get the message.

The war in Ukraine has at least one fortunate outcome in de-coupling the West from its dependence on Russian fossil fuels and accelerating Europe into greater exploration of alternative sources of energy. It has been a massive boost to the roll-out of renewable technology and carbon-free energy sources, including a re-think on nuclear power. In America, President Biden has initiated an enormous stimulus package through the Inflation Reduction Act, which offers big subsidies to green technologies and advanced IT systems. This legislation is, in part, to put a check on the industrial capacity of China and Western dependence on Chinese exports. Europe is reacting to the American stimulus with their own initiatives.

China has been facing its own economic challenges, the impact of which have been felt in the West. This was partly to do with their particular policies in addressing Covid-19, with repeated lockdowns within an essentially closed society, which further impacted on the balance and quantum of trade. The Chinese leadership's battle to control Covid became a cause *célèbre* which was set to show how ineffective and weak the Western democracies were in tackling the crisis. It would ultimately de-rail. For the Chinese people, it couldn't have come at a worse time, as it coincided with their leader's battle to clear corruption and graft from the Chinese economy. The construction industry bore the brunt of the government actions. The wider impact was a dramatic slowing of the Chinese economy, and that would exacerbate unfavourable economic conditions in the West and particularly in the UK, which was underperforming all of the richer western economies by the end of 2022. The Chinese economy recovered in 2023 after a *volte face* by the government on its Covid containment policies, although the woes of its property sector would continue.

ECONOMIC SUSTAINABILITY –
THE LAND VALUE CURSE AND THE REGULATION CURSE

Having been steady and predictable for almost two decades, buoyed by 12 years of almost zero interest rates, the cyclical nature of the UK property market was about to re-assert itself. Residential developers in the UK in late 2022 were facing a perfect storm. Geopolitical events, emanating largely from the war in Ukraine, were pushing inflation to levels not seen in a generation. The effects of Brexit on the supply of human resources and materials were continuing to bite, even if the Government remained in denial that any downside existed following the schism with Europe. In early 2022, a rent cap was proposed by the Government on Registered Providers, which would further constrain their capacity to develop new housing of any tenure, let alone affordable housing. The Conservative Government entered a re-election cycle which caused calamity in the financial markets to the point of international contagion. All this, together with a raft of new legislation rolled out in 2022, added to general cost pressures.

When the French economist, Thomas Piketty, published his book *Capital in the Twenty-First Century* in 2014, it became an unlikely international bestseller and provoked wide discussion, drawing both praise and criticism. Picketty's position was that wealth grows faster than economic output, to the detriment of society, and he railed against the inequality that this tendency makes prevalent within Western economies. He recommended that governments should intervene to re-distribute the inevitable accumulation of wealth by a relatively small number of individuals.

The Chinese leader Xi Jinping must be a fan of Thomas Piketty. His efforts to clean up the Chinese property market are part of a wider effort to more equally distribute wealth across the country by heavily restricting the commercial success of high wealth individuals and certain corporations. The technology and construction sectors were prime targets. In August 2022 the leadership introduced a "three red lines" policy to curb the excesses of the residential property sector, by firstly limiting liabilities to a percentage of assets, then by limiting debt to be no greater than 100% of equity, and finally through ensuring that cash reserves must be at least 100% of short-term debt. The policy exacerbated a housing crisis and resulted in one of the largest developers, Evergrande, to default. Numerous other large developers had similar difficulties. Not even the mighty Chinese Communist Party can resist the power of a property boom and bust cycle.[17]

As has lately become the case in China, much of the wealth in Western society is tied up in land. Real estate is the largest asset class in the world, making up approximately 68% of the world's non-financial assets. In the UK, the value of land has escalated sharply, increasing from 39% of non-financial assets in 1995 to 56% in 2020.[18]

Why does this matter? It matters because it provides further background to the UK property sector and its long-term comparative prosperity on the themes explored in Chapter One and it is something that long-term BTR investors must consider. As well as the tendency to inequality, many economists argue that high land value and the high cost of the property sitting on this land is not only harmful to society, it is ultimately damaging to the economy. They believe that rising land prices can throttle beneficial economic activity. It does this by diverting capital away from innovation and creativity and into a property asset bubble. It prevents mobility of the workforce and reduces its relative wealth because of the high cost of renting or purchasing property and, as it becomes an increasingly important political issue, rising or permanently high land prices can fall prey to party political policy-making which can hinder the economic prosperity of the country. This is a contributing factor to the UK's productivity being one of the lowest amongst rich Western economies and has been at that level for many years. The English obsession with property ownership may come at the expense of meaningful, beneficial investment, including vital research into advanced medicine, ecological preservation and life sciences. These are areas where the UK is strong but for how much longer? Research in America suggests that "the housing cycle is the business cycle" and that housing slowdowns have preceded eight of the last ten recessions.[19] So, the price of land matters a great deal.

There is a condition called the "resource curse", which is the argument that certain countries endowed with abundant natural resources become plagued by poor economies and corrupt political systems. A similar thought process has recently been extended to something called the "tech curse" in relation to California. The American state, home to Silicon Valley, is incredibly wealthy and yet areas of downtown San Francisco have been compared to a run-down illegal drugs market. More people leave the Sunshine State each year than flock into it. Thousands of homeless are concentrated in one district. The city centre's problems are compounded by the non-return of office workers following the pandemic. A vacancy rate for office buildings of 30% is amongst the highest across North American cities.[20]

This line of thinking can be extended to what might be called the "regulation curse". This is in play in the UK today and is influencing the economic sustainability of residential projects. The regulations themselves are not the problem. Rather, it is the consequence of their introduction that is the curse.

A raft of new legislation has come our way since the Grenfell tragedy of 2017, which resulted in the deaths of 72 people, to transform our approach to fire safety. This legislation is clearly needed, as the Hackitt Review concluded. More is to follow as a result of the enactment of the Building Safety Act in mid-2022. Other regulations have been introduced as part of the UK's commitment to decarbonising all sectors of the UK economy to meet our net zero carbon target by 2050. Precise requirements of the new carbon commitment regulations are explored in greater detail in Chapter Five. Other guidance, such as the recently introduced Part O of the Building Regulations, has been brought forward as part of a requirement to embed climate change resilience within our built fabric and prevent overheating within buildings. This is timely, given that excess deaths in the UK amongst over-65s during the hot summer of 2022 approached 3000 in number.[21] The amount of technical data and analysis required to accompany even straightforward planning applications is all-encompassing. When so many regulations coalesce, it takes time for experts to agree amongst themselves the most practicable solution to the overlapping compliance requirements.

On top of this, the UK's health and safety legislation has become the most stringent on the planet. On a trip by a group of PRP staff to Berlin in September 2022, we visited a live mixed-use building site that would be shut down if it were in this country, such was the high number of basic safety breaches. This in the land of "Vorsprung Durch Technik", as the famous slogan from the Audi car advertisement campaign had it – we are more regulated than the Germans.

However, we have fallen down the league tables when it comes to the requirements for second staircases in tall residential buildings. Much of the Western world legislates for them in buildings as low as three storeys. The sudden imposition of new regulations, requiring enhanced safety measures, including second staircases, in early 2023 caused temporary paralysis in the UK residential sector. The consultation period alone, where the Government sought the views of the sector on the proposed changes, caused chaos, with major building programmes halting across England. Clients, contractors and architects scrambled to try to figure out acceptable solutions, including retrofitting additional staircases within buildings under construction and where fire safety and means of escape strategies had already been approved by the municipal authorities. That this happened almost six years after Grenfell, a tragedy made much worse by the lack of an alternative means of escape, points to the glacial nature of reform in the construction sector. The stark details that led to the tragedy are solidly captured in a book by Peter Apps entitled *Show Me the Bodies: How We Let Grenfell Happen*.

In the middle of 2023, further policy change came with the publication by the GLA of new housing design standards for London.[22] The timing of this new design direction could hardly have been worse. Whilst this is released as best practice guidance, there are a number of worrying changes around composition of floorplates, with increased requirements for homes to be dual aspect, fresh restrictions on the number of dwellings per circulation core, increased corridor widths, a big increase in minimum floor to floor dimensions to create higher ceilings in dwellings and some nonsensical restrictions on building heights. The authors of the document appear to have developed some built-in immunity to the effect that current regulations and standards is already having on the residential sector. Even without the regulation curse described above, the guidance, if it could be met on the drawing board, would render most large-scale housing schemes in the capital unviable and could prove the final death knell for social housing in London. The doughnut around London will reap the reward as new development migrates outwards beyond the Mayor's reach, unless the guidance is wholly ignored by its target audience.

One of the consequences of the new regulations is that certain residential developers have become so beleaguered by the time commitments, the technical oversight required and the financial uplift of compliance, that they are once again cutting corners in relation to perceived quality in order to protect profit margins. One would think with the lessons we have learned about fire safety and the on-going programme of remediation of dangerous cladding on multiple tall buildings that we would be more mindful of the consequences of being blind to quality in design and construction. The regulation curse dictates otherwise. It is cursing housebuilders, who are attempting to protect margins in the face of a high inflation environment, to cut back on *"ornament"* within their housing schemes – architectural features on buildings and general specifications within the landscape and public realm. It is affecting other developers and housing associations who, in an effort to achieve financial viability, are reducing the external appearance of their new homes and neighbourhoods back to what they were building in the 1980s. In both cases, fire safety is not necessarily being compromised, because it is being legislated for, and the consequences of non-compliance are serious. But the quality of expression of built form is not something that can be readily addressed through legislation.

The results may well be pitiful.

With certain noble exceptions, including the majority of BTR developers, the regulation curse is breaking the line of commitment to quality that should run like a golden thread from project initiation through to building handover. The gatekeepers of quality within some organisations are becoming *personae non gratae* because of a mistaken notion that they will add to overall costs by insisting on quality. Instead, penny-counters are running the rule over delivery. They have only a passing notion of what constitutes quality and have little grasp of where risk sits within their project. The law firm Trowers and Hamlins have conducted research into procurement of buildings in the UK, based upon the relative price evaluation models which dominate the industry. Such models dictate that lowest price becomes the only selection criterion for choosing a contractor, even though other measures such as social value and construction quality are supposedly in the mix. This creates a race to the bottom which is seemingly unavoidable and where quality in design and construction are seriously compromised.

> *In December 2020, Trowers and Hamlins launched a white paper on alternative price evaluation models, based on a series of workshops attended by clients, contractors and industry advisors, and setting out a range of*

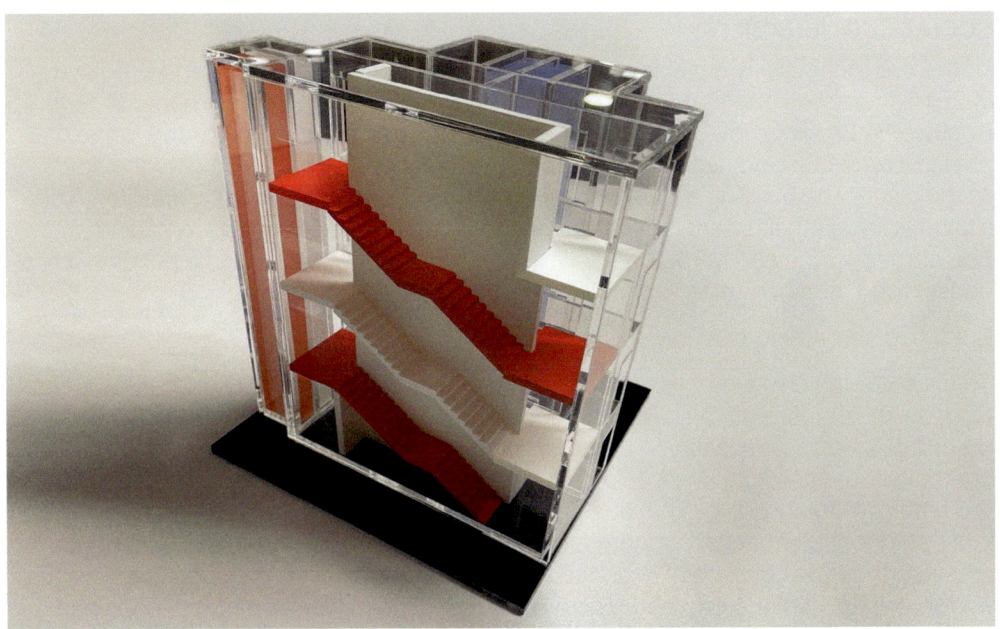

A model produced by PRP to suggest an efficient solution to the two-staircase conundrum.

> *alternatives to lowest-price assessment. Designed as a "conversation starter," it was hoped that contracting authorities and bidders would recognise the problems caused by relative-price evaluation models (where the lowest price bid is then used as the evaluation marker for all other bids, thereby creating the race to the bottom) and adopt one or some of the alternative models set out in the white paper. Put bluntly, we have achieved minimal traction: although everyone recognises the problem, no-one thinks it is theirs.[23]*

We may be over-regulated in this country, but this need not be a curse. There is a sound reason for compliance with most of the regulations we face. Some aspects of legislation will require a common-sense reaction to kick in, in due course. We like regulations, as they imply order. We think we like quality but we find it hard to measure. But we must find a way of preserving it, and it need not cost more. Designers enjoy challenges and can rise to do what is needed in a financially constrained environment. But housing developers need to be resilient. New neighbourhoods that should be with us for a hundred years or more need to be designed for future generations to be proud of, and that requires a re-commitment to quality, from inception to handover and beyond.

The regulation curse can be lifted with the foresight that is required for long-term investment. It can be stepped over by the BTR sector. Looking further, BTR can be a force for good in addressing the land value curse and in assuaging the iniquitous inequality fears of Thomas Piketty. After all, rent levels tend to increase as recessions loom and can be more resilient than rent from other types of property when economic times are tough. In certain market conditions of course, rent levels may continue to rise to the point of unsustainability and this can attract summary rent control policies, the bane of any rental corporation. Taking a broader perspective though, by diluting the property asset reservoir and providing society with a greater degree of choice in how to live, as well as reducing the proportion of individual income tied up in property, the economic benefits to society should be evident.

SOCIAL SUSTAINABILITY

Of the five multi-family developments that PRP visited in Manhattan and Brooklyn in 2016, there was one that stood out. This is a building of 326 apartments at 66 Rockwell in Brooklyn. But it was not the architecture of the building or the range of physical amenities available that provided this distinction. Instead, it was the spirit of the place. The building had the usual provision of amenities of a typical New York multi-family establishment – communal dining provision, external cinema with a pop-corn machine and barbeque facility, a coffee shop for residents, a poker room, a dance/yoga studio, rooftop lounge and bar.

But it had something else too.

This something else was the atmosphere or vibe of the place which largely emanated from a very charismatic building manager or development steward, to use a more meaningful term. This is a new breed of manager with the ability to attract new customers, to interact with people on a one-to-one basis and to gain the trust of all the renters in the building. This goes far beyond the role of a footman or a concierge in a traditional Manhattan condominium. This development steward is an empath and a confidante. Loneliness is banished. His ability to attract spans generations, for there were downsizers living here as well as first-time renters. The older ones had raised their families on the outskirts of the metropolis and had moved back, closer to Manhattan and closer to the next phase of their lives, where the cultural attractions of the city were now freshly within unfettered access. The Brooklyn Academy of Music is in the vicinity. The mix of ages brought an equilibrium and a sense of order which seemed to permeate the building. Nothing happens in the building without the development steward knowing about it. He also knows how you take your coffee in the mornings. This knowledge anchors and brings comfort to the place. It helps make the community.

Here is an example of the importance of high-quality curation and a warning of the pitfalls for ignoring the need for professional care and maintenance. Peter Cooper is an expert in town centre regeneration and is a former Director of Hammerson, a property company specialising in retail development. Peter speaks with detailed knowledge about the Brunswick Centre, a brutalist architectural icon in Bloomsbury, London, built by Camden Council in the early 1970s, as he lived in one of its apartments for a spell.

> *Longevity is crucial in community investments. If you don't invest in ongoing management, you're not truly investing in the community. In 1999, I was working for a company called Allied London, which managed Spinningfields, among other shopping schemes across the country. We bought the Brunswick Centre for £12.5 million because it was failing. Homeless people were living in the basement, and Camden Council had all the flats on a single lease. The centre had 560 flats, but the retail spaces had failed, and it was desolate. Only a Safeway supermarket and a closed laundromat were there, the latter being used by Smirnoff to film adverts. We made more money from filming projects like Clockwork Orange.*
>
> *The building was beautiful and got listed halfway through our ownership. We sold it in 2006 for £112 million after investing £60 million, creating a new community in the process. There were 100 flats sold off on long leases, and I bought one. If Camden Council had been more strategic, they could have made a significant profit. I bought my flat for £170,000 and sold it six years later for £650,000. That's the impact of regeneration.*

The Brunswick Centre, Bloomsbury, London.

The issue around poor management and curation arose when Allied London sold the building to an institutional owner who didn't know how to manage the apartments above a mixed-use building that was 30 years ahead of its time. It was a listed building and you had to deal with Camden Council. They then sold it to another company with similar issues, interested only in making a profit. As a result, the building will never reach its full potential because it's not being curated properly. There was no plan; the goal was to sell it and cash out. We made a net profit of £45 million. However, what we left behind was not a legacy but an impending problem. Please, don't make the same mistake.

In our post-pandemic environment, we have come to increasingly appreciate the need for access to and the exemplary curation of good amenities and open space and the value of socialising for one's mental health and wellbeing, This is especially understood by the core BTR demographic. If BTR private amenity spaces could be managed to be part open to the public, much like the grand Georgian squares of London which are secured at dusk, then the links to the community placemaking become so much stronger. Play facilities and nurseries and other amenities could be shared in a similar fashion.

BTR developers are not immune to economic cycles. They face the same construction cost inflation as other residential developers and similar costs in relation to long-term servicing and maintenance, but a long-term investment mindset can look beyond an economic crisis, even one as daunting as that facing the UK residential sector in 2024.

MIXED AND BALANCED COMMUNITIES

A strong aspect of good placemaking is a truly mixed community with a variety of housing tenures. Mixes of genders, ages, cultures, abilities and backgrounds in one location can not only create rich and vibrant areas that are sustainable and long-living but additionally, such diversity enhances social experience, opens the mind, forges stronger, more tolerant bonds and can lay the basis for more productively active neighbourhoods.

Conventional residential developers often struggle with mixing tenures, for fear of affordable elements of the tenure mix de-valuing the private sale elements of a development. Typically, in residential design, mixed tenure has been implemented at masterplan and urban level but has never really gained traction within a single building. Conceptually it should be the easiest of things to achieve. Student, Co-living, Build To Rent and Later Living (without care) are all institutionally backed, stewarded rental products with enhanced amenity spaces and a focus on user experience and lifestyle. These tenure types focus on engagement and a shared communal experience. They require similar facilities such as lounges, quiet spaces, wellbeing spaces, postal and delivery rooms, cleaning and maintenance and they look to provide their tenants with high quality, external living and amenity. All share a service charge, which is lower the more people there are living within the development.

Build To Rent and other stewarded housing providers have the internal skills and infrastructure, to bring thoughtful consideration of community creation and the long-term view to implement and manage it. Their organisations often cover all of the different tenure types. This is important, because we are building some very large residential buildings in our towns and cities. PRP's first mixed-use, mixed tenure social regeneration scheme in the late 1990s contained 348 dwellings across six sites on an estate in Islington. The tallest of the BTR towers at Coppermaker Square, in Stratford, contains 349 within a single building, all of the same tenure.

It is commonly accepted that mixed and diverse communities create better social environments. Therefore, investing and managing more inclusive models should bring truly socially sustainable communities to the benefit of society. However, as the BTR asset class matures, some operators are demanding clear ownership demarcation, creating mono-tenure rental blocks with complete control over servicing, plant and car park access for ease of future management. Perhaps this is one barrier that will remain in place, even for the enlightened exponents of Build To Rent. Peter Bishop sums up the challenge.

> *Successful places might be defined as popular places in which to live (as evidenced by a range of indicators from health to house prices) and as places that are likely to mature and improve over time. In this respect the concept of community is important. A resilient and well-balanced community is based on more than the sharing of a specific geographic community. It is based on a degree of shared interest. If one can create the conditions for powerful shared interest then a stable and successful community, one that continues to develop over time, might be created.*[24]

FINANCIAL SUSTAINABILITY

One of the attractions of BTR for investors is that as well as receiving a residual income stream from the rent on a property, that property is also subject to capital growth, assuming a healthy property market or a perpetual shortage of housing. It is not for everyone, as rental yields need to be accrued over long periods of time. The rental yield is one of the key metrics for measuring potential commercial success. It is calculated by taking the annual rental income of a property and dividing it by the purchase price of a property. So, a property which is on the market for £400,000, which could attract a monthly rent of £1,800, will give a rental yield of 5.4%.

BTR as an asset class attracts significant investor interest, with the amount of available funding in the sector often outstripping supply. Over the last ten years, investment into BTR has doubled from £2.25bn in 2012 to £4.25bn in 2022.[25] However, as a percentage of overall housing stock, BTR comprises just 1%, with circa 260,000 homes in the sector. The potential for growth therefore remains high. As at the final quarter of 2024 there are 100,300 BTR homes in operation, 60,000 under construction and 112,500 in the planning pipeline.[26] Since the uncertainty of the November 2022 mini-budget, BTR has outperformed other asset classes within the UK living sector (hotels and student accommodation), as well as in traditional core asset classes of office, retail and industrial, notwithstanding economic headwinds such as rising construction costs and rising interest rates.[27]

The sector is underpinned by strong demand for good quality homes, whilst more and more municipal authorities are activley encouraging BTR activity within their jurisdiction. Its appeal as an asset class has remained strong at a time of rising interest rates, which place greater affordability constraints on the options of home ownership described in Chapter One. These manifest themselves in greater demand for product and, subject to affordability constraints, rental growth.

It is recognised that the funding of individual projects necessarily requires bespoke solutions that are financially sustainable. This section of the book seeks to identify and highlight common themes that reflect the investment structures that have supported delivery of BTR in the UK.

As with all real estate asset classes, money is available with varying degrees of risk appetite. In the case of BTR, that broadly breaks down to planning and land assembly, construction and the operational phase. Investor appetite also varies by reference to the scale of the opportunity, such that it is sufficiently large to justify the investment of time and resource as well as geographical location, connectivity and local demographic. As the market has matured, so too has investment spread beyond London to regional hubs like Birmingham, Bristol, Manchester and Leeds.

As reflected on at the beginning of this chapter, crucial to the success of the longer-term investment will be the operational platform, brand, management proposition and provision of additional services to the building that meet the expectations of increasingly discerning tenants. Long-term investor appetite is for stable revenue streams and minimal voids where the breaking up of an asset for onward sale does not ordinarily form part of the exit strategy.

The need for BTR developers to compete to assemble land with their open market competitors has meant that margins can be lower in BTR than in traditional housebuilding. This reflects the fact that the viability of the BTR model is predicated on long-term revenue growth rather than short-term capital receipts. That said, those lower margins may reflect that BTR stock is often pre-sold to, or forward funded by, the long-term owner.

In the fledgling days of BTR, some real estate funds looked to deploy capital by way of development finance, in return for a guaranteed commitment from the tenant (of appropriate financial strength) to pay rent over the term of a lease. One such example, which was completed not long after publication of the Montague Report in

Aberfeldy Estate, Tower Hamlets, London.

2012[28], was the investment of capital from the M&G Secured Property Income Fund by way of development funding for a project named Aberfeldy New Village at East India Dock by the developer be:here, at this time a subsidiary of the property and construction group Willmott Dixon.[29] A 30-year lease was granted by M&G to Poplar HARCA, at the end of which ownership of the social and affordable units passed to Poplar HARCA, with the private rental units retained by M&G.

Typically, in such transactions, the developer receives a margin in recognition of its delivery of the scheme on time and on budget and the cost of funds is reduced to reflect the long-term commitment by the tenant to pay a pre-agreed indexed rent, in the above example, for a 30-year term. The tenant is therefore absorbing the void and bad debt risk but is also able to make a margin should it secure a net rental stream from occupiers that is higher than that payable under its head lease. One other risk which the tenant needs to consider is increased regulation and potentially capped rents, which need to be considered when agreeing the "guaranteed" rent at the outset.

As noted in Chapter One, the BTR model has not proved particularly popular with housing associations and the same might be said for some local authorities. Nevertheless, the covenant strength of such organisations means that this model remains an attractive proposition for long-term income funds seeking index-linked returns.

One recent example is Fifth Capital's re-development of Trocoll, House close to Barking & Dagenham train station in East London. The £35bn Railways Pension Scheme is investing £92m in the acquisition and development of the site to provide 198 BTR apartments, 35% of which are to be let at discounted rents.[30] The London Borough of Barking & Dagenham will take a 50-year lease on all units, following practical completion of the scheme, at a pre-agreed index-linked rent. It is typical in such models for ownership of the asset to pass to the tenant at the expiry of the term for £1, once the investor has received its anticipated return.

Various alternative models exist for funding BTR schemes, leveraging debt alongside an equity commitment, forward purchase and forward funding. A forward purchase takes away any speculative element of development risk (and in practice speculative development of BTR is not common), providing the developer with the comfort of an "exit" on practical completion of the scheme. For the developer, a forward purchase and a forward funding model offer the advantage of a pre-agreed commitment to buy the asset, whereas there is no such exit directly associated with the development or investment debt model.

In the BTR debt market, one of the largest debt deals has been Quintain's £800m corporate development facility for Wembley Park, which was first announced in 2016 following the acquisition of Quintain by Lone Star.[31] The loan was provided by three global lenders: Wells Fargo, AIG and the Canada Pension Plan Investment Board. As well as refinancing Wells Fargo's original loan for the acquisition of Quintain, it has enabled Quintain to continue delivery of the Wembley Park Masterplan. Over the last seven years, that project has delivered over 3,500 new homes of differing tenures, a permanent base for its Community Centre, as well as Boxpark and the Troubadour

Wembley Park, London.

Theatre. In 2022, construction work began on the North East Lands, where Quintain has secured a loan of £277m from JP Morgan for two BTR buildings. Most recently, Quintain committed to achieve Net Carbon Zero by 2040.[32]

Continuing the debt theme, but this time outside of London, Moda Living secured £188m of development finance early in 2023 for its Great Charles Street scheme in Birmingham. The five-year facility from Precede Capital will enable delivery of 722 apartments alongside extensive amenity provision. Equity for the scheme was provided by Apache Capital, Harrison Street and NFU Mutual.[33]

Many BTR projects adopt a forward funding model by which an investor agrees to purchase a site and provide development finance up to an agreed cap. The forward funding vehicle may itself access debt in order to do so. Once the site has been sold to the forward funder, funding is drawn down by the developer against certified expenditure. Over and above the funding cap, the developer will meet any cost overrun, but should it deliver the project for less than the cost cap, this will generate the developer's profit margin. The appetite of the investor for risk will usually determine the point at which it is willing to commit to the scheme and the point at which the developer is entitled to its profit margin and exit.

By way of example, in the forward funding model, pension funds may be reluctant to assume planning and land assembly risk, leaving that to those seeking a higher risk/reward profile. Once planning is secured and construction prices are (so far as possible) fixed, an institutional forward funder can be brought on board. The funder secures a full suite of warranties from the main contractor and professional team and a condition precedent to practical completion will be the handover of a significant pack of completion, health and safety, and future management documentation.

Whilst the UK BTR market remains relatively immature in comparison to other commercial asset classes, the sector has yet to see strong demand from forward funders for achievement of an agreed level of net rental stream (known as rent stabilisation) to be a pre-condition to developers accessing their profit margins. There are nevertheless some developers who will retain an equity stake in, or management responsibility for, the operational asset, therefore spreading their risk over a longer timeframe, giving an added incentive, if one were needed, to timely delivery of the development phase. Of course, where developers are willing to defer some profit margin (or occasionally for that matter an element of the initial land receipt) beyond practical completion to a position of rent stabilisation, there should be a commensurate increase in the margin sought.

Investors seeking to acquire Buid To Rent assets are increasingly focusing on sustainability and are asking questions of contractors, developers and BTR operators about their carbon strategies. Green financing is increasingly diversifying flows from banking, insurance and investment bodies to appropriate development vehicles or organisations which have proven environmental aspirations and capabilities. Going forward, liquidity risks are likely to be attributable to operators who lack provable environmental credentials or who are greenwashing their commercial activities.

WELLBEING

One of the effects of the global pandemic was to unleash a whole world of "wellness" on everyone. From the endless debates on the benefits of working from home to in-office mental health and wellbeing tutorials, the lived environment turned on its axis. Employers now feel obligated to address their employees' physical, mental, financial and social health in addition to merely providing employment. But what of the residential sector? The increasing demand for rental accommodation means that the BTR sector can significantly impact the wellbeing of users. We have touched on the importance of well-designed homes within a well-serviced, well-located environment and it cannot be overstated.

> *The home is where dreams are formed, nurtured and developed but which, in the wrong environment, can be snuffed out. The precise location of the home, its immediate environment and connection to a viable and thriving community, its access to infrastructure, transport, green space amenity and beauty will impact on how much of a nurturing environment it can provide. Location is the key.*[34]

On the flip side, the downside to a lack of decent housing provision is debilitating to society. Few commentators have experienced the failure of the housing system in the UK to the extent lived by Hashi Mohamed, the former refugee who we came across earlier in this chapter and who, against considerable odds, became a planning barrister.

> *One of the things about poor housing is that it amplifies – and is itself amplified by any other problem you might be facing. Living in inadequate housing is stressful in a way that puts pressure on your physical and emotional health and also on your relationships.*

Hashi expands on the potential for widespread harm.

> *Just as wealthier families are able to pass down housing security to their children, the kind of trauma that comes with precarious housing arrangements can act almost like some kind of inter-generational undiagnosed post-traumatic stress disorder.*[35]

The World Health Organisation defines health as a state of complete physical, mental and social wellbeing. Mental health goes beyond just the absence of mental illness: it encompasses positive issues such as peace of mind, contentment, confidence and social connection. Social wellbeing is affected by the quality of an individual's relationships and the way in which they function within their community.[36]

Design features, such as good daylight levels, ventilation or open space provision, can positively impact people's mental wellbeing and physical health. It is essential to consider these aspects from the early design stages. Incorporating such specific features not only positively impacts wellbeing but also allows for reducing energy consumption and carbon emissions. As we spend around 65% of our time at home, the internal environment can greatly impact our health and wellbeing. The design of the residential areas is critical, as it provides opportunities for social interaction, exercise, and access to nature and inner amenities. Access to external amenity, with provision for food-growing, promotes biodiversity and eases the carbon footprint of sourcing food. All of these features impact on how much residents will enjoy living in their community, and therefore benefit their own health and wellbeing.

The clubhouse at Canada Gardens, Wembley Park, London.

BTR can also help address loneliness, particularly in the older generation (see next section). The way in which Council Tax, a banded tax on the size of a property levied by all local authorities, has been levied has not changed in 30 years and the most expensive homes are taxed relatively lightly and, more often than not, are chronically under-occupied. At the other end of the scale, the number of people living alone in the UK has increased by 4.0% over the last ten years and constitutes almost a quarter of households in London.[37] The communal experience of a modern BTR environment can act as a tonic to solitary existence. The progressive BTR operators have realised that a building's design will affect the behaviours and lifestyles of their residents in many ways and if such behaviour is communally infectious then everyone benefits.

THE SUSTAINABILITY OF LATER LIVING

The later living sector is another area of massive potential for BTR. More providers are showing interest and there are new entrants to the market, not least because there is a substantial lack of suitable private accommodation for older people in both sale and rental tenures.

Ninety-three per cent of people in the UK aged 55 and over live in mainstream housing as owner occupiers or tenants.[38] These homes are often situated in a community that they have lived within for most of their adult lives, in dwellings which are often unsuitable to their specific needs or degree of disability. Despite this, research into Development Plans in England, Scotland and Wales found that only 7% of local authorities have allocated housing sites for the older generation within their adopted planning strategies.[39]

Only 0.6% of over 65s in the UK live within a retirement community compared to between 5 to 6% in the United States, New Zealand and Australia.[40] However, things may be changing. The developers, investors and operators who are delivering private retirement living are beginning to respond to market challenges providing homes with flexible tenure options allowing for sale or rent within their care villages and retirement communities. AEW, a global property investment manager, envisages a shift away from the prevalent UK purchase model where people buy a retirement apartment and instead move towards renting one in a retirement village. This releases capital that they can pass on to the next generation or use to fund their rent.[41]

The state, in the past, has shouldered much of the care provision for older people within the social sector. Today, however, the provision of social rent accommodation for the older population in the country faces serious challenges. Over a quarter of tenants within the social housing sector are aged 65 or over and whilst many receive some sort of care support, only one in seven of this group live in specialist, integrated housing with care.[42] Even though the affordable providers have led the later living market for many years, there has been a marked reduction in the quantum of dwellings being developed since the boom years of the 1980s and 1990s with London in particular suffering from this decline in provision. The burden of support for the elderly falls to adult social care at local authority or county level and continues to be woefully underfunded.

In the past, housing associations, as Registered Providers, responded to the need for housing with care solutions for their older residents by working alongside housing and social care departments as joint commissioners. However, government cutbacks have significantly reduced the amount of new housing with care accommodation being provided by Registered Providers, as the revenue funding for those living within these developments has come under intense pressure.

In the ten years since 2010, the funding of local authorities fell by half in real terms and whilst the loss of revenue has been partially offset by increases in Council Tax and a social-care levy, spending on care has dropped from £514 per adult to £478 per adult in these ten years.[43] This partly explains why it is so difficult to get state-sponsored care in the UK. Someone seeking social care needs to be judged by their local authority to have high needs whilst having assets less than £23,250.[44]

There is also a lack of clarity about the role that Registered Providers can play in addressing growing needs as the volume of a ticking demographic timebomb looms louder. There has been scant recognition of the role that Registered Providers or potentially BTR operators could provide to help address a growing crisis.

> *The benefit of effective housing with care offers are many. For Registered Providers, supporting their tenants to maintain tenancies for longer is not only the right thing to do, but it also makes good business sense. For government, there is the potential to reduce the costs to the NHS attributed to poor housing among older adults – currently estimated to be over half a billion per year, or around 8% of the total social care bill for older people.[45]*

PRP's later living development at Pilgrim Gardens, Evington, Leicester.

Added to this is the depressing statistic that the National Health Service, under as much financial stress as it has ever been, has one in ten of its hospital beds occupied by people who are well enough to be discharged, restrained unnecessarily by a Kafkaesque administration system.[46]

Whilst the evidence around the savings that the housing with care models bring to the NHS and Adult Social Care budgets is compelling, the fundamental issue remains that these savings are retained at social care level, which has incentivised local authorities to develop and disincentivised housing associations.

The particular privations of the Covid-19 pandemic within institutional care homes has brought Government attention to the sector and helped to underscore the importance of housing providers in the successful delivery of good social and sustainable care outcomes. This is evidenced by the 2021 social care white paper, People at the Heart of Care. It is estimated that 50,000 homes per year need to be built to tackle the UK's health and social care crisis. The annual delivery is woefully short of this number and is currently around 7,000. Projected forward, the UK will need to allocate up to a quarter of all new homes to later living in order to cater for an estimated 17 million people who will be aged over 65 by 2030. These figures come from the *Mayhew Review: Future-proofing Retirement Living*, which advises that targeting this level of growth would give lengthened periods of independence to older people living in their own homes but would also encourage downsizing into more suitable forms of housing, thus freeing up family homes for younger generations.[47] The Mayhew Review takes the correlation between housing and care one step further, stating that "fundamental change is needed in the way we provide care to older people and in their housing options".

Despite such sound recommendations to stimulate this part of the market, the policy focus remains on the first-time buyer and a continued focus on home ownership as explained in Chapter One. It wilfully ignores the fact that older people, particularly those in their 80s, are the one demographic who would readily consider coming off the property ladder to rent in their later years if they had the incentive. One such incentive would be the retention of stamp duty costs by these last time buyers within their family to supplement their pension or to help their children financially. Incentives to downsize could also happen through changes to the planning system or through assistance from Government, for instance by changing the way Council Tax is levied, as it currently offers no incentive for older people to move out of their often large homes.[48]

But perhaps the Government is stirring after all. In early 2023, it announced details of an Older People's Task Force, which is to operate for 12 months to arrive at a set of recommendations which will drive an increase in the volume and range of housing options for older people.

The private market in the UK is fairly regional and is dominated by a few key players, such as Signature Senior Lifestyle, a developer and manager of high-end care homes and McCarthy Stone, a developer of retirement communities with both rental and sales product. This organisation was acquired by Lone Star Funds in 2021, the same funder who acquired Quintain in 2016, leading to the explosion of BTR provision at Wembley Park.

Some private operators within the later living sector share similar incentives and ethos to the BTR providers and have been refining their products to respond accordingly to their target markets in terms of the provision of amenities and services provided, both aimed at improved health and wellbeing outcomes for their customers. Most providers are now offering private rental accommodation either as a BTR option or pepper-potted within a for-sale development and sometimes on a "try before you buy", basis. The private rental market for older people is seeing rapid growth, with the number of rental properties forecast to increase by 114% in the next five years.[49]

New players are entering the sector, such as Retirement Villages Group (RVG), with a sales and care support offer which resembles BTR in many respects. RVG typically develop large projects within town centre locations, which would equally suit BTR operators. Their approach is one which is supported by the Mayhew Review, which recommends that *"integrated retirement living should include more developments in town centres as part of the levelling up process and local regeneration programmes".*[50] However, it must be remembered that most providers are aiming at the higher end of the market, where they can charge the level of fees that are needed to fund such development in the first place, another reason for the lack of intermediate product in the sector.

One of the few bespoke BTR providers is Birchgrove, a developer of assisted communities operating around the fringes of London. It is backed by Bridges Fund Management, a specialist fund manager focused exclusively on sustainable investment goals such as health and wellbeing, education & skills, sustainable living and what they refer to in their marketing material as "underserved markets". They provide a model of what is possible and are doing their bit to expand choice within the sector. The gap in the market for BTR operators here is considerable, although it may need some further government support to help fill the gap and consider the issue more strategically. Directions for government may accrue from the Older People's Task Force.

PRP's scheme for RVG at West Byfleet, Surrey.

Not only are demographics changing. Family units, as well as living longer, are living differently from how we have lived in the past. More people are living alone following the death of a loved one, or because of separation or divorce, or simply out of choice. Whilst households containing multiple families represent the smallest share of all households (1%), they are the fastest growing type of household over the last two decades, having increased by two-thirds to an estimated 278,800 households in 2020.[51] The design of new housing and communities needs to adapt to respond to these new family structures and the emerging social challenges associated with everyone living longer.

As an architectural practice, PRP has been at the forefront in promoting multi-generational living and inter-generational masterplanning. Here, too, exists a unique BTR or single-family opportunity for enhancing communal harmony, banishing loneliness, and improving health and wellbeing amongst generations which are growing older. Six multi-generational homes have been delivered on the first Olympic legacy housing development site at Chobham Manor, Stratford in East London. They have proved to be the most popular dwelling typology, within a family-oriented masterplan comprising 850 homes. These typologies, which have been further evolved into apartment variants, allow generations of a family to stay together within interlinked compartments of an extended family home. The typology was originally designed as an affordable typology but contemporary levels of grant funding make such large homes difficult to deliver for housing associations. The "multi-gen" houses on the Queen Elizabeth Olympic Park have all been sold privately. As masterplanners, it became clear that many more of these unique homes could have been placed within the masterplan, such was the level of interest from purchasers. We had discovered a hole in the market for this type of accommodation, where elderly relatives can remain part of the family and are not shipped off to a home, where they can enjoy retained independence with family support close at hand. We had touched on the chronic lack of choice within the wider later living sector, much as BTR has done within the private rented sector.

Our growing older population, rather than being a burden on public services, can play an important role in enhancing the communities they live within. With a wealth of life experience and time on their hands, they are becoming the community volunteers, part-time professionals, informal carers for grandchildren, receivers of deliveries for their working neighbours and shoppers for themselves and others on the high streets, who can use all the help they can get in the current retail environment. They contribute to the local commercial and leisure economy, part of a longevity dividend that is barely recognised but which can offer so much to a community, including BTR. As we have discovered, choice of home and lifestyle needs to be enhanced. Funding is certainly required to address the needs of those without the income to support themselves and more design initiatives are needed which encourage inter-generational support for the benefit of society.

The multi-gen house, Chobham Manor, Stratford, London.

CHAPTER FIVE
The Climate Challenges Facing the Sector

CLIMATE CONTEXT

The need to embrace regenerative design practices, ensuring that the built environment has a net positive impact on natural systems, has never been more pressing, given the immediate threats that climate change and global warming represent. It is now widely accepted that in order to avert the worst impacts of climate change and preserve a liveable planet for humanity, global temperature increase needs to be limited to 1.5°C above pre-industrial levels. Currently, the Earth is already about 1.1°C warmer than it was in the late 1800s, with emissions continuing to rise. To keep global warming to no more than 1.5°C, emissions need to be reduced by 45% by 2030 and reach net zero by 2050.[1]

Recent changes in legislation are already having a significant impact on the residential sector, as referenced in Chapter Four. Much of this regulatory change for the London context is set out below, but it should be noted that what starts in London is usually subsequently fed out to the regions. The threat to how we live our lives and how the ecology of the earth is being irreparably damaged is finally being recognised. The international community has been taking various steps to attempt to address the climate emergency, the most notable being the Paris Agreement of 2015, an international treaty on climate change signed by 179 countries, including the UK. The international indicatives to which the UK is responding are also set out below.

Recent studies from the United Nations Energy Programme indicate that buildings use about 40% of global energy, 25% of global water, 40% of global resources and emit up to one-third of greenhouse gas (GHG) emissions.[2] Specifically, it is known that the building sector, including both residential and commercial premises, accounted for 30% of global delivered energy consumption in 2020.[3] Hence, the significant impact that the built environment, including the housing sector, might have in reducing emissions and helping protect against climate change.

In the UK, a study in 2017 by CBRE indicated that the residential sector is responsible for 29% of the nation's annual energy consumption.[4] This is a significant enough statistic, but a real cause for concern is that the sector has failed to achieve reductions in its emissions compared to other areas.

FACING PAGE The Mercian, Birmingham.

A significant part of energy demands in residential buildings comes from the need for space and water heating. Currently, 90% of homes in England use fossil fuels, with 85% connected to the gas grid.[5]

The UK Department for Business, Energy and Industrial Strategy provided statistics on environmental performance, which showed that the residential sector is responsible for 13% of GHG emissions in the UK, with over 27% of the UK's carbon dioxide (CO_2) emissions coming from the residential sector.[6]

Furthermore, according to the Committee on Climate Change in the BTR breakthrough year of 2016, 40% of UK emissions came from households.[7] The direct emissions from fossil fuels, primarily gas for heating, make up almost half of buildings emissions. The other half is electricity-related, from lighting and the use of appliances, as well as some electric heating which has seen gradually increasing usage in the private for sale sector. However, this split is changing quickly due to the recent updates to the UK Building Regulations and Government direction to move away from the use of fossil fuels.

LONDON

London has become the main attraction to investors in BTR, given its size and prospect. Its mid-year population in 2021 was estimated to be 8.8 million, making it the third most populous city in the European continent, and this is projected to reach 10 million by 2038, according to the GLA City Intelligence Unit.[8] The 2022 surge in immigration as a result of the war in Ukraine, the influx of citizens exiting Hong Kong for good, together with the Government's current immigration policy to attract key skills is largely centred on London. Faced with this, the capital has ambitious plans to combat climate change and protect its growing population.

According to studies shared by the GLA, in 2020, London's CO2e emissions were 28.1 million tonnes, a reduction from 31.5 in 2019. This represents a 38% reduction from 1990 levels and a 45% reduction since peak emissions in 2000. London's per capita emissions have reduced by 53 per cent, from 6.7 tCO2e in 1990 to 3.1 tCO2e in 2019.[9]

The Mayor of London published the 'London Environment Strategy and Zero Carbon London: A 1.5°C Compatible Plan', which presented a range of energy system scenarios for London consistent with a 2050 net zero target.[10] In the Plan, the Mayor committed to bringing forward London's net zero targets from 2050 to 2030. At the time of publication of the 1.5°C Plan, the UK's ambition was to achieve an 80% reduction in emissions by 2050. Since then, both national and local climate ambition has increased. At a national level, the UK has committed to reaching a 68% reduction in emissions by 2030 and net zero emissions by 2050.

Moving forward, a net zero target for 2030 represents a substantial increase in ambition relative to the target remaining as 2050. This also means that action at a London level would be required in a timeframe beyond that supported or funded at the national level. With this high ambition in place, efforts will be required in all key sectors, including transport, finance, energy and buildings. BTR investors will need to consider a new financial variable for schemes delivered in London compared with those outside the capital.

The London Plan provides the spatial development strategy for London and deals with matters of strategic importance to Greater London. The three principles for the Greater London area, which form the focus of the London Plan, are to promote economic development and wealth creation, social development, and environmental improvement. In this context, several policies within the London Plan provide an environmental framework for the development of the capital.

The Plan mentions a number of requirements relating to minimising greenhouse gas emissions.[11] It states that major development should be net zero carbon, which requires reducing gas emissions in operation and minimising both annual and peak energy demand. This should be achieved in accordance with the energy hierarchy, which evolves four principles to be followed in order of priority; be lean, clean, green and seen. 'Be lean' relates to decreasing the amount of energy being used and managing demand during operation. 'Be clean' requires the use of local energy resources (such as secondary heat) and an efficient and clean supply of energy. 'Be green' calls for maximising opportunities for renewable energy by producing, storing and using energy on-site. The last principle, 'be seen', relates to post-occupancy monitoring, verifying and reporting on the energy performance of the development.

It also states that major development proposals should include a detailed energy strategy to demonstrate how the zero-carbon target will be met within the framework of the energy hierarchy.

The Plan requires a minimum on-site reduction of at least 35% beyond Building Regulations for major developments. Residential development should achieve 10%, and non-residential development should achieve 15% through energy efficiency measures. Where it is clearly demonstrated that the zero-carbon target cannot be fully achieved on-site, any shortfall should be provided, in agreement with the specific London borough, either through a cash-in-lieu contribution to the borough's carbon offset fund or off-site, provided that an alternative proposal is identified and delivery is certain.

In addition, it is stated that major development proposals should calculate and minimise carbon emissions from any other part of the development, including plant or equipment, that Building Regulations, i.e. unregulated emissions, do not cover.

Lastly, the policy mentions that development proposals referable to the Mayor should calculate whole lifecycle carbon emissions through a nationally recognised Whole Life-Cycle Carbon Assessment and demonstrate actions taken to reduce life-cycle carbon emissions.

The GLA have led the line over the years in promoting the incorporation of high levels of cycle parking in new residential buildings. The Plan encourages active travel, with convenient and inclusive pedestrian and cycling routes, including cycle parking and legible entrances to buildings, aligned with the users' desired lines and movement patterns in the area.

THE BUILD TO RENT SECTOR

Despite the politicisation of home ownership covered elsewhere in this book, a significant part of the population is renting instead of owning their home. Out of approximately 23.5 million households, over one-third are either private or social renters.[12] Therefore, the private rental market is increasingly important in meeting the UK's housing needs. Today, over four million households privately rent their homes, which is double the number of households who were renting at the turn of the century.

For London, this figure will soon reach 40% of its households renting, meaning that the BTR sector will play an increasing role in housing delivery and design. But more than that, and as we saw in the last two chapters, the sector represents a potentially important role in the wellbeing of residents in London and across the country and has a crucial and potentially leading role in the environmental impact of the building industry.[13]

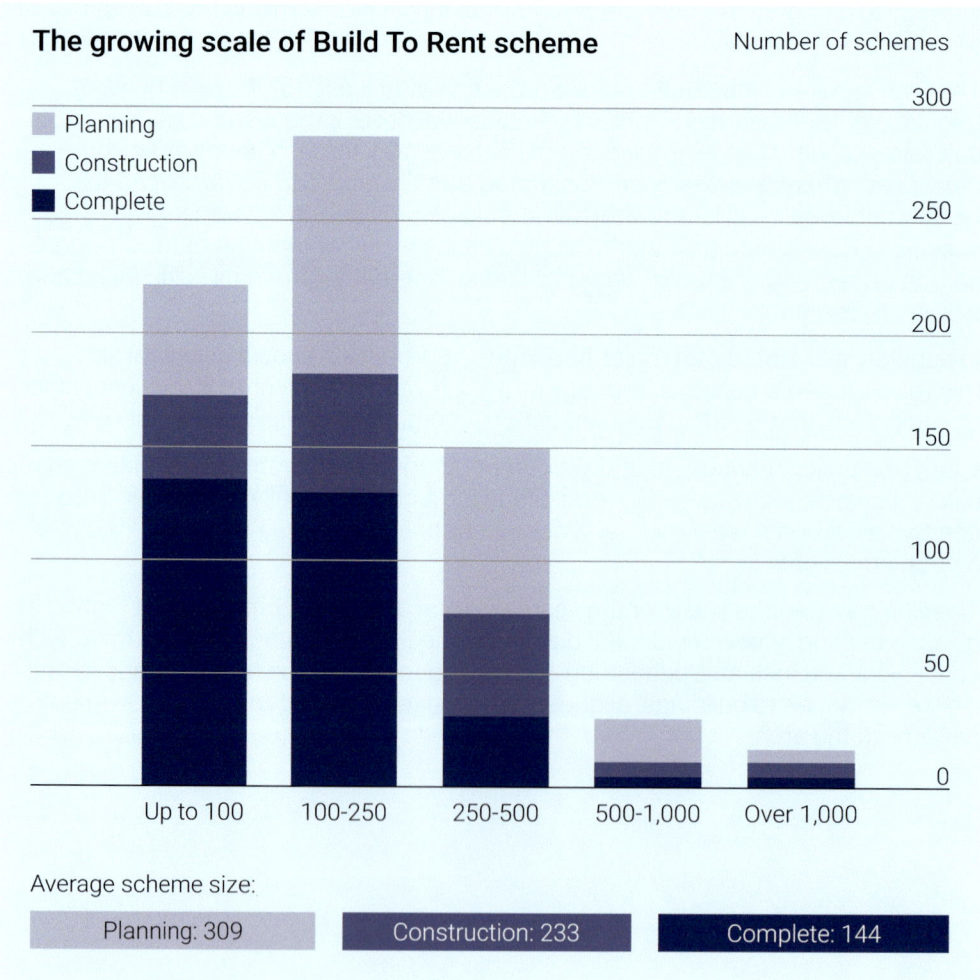

SOURCE Savills Research, British Property Federation, Molior

In light of the UK's rapidly growing demand for rental accommodation, shifting to more sustainable development for the BTR sector will require a proportionate increase in investment. Through the principles that have been set out in this chapter, there is a real opportunity for the sector to contribute to the UK's efforts in tackling climate change as the country aims to meet the net zero targets and can help deliver some of the Government's key environmental policies. BTR developers could also do more to invest in existing stock and engage in more adaptive re-use of redundant buildings. An estimated £41 billion worth of property is sitting void in London – more volume than exists within the entire city of Liverpool. Some of this capacity should interest progressive, sustainability-focused rental funders in meeting environmental, social and corporate governance commitments. A bespoke multi-family developer operational in the North-West, Placefirst, have shown that this is possible, with a 300 homes refurbishment project in Welsh Streets, Liverpool, where existing homes have been remodelled and made larger.[14]

SUSTAINABILITY – BACKGROUND & INITIATIVES

The Kyoto Protocol was an international treaty which extended the 1992 United Nations Framework Convention on Climate Change. This convention, which was signed in 1997, commits state parties to reduce greenhouse gas emissions, based on the scientific consensus that global warming is occurring and that human-made CO_2 emissions are driving it. In terms of greenhouse gas emissions targets, the EU and its Member States, Iceland, the UK and Norway, collectively made a first commitment period under the Kyoto Protocol to reduce greenhouse gas emissions across the EU by 8% on 1990 levels by 2012. As part of this, the UK also committed to reducing total greenhouse gas emissions by 12.5%. For the second commitment period of the Kyoto Protocol (2013–2020), the target was set to reduce emissions by 20%. This is being fulfilled jointly in accordance with Article 4 of the Kyoto Protocol.[15]

Within the residential sector, several measures and programmes have been implemented in recent years as part of the UK Government's Climate Change Agenda to improve energy efficiency within homes. These have included regulatory guidance and financial incentives such as the Green Deal and the Code for Sustainable Homes, aiming to enforce improvements and decrease the residential sector's contribution to the UK's overall gas emissions.

When it comes to residential buildings, the UK is also following energy and carbon targets set by other initiatives such as the Royal Institute of British Architects (RIBA) 2030 Climate Challenge, London Energy Transformation Initiative (LETI), and a network of built environment professionals working together to put London on the path to a zero-carbon future. RIBA developed the RIBA 2030 Climate Challenge to support architects and the wider construction industry in meeting net zero carbon. The RIBA 2030 Climate Challenge Version 2 (2021) has refined and updated targets that encompass development in the knowledge base of performance trajectories. The embodied carbon targets are aligned with LETI and the Whole Life Carbon Network, among others, to follow the latest jointly authored guidance. It is already becoming an industry norm that the energy use intensity should progressively regress to <35 kWh/m2/yr and Embodied Carbon: <625 kgCO2e/m2.[16]

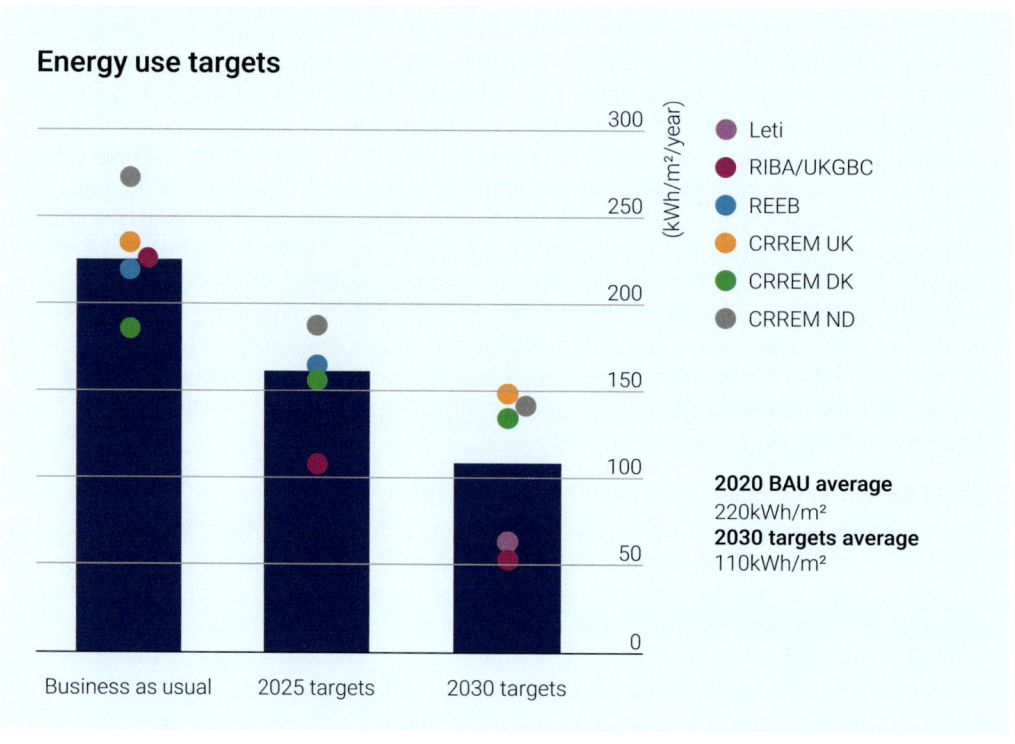

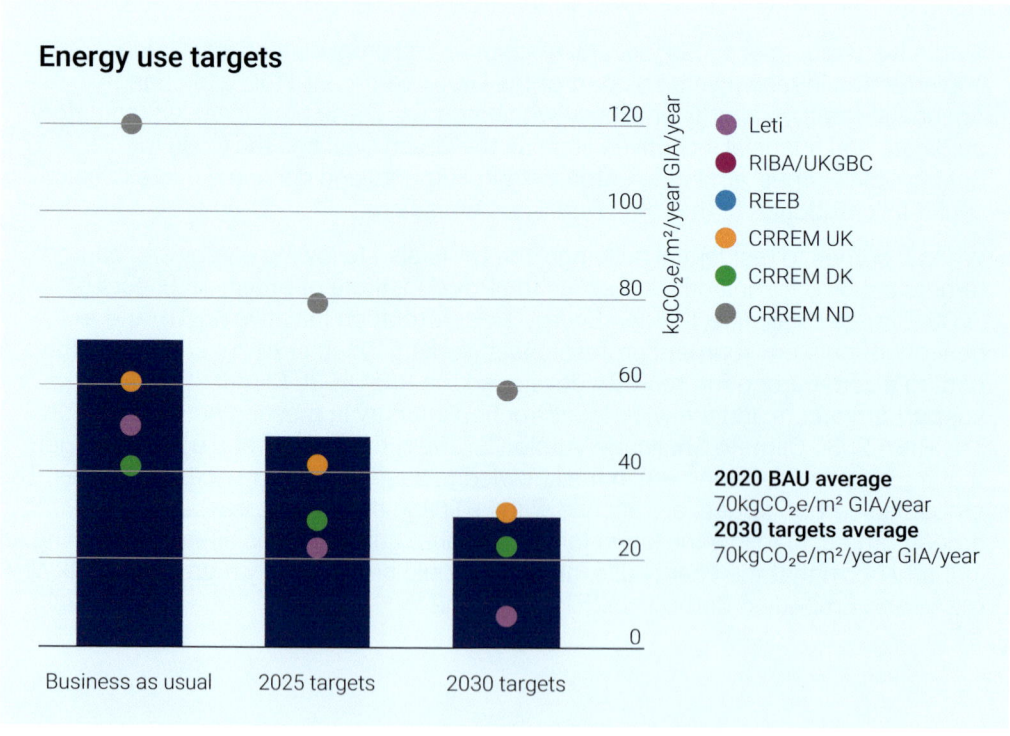

SOURCE GLA. (2022) London Plan Guidance - Whole Life-Cycle Carbon Assessments. London: Greater London Authority. Available at: https://www.london.gov.uk/sites/default/files/lpg_-_wlca_guidance.pdf[17]

NET ZERO

The United Nations has defined net zero as *"cutting greenhouse gas emissions to as close to zero as possible, with any remaining emissions re-absorbed from the atmosphere, by oceans and forests, for instance."* [18]

The built environment is a critical sector to tackle if we aim to reach the climate mitigation targets set out in the Paris Agreement as it represents close to 40% of global energy-related carbon emissions. Such high emissions offer real hope of easy wins in the climate challenge using proven and commercially available technologies. Existing as well as future residential projects, including those within the BTR sector, must do more to meet this challenge and help the transition to zero-carbon. A net zero building can be understood to be a building that has no net carbon emissions during its construction and operation, and if leftovers of energy demand were to be needed, these should be balanced by renewable energy or carbon offsets.

WSP, an engineering consultancy, has defined the following three main categories that evaluate the operational and embodied carbon emissions of a building: net zero in operation, net zero in construction and net zero in whole-life carbon.[19]

To achieve net zero in operation, which means that no operational carbon emissions are produced, a building must be highly energy efficient and powered by renewable energy either on or off-site, with any remaining annual carbon emissions offset.

Net zero in construction requires that the carbon emissions associated with the building's production and construction stages, up to practical completion, are offset through the net export of onsite renewable energy or by offsetting the emissions.

However, a truly net zero building must achieve net zero in whole-life carbon. This means that the building operation and embodied carbon, including its disposal, are zero or negative over its lifetime.

Net zero aims to improve all buildings regardless of their use class. Even though it has been aimed more at new buildings, the opportunities to adapt existing structures to be net zero would represent a more significant impact on the current carbon emission reductions produced by the built environment.

BTR operators should be aware that the UK Government will be introducing the Future Homes Standard in England from 2025, the chief aim of which is to considerably reduce carbon emissions from buildings. Unfortunately, the precise metrics of the new standard have yet to be agreed.

PASSIVE DESIGN FEATURES

Following passive design principles is the primary step towards achieving a net zero-energy building. A good definition of passive design is *"the fundamental principle of utilising the external climate to maintain a comfortable environment with minimal or no active lighting, heating, cooling or ventilation systems."* [20] As the built environment is estimtated to consume 40% of global energy, 40% of global resources, and emit up to one-third of greenhouse gas (GHG) emissions, it has become crucial to incorporate passive design strategies that can help to reduce the energy consumption that our residential buildings generate.

Clifton Green, part of PRP's Passivhaus scheme in Salford, Manchester, for Salford City Council.

The concept of net zero-energy buildings has emerged in the last three decades as an aim to reduce energy use and only make use of renewable energy systems to meet the remaining energy needs. Passive design strategies have also started to be innate characteristics to the form and design of a building to ensure the users' thermal comfort alongside minimising energy use. These climate-specific approaches based on sun, wind, light and micro-climatic considerations can be efficiently employed to design energy-efficient buildings. The consideration of these characteristics should start from the very beginning of the design of the building form and its façade, as this is the intersection between the building and the external climatic conditions, where it can harness solar heating and daylight passively, fresh air for breathing and remove heat gains in addition to restricting heat losses and optimising internal thermal comfort.[21]

To take this advantage of nature and site surroundings, it is crucial to study and understand the climatic benefits that can be harnessed and which will allow appropriate decision-making to translate the passive design into project-specific factors relating to: building form, orientation, glazing ratio, choice of materials, natural ventilation, and the decision on the level of adaptive thermal comfort that could be provided to the users with an aim to achieve comfort by using as little active cooling and heating as possible. By implementing this approach, an important reduction in the cooling requirement during the summer and heating for the winter can also be achieved. Regarding a building's façade, preliminary design considerations on walls, windows, shading features and the roof can help moderate the climate's effect.

Maximising the performance of the components and materials that make up the building fabric also plays a key role in reducing energy use in buildings. The building fabric constitutes elements such as walls, floors, roofs, doors and windows that work as a way of physical access to daylight, provide natural or mechanical ventilation and supply services, amongst other things. Further consideration of the building's envelope can also include the use of thermal mass and appropriate colour specification of external finishes to minimise the number of hours when heating or cooling is required to maintain comfort for current and future climate scenarios. We have probably arrived at the point where designers need to carefully consider the selection of external materials in new buildings in order to communally ameliorate a built-up area's urban heat island, an urban area that is significantly warmer than its surrounding rural areas due to human activities, by specifying lighter colours in façades, solar reflective roofscapes and by incorporating specific landscape elements which help moderate higher temperatures.

TACKLING OVERHEATING IN BUILDINGS

2022 has been confirmed as the UK's hottest on record. The average annual temperature passed the 10 degrees centigrade mark for the first time, assisted by a record temperature in July of that year which exceeded 40 degrees for the first time, smashing the previous high of 38.7C. Government experts advise that such heat extremes are now expected every three to four years and are a direct result of greenhouse gases emitted by human activity. Without this activity, such a warm year would be expected only once every five centuries. The 10.03C temperature reading beat the previous record of 9.88C set in 2014, and is 0.89C above the average of the last three decades.[22]

In developed nations, the majority of fatal heat exposures occur indoors and the average number of deaths caused by heat in the UK is expected to more than triple to 7,000 a year by the 2050s. Older people are particularly vulnerable and suffer increased fatalities from cardiac and respiratory disease during heatwaves.[23]

In the UK's current temperate climate, where air-conditioning in dwellings isn't standard, the occurrence of summertime overheating is increasing. A recent study by Loughborough University indicated that in the hot summer of 2018, 15% (3.6 million) of dwellings in England had overheated living rooms and 19% (4.5 million) overheated bedrooms.[24] With the average global temperature increasing, the frequency of this risk in buildings is bound to surge, especially in buildings not robustly designed to mitigate the overheating risk. The combination of higher outdoor temperatures, plus the Urban Heat Island Effect in large towns and cities, combined with the highly insulated building envelopes and increasing airtightness in new buildings utilising the efficient, compact forms of modern apartment complexes, all increase the risk of homes overheating. This risk is greatest in London and the South-East.

Overheating in buildings in a climate like the UK's can be mitigated if appropriate design measures are applied. This can be achieved through the design by ensuring that the excess heat can be dissipated and that solar gains are controlled in the warmer summer months. The main passive measures in order to reduce the risk of overheating in homes include effective ventilation and solar protection. In addition, the optimisation of glazing ratios to find a balance between daylight levels, winter performance and summer performance is essential and needs to be considered during the early design stages. Designers can also look to the colourful sun-breaks and shutters employed from Nice to Nicosia for lessons on mitigating solar gain.

Passive cooling is far more challenging in noisy urban environments and may drive proposals towards mechanical cooling for particular buildings. Therefore, it is essential to consider all interlinked factors early on and develop a well-integrated environmental strategy.

The recently introduced Part O of the Building Regulations has been developed specifically to help address this environmental issue and will significantly affect the façade design of medium to high-density residential schemes, particularly in our large towns and cities. It has been developed to safeguard the health and welfare of occupants of the building by reducing the occurrence of high indoor temperatures, especially during the summer months and typically requires a dynamic thermal modelling method for predicting overheating risk in demonstrating compliance with the regulation.

Part O defines the key design strategies to reduce the overheating risk and also includes guidance on detail, such as setting the indoor temperature limits for operating windows during the day and night, defining a methodology for evaluating the free areas of window openings, and aligning with factors such as acoustic attenuation, security and protection from falls. However, as passive design strategies for individual buildings might not be enough to deal with extreme future weather scenarios, strategies that can positively influence at a wider urban level would need to be considered and integrated into a regenerative masterplanning process at early design stage. This could include features such as extensive greening of areas of the masterplan, the creation of zero-emission transportation zones or perhaps even the deliberate targeting of prevailing winds to be channelled as as a cooling agent.

DESIGN OF MECHANICAL, ELECTRICAL AND PUBLIC WASTE SYSTEMS

It has become clear in recent years that energy efficiency needs to be considered early in the design of new buildings to help reduce energy consumption. Currently, some Mechanical, Electrical and Public Waste Systems (MEP) technologies are starting to be implemented in the built environment to help achieve more sustainable systems.

Trimble, an American software, hardware, and services technology company, consider that Heating, Ventilation and Air Conditioning (HVAC) systems that make use of Artificial Intelligence (AI) learning to make automatic adjustments have the potential to increase energy efficiency and reduce waste.[25] These systems leverage internet data to adapt air conditioner settings to predicted weather conditions. Certain sophisticated systems even have the capacity to adjust heating levels by monitoring human activity in a given room by measuring floor temperatures.

High-efficiency heat pumps are beginning to be introduced across the UK at scale. They have a remarkable coefficient of performance given the ratio of resources needed to work the plant and the heat produced, delivering more yield with less waste. It is estimated that heat pumps are four times more efficient on average than gas boilers if used in well-insulated and airtight spaces, making them an affordable, sustainable energy source to consider for residential developments.

Other systems, such as ventilation with heat recovery, constitute eco-friendly ventilation systems as they are able to ensure minimal heat loss while providing efficient airflow. These systems use heat from machines and human activity to warm up air blown in from outside. This brings the significant advantage that no heat is wasted and ensures a sustainable/low-energy demand air circulation.

Smart control units and sensors are other technological installations that can increase energy efficiency in residential buildings. This technology allows one to monitor energy consumption in buildings and control heating and cooling systems, even from smartphones or tablets. This allows for the monitoring of energy peaks which occur in large apartment complexes along with the ability to regulate them.

Even though some of these technologies might represent an additional investment for a project, in general, power is one of the largest operating expenses for buildings. This can be translated into a long-term cost saving for electricity expenses and a substantial improvement in a building's energy efficiency level.

Once a MEP system is fully operational, the maintenance team can utilise Digital Twin integration to uncover strategic improvements to boost efficiency on day-to-day operations and building management levels. Technological advancements in eco-friendly MEP systems and BMS can allow buildings to improve their environmental credentials and do their part in reducing the carbon footprint of buildings.

Mechanical and digital installations, however, are only as good as their commissioning and maintenance regimes, and passive systems should be employed wherever possible. The larger BTR organisations are adapting quickly to this new paradigm (see Chapter Six).

WHOLE LIFE-CYCLE ASSESSMENT

According to Greater London Authority "Whole Life-Cycle Carbon (WLC) emissions are the carbon emissions resulting from the materials, construction and the use of a building over its entire life, including its demolition and disposal".[26] They capture a building's operational carbon emissions from regulated and unregulated energy use and its embodied carbon emissions associated with raw material extraction, manufacturing, transport of building materials and construction. They also cover the emissions associated with maintenance, repair and replacement, as well as dismantling, demolishing and final material disposal.

A WLC assessment studies all the carbon emissions of the base case scenario of a project through its lifetime and evaluates the potential savings from the reuse or recycling of components after the end of a building's useful life. It provides a true picture of a building's carbon impact on the environment and allows it to target in which stages the building could be generating more carbon emissions and helps an environmental team to propose solutions for them.

Following this approach results in a high level of resource efficiency and cost savings by encouraging refurbishment instead of demolition, identifying the carbon savings from using recycled material, the minimisation of mechanical plant and services in favour of natural ventilation, the categorisation of the impact of maintenance, repair and replacement over a building's life cycle, the improvement of lifetime resource efficiency and reduction of lifecycle costs. It encourages local sourcing of materials and short supply chains as well as durable construction and flexible design, which contributes to greater longevity.

According to Statista, an online platform specialised in market and consumer data, the British Government spent 10.3 billion pounds on waste management in 2021/22.[27] The phase in the lifespan of a new-build BTR scheme that contributes the most to climate change is construction. One way to reduce both carbon emissions and waste during the build phase is modular construction.

Modular construction is a process in which the building's parts are constructed off-site under controlled conditions and then transported to site. The construction of modules in controlled factory conditions limits the amount of waste brought to the site and discarded. This can decrease carbon emissions from transport as it reduces the number of deliveries to the site that are needed, and also has the benefit of lowering on-site disturbances. In addition, the various building parts can easily be dismantled, which means that if refurbishment is required, the process will be more straightforward. Despite modular construction being more expensive than conventional construction methods, the speed of construction is higher; this can have significant financial benefits for the rental sector, as the faster the construction period, the more accelerated the commencement of the rental income stream.

CIRCULAR ECONOMY

Some nations are beginning to address the need to reduce the adverse impacts that people have on the environment, which requires a fundamental cultural and economic shift in how we consume resources and embrace a sustainable mindset. The shift begins with re-evaluating the standard of a "take-make-dispose" linear economy and transitioning towards a "regenerative" circular economy (CE) that considers long-term impact. The concept of CE seeks to encompass the principles of reducing, reusing and recycling and applying them in practice. It also looks forward to bringing cleaner production from the manufacturing systems and how the materials flow. Here, products and assets are designed and built to be more durable and to be repaired, refurbished, reused and disassembled. For the built environment, the circular economy can be applied by approaching it through a "building in layers" concept, where each layer has its own life cycle, life span and maintenance.

The built environment is a major consumer of natural resources. The sector recognises the need to fundamentally transform the supply chain, its components and systems to reduce waste and increase efficiency. Arrangements to incentivise the return of products are starting to emerge, but there is yet to be a clear articulation of exactly how processes will need to change in order for them to be implemented. Once again, the long-term view of BTR operators should sit easily with the embedding of circular economy principles within up-coming construction projects and the management of the buildings thereafter, particularly those higher density projects depicted in this book. This aligns with how Arup, an engineering consultancy, attempt to define CE.

> *Co-location, shared and flexible working spaces are becoming increasingly common in densely populated cities. By occupying less space and minimising the time an asset is idle, fewer resources are needed to deliver the same function or service, and thus less waste is produced.*
> *This includes housing more people within a smaller footprint, making greater use of offices and workplaces throughout the 24-hour cycle, and sharing facilities and vehicles. Shared ownership, sharing platforms and the 24-hour economy are enabling a shift in the way that space and services are used and accessed. The approach can also provide additional revenue and cost savings for owners and operators.*[28]

The GLA has led on policy direction in this area through the London Plan, the statutory spatial development strategy for the Greater London area. It encourages new developments to minimise the use of new materials by following the principles of circular economy, which should be considered at the start of the design process. The fundamental principles involve building in layers, which allow for different parts of the building to be accessible and maintained and replaced where necessary. Consideration of standardised components, modular build and re-use of secondary products and materials is required. Designing for longevity, adaptability or flexibility and for disassembly is also encouraged as well as using systems, elements or materials that can be re-used and recycled.

The London Plan also promotes principles that improve resource efficiency and innovation by ensuring the future durability of materials. It encourages waste minimisation and prevention through the reuse of materials by using fewer resources in the production and distribution of products. Additionally, it asks to design developments with adequate, flexible and easily accessible storage space and collection systems that allow the separate collection of dry recyclables (at least card, paper, mixed plastics, metals, and glass) and food.

The Plan has policies relating to waste reduction in promoting a circular economy approach and aiming to be net zero-waste. It also requires a Circular Economy Statement to be submitted to demonstrate how all materials arising from demolition and remediation works will be re-used and/or recycled and how the proposal's design and construction will reduce material demands and enable building materials, components and products to be disassembled and re-used at the end of their useful life. It needs to cover opportunities for managing as much waste as possible on site and to provide for adequate and easily accessible storage space and collection systems to support recycling and re-use have been put in place. A definition is required describing how much waste the proposal is expected to generate, and how and where the waste is to be managed, together with how performance will be monitored and reported.

CHAPTER SIX
The Key Design Ingredients for Success

This chapter takes BTR from the viewpoint of the designer. It examines the considerations that are critical for successful operation and examines elements which lift the experience beyond conventional sales-led projects to address the human emotions of happiness, comfort and security. It also looks at certain features of a contemporary offer that need further management review.

The complexity of regenerating any sizeable portion of land for residential use within a UK urban context is formidable. The drawing below gives an indication of the range of considerations that the designer must address at a macro level, and the developer must cover in the project funding stream, to realise the proposal.

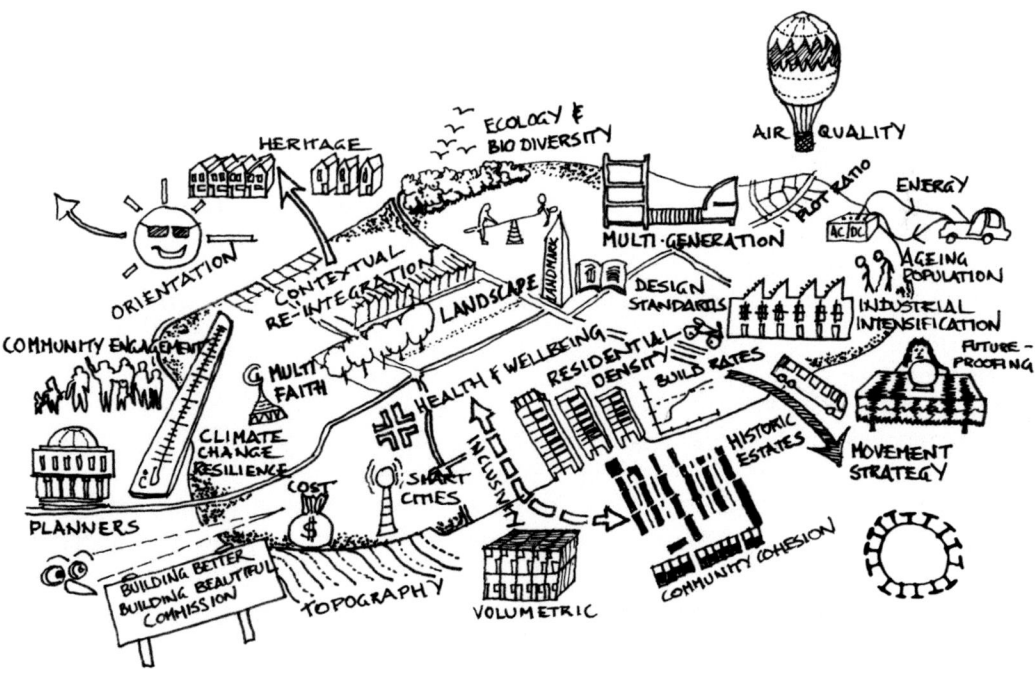

ABOVE Some of the many considerations within estate regeneration.
FACING PAGE Coppermaker Square, Stratford, London.

The advent of BTR represents an exciting shift for architects and designers on many fronts. One of them is the requirement to design for longevity and operational efficiency rather than simply aiming at optimising floor area ratios in order to maximise the commercial offer for a developer. This shift requires the design of flexible amenity facilities that can be programmed, curated and owned by the community and the creation of neighbourhoods with cross-district connections that embrace inclusivity and diversity rather than sterilising it. The shift means designing buildings that have a lifespan beyond the time it takes to sell the last dwelling on the project. The inherent sustainability of this form of living is important to designers and it is becoming increasingly important to prospective occupants. Moda Living, for instance, were one of the first BTR operators in the UK to tap into the environmental concerns of its residents and a wider realisation that more and more of their potential customers are becoming knowledgeable about the climate challenge and wanting to do something about it. This sustainable undertone forms a key part of the Moda Living brand, perhaps the most recognisable of any within UK BTR.

The overall design should be diverse and it should be flexible. The ability to live, grow, age and evolve in a sustainable manner is likely to be a measure of success. In order to copper-fasten this success there is a need to incorporate a facility for refreshing and adapting in future the buildings that are being designed now. This facility needs to allow for change and needs to incorporate the circular living described in Chapter Four. This applies equally to a designer's consideration of both urban and suburban conditions, for multi-family and single family, which have parallels but present different challenges. These challenges were exacerbated by the pandemic and the flight from certain urban areas to more suburban and non-urban locations. At the heart of this consideration is the provision of public realm – the amenity of the community - which should be accessible and inclusive for all and proportionate in its amount to residential density, joining the dots between individuals and generations and between adjoining neighbourhoods with transport strands and green linkages which respond to the seasons, emanating from and connecting to other green realms.

THE DYNAMISM OF PLACEMAKING

The concept of placemaking is one which is relatively recent within the UK context. It arose primarily as a response to inner city urban decay, including the decline of the great estates referred to in Chapter One but also as a reaction to the prevalent and largely soulless product of the volume housebuilders from the 1980s onwards.

The Urban Task Force was established in 1988 under the then Labour Government following the publication of a government policy paper entitled "Planning for the Communities of the Future". A government-sponsored report under the chairmanship of the renowned architect and passionate urbanist Richard Rogers, "Towards an Urban Renaissance", set out the principles for the revitalisation of English towns and cities, demanding that housing be built to higher densities in walkable neighbourhoods with access to local goods and services, reducing the need for travel and fostering community interaction.[1]

> *The importance of high-quality urban design and architecture, and of placemaking, was central to the thinking set out in the report. In particular, it was recognised that if people were to be persuaded to accept the benefits of living in higher densities than they might otherwise have chosen, this would only be achieved if the new neighbourhoods were attractive. They would need to be*

well designed, in order to overcome problems such as overlooking and noise disturbance, which become more acute as densities increase. All this would have to be sold to a sceptical public with the promise of specific benefits – not just to society, through reducing the use of cars, but to individuals and families through the creation of a more engaging form of community and community life.[2]

Placemaking is boosted when good quality urban design principles are embedded from the outset. In London, most large-scale developments, including the London-based case studies contained within this book, are apartment-based, high-rise and high-density projects. Densification has become second nature to designers and developers in our larger towns and cities and yet research on its appropriateness is relatively scarce. In 2020, LSE London, part of the London School of Economics and Political Science, published an insightful study into the suitability and experience of living in high density development.[3] It has many lessons for the BTR sector. The report finds that a critical mass of long-term residents seems to contribute to a sense of community and security in a development. Residents seem also to have a utilitarian relationship with their surrounding neighbourhoods, focussing on transport proximity and services. A key finding is that density alone does not determine whether these environments provide successful homes or not but instead it is the interaction between density, design, build quality, location and people that creates a sense of place.

A simplistic outline for a successful Build To Rent scheme, with placemaking at its heart, would describe a development located on a site like 66 Rockwell in Brooklyn, close to transport infrastructure and good local facilities with a single 24-hour entrance lobby that restricts access to the secure residents' amenities. This basic description hints at an order of exclusivity akin to some of the large private residential blocks recently constructed across London, Nine Elms being a prime example. But the difference between the bolthole for the exclusive and BTR is the potential that the long-term curation brings. The more progressive BTR investors care about the wider offer, their place within the local community and the on-going success of their developments for the long term. It is an antidote to a lot of large developments in large UK cities which the housing expert Paul Bridge alluded to in his essay entitled "Regeneration, Turning Threat into Opportunity".

> *It is commonplace to see vast numbers of small flats replacing outdated small flats or houses and thereby reducing the chance that the families of the future, created by both new and existing residents, will be able to stay and create a multi-generational community. This ill-documented effect is exacerbated by the generally low provision of social housing and housing for those who require community support.[4]*

Imagine that we transport ourselves back to 2016, the breakthrough year for BTR, and take a walk south from Wembley Park underground station directly south to Wembley Stadium. You are walking along Olympic Way. It was historically laid out to allow thousands of fans to make their way to the big games and events at the national stadium. It was functional and robust and there was little to see to make you linger or to which the word design could be ascribed. Walk further along Olympic Way through to Wembley Park Boulevard and the upgrading of Wembley Arena, Arena Square and the developments adjacent, some of the first interventions in this barren hinterland, are a whisper of what might follow. Water fountains for children to play in, a hugely popular secure play park that soon followed, alongside the launch of London Designer

ABOVE Olympic Way, Wembley Park, London.

Outlet, bringing retail and food and beverage to the neighbourhood. But even these pockets of promise had little effect on the promenade of Olympic Way, particularly as you approached one of the finest sports stadia in the country, a national icon.

If you take the same walk today, the wide thoroughfare remains and still delivers the functional need, to channel matchday fans or gig attendees in their thousands. However, the place has been utterly transformed, with retail outlets, café culture and wide-open tree-lined streets. The remarkable catalyst for change has been the culmination of the large-scale development of primarily residential buildings with retail, leisure and restaurants at their base, a key factor for success at Wembley Park, and carefully curated landscape amenity areas in between. This is the power of transformation for well-considered residential-led urban regeneration and BTR is at its very heart.

If you compare the pre-existing conditions at Wembley and at Coppermaker Square, the word "transformative" does not do justice to the quality of "place" that has been carved, sculpted and spirited into reality, within incredibly brief timeframes. If you can make the comparison then you can truly realise the potential of the sector.

The primary interface between any building and the local community is the ground-plane, that founding storey where the building hits the ground which, in recent times, has become one of the greatest challenges to good urban design and architecture. Higher densities are placing massive pressure on the ability of a building to activate the street. The greater quantum of development above increases back-of-house facilities at ground floor level, creating dead activity zones and reducing the designer's ability to create active frontages. Space for bicycles, refuse, plant, and wheelchair standard parking spaces compete with each other for what space is available. Who had heard of cargo-bikes five years ago, yet these too must now be catered for. Excavation and construction costs preclude basements in many locations and placing facilities above ground floor level is technically and functionally challenging. Contributing to these dead zones is the ever-present pressure on the high street from the surge in online shopping, the work-from-home revolution adding to the mix. All are impacting ground floor activity to a point where many of our streets and spaces are in danger of being permanently boarded up. A lack of active frontages is a significant barrier to achieving good placemaking.

This is where BTR comes into its own. Rather than providing facilities buried deep within the floorplate or high up in the building, exclusive for the residents only, one of the solutions is to push this ancillary space to the ground floor, outwardly looking and open to all. Some forms of curated rental products such as Co-living or the various forms of bespoke accommodation on offer to the older population are doing this regularly with co-working space, cafes and elements of bespoke ground floor commercial and retail space open to the wider public. BTR can also embrace this ethos and make it the norm. These so-called "exo-amenities" can provide cafes, restaurants and work spaces which cater for the local neighbourhood as well as the residents of the building. Some UK developments and many American ones are taking tentative steps in this direction, particularly where commercial viability concerns can make the difference between having these facilities or not.

Whilst this may entail a greater management challenge, the benefits of wider integration are obvious. The wider neighbourhood can gain access to carefully managed and curated amenities whose long-term success is part-secured by the development's sponsorship and stewardship. Local residents interact with the new tenants, welcoming them into their community. The tenants also gain from this arrangement. They can access vibrant amenities that, because they are shared, reduce development overhead and, therefore, potentially their expenditure on rent. Further, the risk of the wider public being excluded from these facilities as can often happen in non-BTR developments, is removed. The traditional introverted BTR development, with its stage-sets and themed amenities, is replaced by a more authentic place-specific set of facilities. The residents feel that they are part of the local community and that they contribute to a truly socially sustainable place.

Peter Bishop, a professor of urban design at the Bartlett School of Architecture, UCL recognises the importance of integrated, vibrant communities in his essay "Housing Regeneration – Why Is It So Difficult?"

> *Neighbourhoods change over time and high levels of "churn" are not necessarily a bad thing. Many city dwellers might choose to live in areas of transient population, but others value knowing their neighbours and recognising people in the street. In such areas, a variety of housing types, sizes and affordability offers opportunities to up-size and down-size as personal circumstances change. In this way personal networks can be retained and social institutions can become well established. Ultimately, a community that values its area is more likely to work to maintain it.[5]*

The BTR approach is capable of more dynamic evolution than conventional residential development. It is more flexible and responsive to need. This suppleness means that the boundary of what is possible for the ground floor can be stretched and re-imagined. In the end, an outwardly facing, active ground floor environment is a force for community cohesion and should form part of a designer's toolkit when considering social sustainability and good placemaking. For more detail on this topic, see PRP's publication entitled "Lewisham Town Centre Mixed Use Briefing Document".[6]

DENSITY AND TENURE

Perceptions of residential density change with time and geographical location. The five case studies in this book are dense residential projects. It is highly doubtful if any of these projects would have received planning consent even ten years ago because of their relatively high density. I remember walking across Blackfriars Bridge in London with a young friend from Tokyo, just after the Shard had been completed on the south bank of the River Thames. I proudly pointed out to her the tallest building in Western Europe. "My friend lives in a taller building than that", she nonchalantly replied. So, density is relative. However, residential density needs to be handled with care because the perception of space is important, as is the manner in which the designer deals with a brief which pushes density to the limits.

The demands of clients to optimise residential density to the limits of policy are greater than ever, reflecting the pressure on commercial viability faced by developers. One of our practice's celebrated schemes at Portobello Square in the Royal Borough of Kensington and Chelsea is a model of appropriate density measured against its physical context and the due process of a conservative planning authority. The first phase of development completed in 2017. If this masterplan was being designed today, the density that was achieved back in 2017 would be considered inappropriately low, even though in terms of its urban design and architectural approach, it is beyond criticism. Another of our projects, Geoffrey Close Estate in Lambeth, is pushing the density of an estate regeneration scheme on a confined urban footprint to the limits of what is possible within regulatory compliance and design guidance, in an effort to achieve a viability for a joint venture client organisation made up of a housing association and a private housing developer. In order to re-house the existing tenants on the estate and achieve financial viability, dwelling numbers are increasing by a factor of 3.3. Portobello Square has a

Portobello Square, Kensington and Chelsea, London.

Geoffrey Close Estate, Lambeth London.

Early design sketch showing proposals for Canada Gardens, Wembley Park, London.

Realisation of initial sketch proposals in completed buildings at Canada Gardens, Wembley Park, London.

residential density of 182 dwellings per hectare and Geoffrey Close has 416. Both are estate regeneration schemes in London with planning consents seven years apart.[7]

Higher residential density can only succeed if the space around the buildings is generous enough and carefully crafted. The 2020 London Plan introduced the Urban Greening Factor for major development proposals. Its intention is to prevent over-development and to promote health and wellbeing by encouraging the provision of street trees, rain gardens, green roofs and other bio-diverse provisions. Density and amenity are intertwined. Some experts consider that at least five square metres per person of accessible and useful open space should be provided for residential regeneration and, where possible, aim for at least 10 square metres.[8] It should also be noted that BTR developments usually come with significantly enhanced internal BTR amenities which are typically absent in conventional for-sale housing.

Higher residential density requires a focus on borrowed landscape where podium decks, access terraces and rooftops are drafted in to play their role in an overall amenity offer. This is no better demonstrated than at Wembley Park, where Quintain have delivered a tour de force in external amenity and landscape design, optimising the available space and framing special views across an extensive and abundantly landscaped podium deck.

An often-overlooked advantage of tall residential buildings is the long-range views that are on offer, anchoring the viewer with an urban landscape, often with a superior quality of light and little mechanically produced noise. This affords a faraway view of the buzz of the city as well as a better appreciation of the changing seasons. This is counter-intuitive to the common perception of high rise. The views across the River Mersey from the upper stories of Moda, The Lexington, one of this book's case studies, are as stunning as any view in Liverpool.

The journey home becomes elongated at higher densities. Increased fire safety requirements are adding further thresholds to cross and doorways to navigate. This puts pressure on the designer, who is attempting to make the transition from "district to doorknob" as pleasurable as possible, including minimal waiting times for elevators.

View of Pier Head and ther River Mersey from Moda, The Lexington, Liverpool.

As we saw in Chapter Four, tenure integration is often problematic on new residential projects. Developers often want private sale apartments shielded from affordable or social rent apartments so as not to devalue their sales product. This risks the creation of "poor doors" to aid segregation and the positioning of affordable rent elements of a development being placed in the most disadvantaged locations, "next to the abattoir" so to speak. This in turn leads to planning authorities seeking designs which are "tenure blind" so that there is no visual distinction between different forms of tenure including the design and specification of the external façade. This issue is less problematic in BTR. At Wembley Park, there are nine different forms of tenure across the masterplan including student accommodation. The Discount Market Rent portion of the project, where rents are discounted by twenty per cent of the market rate and which typically accounts for 20% of the total number of dwellings, is pepper-potted through the development. It is a model of tenure integration, breaking down social segregation and allowing social and affordable renters to be part of an aspirational community with access to a range of amenities that simply wouldn't exist in a conventional affordable housing project.

BACK-OF-HOUSE SUPPORT FACILITIES

Often overlooked and undervalued, the design of facilities that support the running of a BTR development needs careful consideration. The design of the reception area, which may also function as a "super lobby" to the entire development, must be an appealing place to arrive in relation to its utility and its interior design. It needs to be a wayfinding station and a refuge point on the journey home. It is the shopfront for the operator and its appearance is a big opportunity to relay the aspirations of the organisation, its values and its competence.

The relationship between the front desk and the post rooms and parcel rooms is also important given the high volume of parcels being delivered from online retail and food orders. Recent BTR developments include parcel unpacking rooms, allowing bulky

Post room at Canada Gardens, Wembley Park, London.

cardboard and othe packaging to be recycled on the spot and not carried up into the building. Consideration needs to be given to offering additional storage facilities to tenants, as these are generally in demand and, rented individually, can offer a better commercial return per square foot of area than a typical apartment.

Staffing levels need to be anticipated. The Mercian in Birmingham can have as many as ten members of staff helping to manage the 481-home facility and they should not be accommodated in an airless closet devoid of natural light. The business of marketing and letting accommodation is an ongoing operation after the construction is complete and should help market the facility in relation to hospitality to would-be renters.

Further facilities depend very much on the nature of the operator and the location of the development. Should a creche be provided? What about a DIY workshop for residents. How sophisticated should bicycle repair and cleaning stations become? Storage for furniture may be required and with good access to a weather-protected loading bay and goods lift. If the development is to be pet-friendly then washing facilities for dogs will be needed. Pet-friendly developments can change the nature of the demography in a building. In one of the BTR projects we visited in New York, a development of 826 apartments, there were three times as many dogs as children. The decisions on many of these issues in the UK context are still evolving as brands grow stronger and more lessons are learned.

One of the biggest management headaches in any residential building at scale is the question of how best to deal with refuse. The legacy of 1960s tower blocks effectively stigmatised the use of refuse chutes for decades but they are unavoidable in tall residential buildings. Black bin bags cannot realistically be brought down in passenger lifts by tenants without degradation of finishes and fittings. How the refuse chute is managed is another matter and how they are streamed for recycling. Pizza boxes and redundant duvets are the bane of any building manager because they cause blockages. How does one deal with serial offenders within the customer group? Cameras above chute hatches to aid identification are a realistic consideration, to stop the few clogging the operation for the many.

THE EXTENT OF LANDSCAPE AMENITY AND PUBLIC REALM

Whilst interest in ecology and nature preservation has been steadily increasing in recent years, as the full scale of the climate challenge has become increasingly evident, it was the global pandemic and the series of enforced lockdowns that gave us a new perspective on the importance of private amenity and accessible open space, and its effect on our health and wellbeing.

The mega-cities of India and China are struggling to deal with air-borne pollution, much as the UK's cities suffered during the early 20th century. In 1956, the needle was shifted in the UK when Sir Hugh Beaver helped pass the Clean Air Act, giving councils powers to control emissions and set up smoke control zones. The centres of our cities were transformed. Smog was reduced and death rates caused by poor air were halved in Greater London. Cities became better places to live and physical health improved. Fast forward nearly 70 years and new regulations are again attempting to do the same thing – to enhance the living experience in our cities, and ultimately, on our planet.

These regulations have focused heavily on built form, with our buildings becoming more sophisticated in managing their environmental impacts. High U-values and airtightness are leading to low energy usage. Highly recyclable materials mean low embodied carbon. In the past, however, regulations have focused primarily on buildings. The spaces in and around are equally important. We are now starting to explore the impacts and contributions of the non-built form in more detail, driven in great part by planning regulations that focus on landscape quality – Urban Greening Factors, Biodiversity Net Gain, amenity provision and play space quantum. These regulations recognise the physical benefits of the spaces around us and the importance of planting that sits within it. We know that a tree reduces the Urban Heat

Podium garden at Canada Gardens, Wembley Park, London.

Landscape at Coppermaker Square, Stratford, London.

Island Effect and cools its surroundings, mitigates wind, provides shade, improves habitat, cleans the air, contributes to carbon offset and reduces noise of busy roads. But it also has more intangible benefits beyond the physical. The view of a tree makes us feel better, the sound of its leaves rustling is calming, patterns of light changing as foliage moves and seasons pass. Where improvements in built form improve the more measurable aspects of sustainability, our immediate landscape environment contributes as much to our wellbeing and mental health as it does to improving the environment and helps drive us to do more to protect it.

A number of BTR developers have recognised this. Landscape quality and quantity has always been key to attracting residents, but now we are recognising that it is essential to improving residents' mental health and wellbeing as well. Gardening clubs, grow-your own allotments, community horticultural events each make for rich life experiences and BTR operators are able to create, manage and encourage this. Providing resident growing space doesn't need to cost a lot but can have an enormous impact on residents' mental health. It provides routine, endeavour and reward, while causing us to think about where our food comes from and how local produce can help in tackling the climate emergency.

LAYOUT AND INTERIOR DESIGN

An efficient BTR scheme will reflect optimal design, often based on Nationally Described Space Standards. These are standards which must be met in new projects and set out the gross internal floor area of dwellings at a defined level of occupancy, as well as floor areas and dimensions for key parts of the home such

Rentable camper vans on the rooftop of The Robbinson, Wembley Park.

Entrance foyer to The Robbinson, Wembley Park.

Sky Lounge at The Robbinson, Wembley Park.

as bedrooms, storage and floor-to-ceiling height. Projects in London will have additional considerations in order to meet the space requirements of the London Plan. The five case studies in this book reflect such efficiencies in relation to numbers of apartments per core and typical apartment layouts. The dwelling layouts vary only marginally from typical homes for sale for studios or one-bedroom flats. As dwellings become larger, the typologies show more variation, principally in relation to bathroom utilisation. A two-bedroom, four-person apartment, for instance, will have bathrooms of equal specification dedicated to each of the bedrooms as opposed to a regular bathroom and an ensuite found in a for-sale version of the same flat. One of the surprises at Wembley Park was how popular a three-bedroom, three-bathroom sharing apartment became. This is because if three people are sharing this apartment in a *Friends*-type of arrangement, it becomes the most economical way of renting within a BTR facility. It also optimises the yield for the operator compared to smaller typologies.

As the sector matures, there is a notable move towards standardisation of layout, not just of kitchens and bathrooms within apartments, but also in relation to bedroom dimensions in order to economise on management and operational costs. This is to facilitate the furnishing of the space with completely standardised furniture from a single supplier, meaning that the rental offer across a BTR development is homogenised. This entails a more streamlined re-fit and up-grade operation for periodic maintenance or between changes of renters, but also that less attention is placed in designing into an apartment complex the need to facilitate ease of move-in and move-out of an individual's own furniture or providing variation for re-letting. The offer is becoming more standardised for more operators.

One of the requirements of the London Plan which is dropped outside London is the provision of prescribed balcony sizes for new apartments, which increase as occupation increases. There is usually little manoeuvre with London's planning authorities, even though many conventional developers would avoid the expense of their provision if they were allowed. At Wembley Park, the local authority agreed to a uniform balcony size for all apartments as long as the average size balcony required by the London Plan was achieved. This had a significant effect on manufacturing and construction efficiencies. At Coppermaker Square in Stratford, the initial design intent was to provide the required balcony area as a "solarium" or permanent winter-garden, in effect an internalised balcony, for the tower elements of the scheme. In the end, these spaces were provided un-demarcated within the dwelling itself, adding to the gross internal floor area but with no dedicated external private amenity.

The interior design of the communal entrances, corridors and amenities is an important aspect of the offer. This varies from the assured, controlled Manhattan vibe of a typical Moda Living development to the exuberance on show at Wembley Park. Here, a flamboyant firm of interior designers, Fossey Arora, have brought three distinct themes to the three phases of development, each one deliberately aimed at a slightly different demographic. Their remit has not been confined to the interior and their design interventions on the Wembley roofscapes have brought dynamism and fun to the communal amenity available to residents. The three design themes offer a palette of choice for renters and the ability to move within the development depending on one's disposition or age. The case studies detailed within this book for Wembley Park and for The Lexington and the Mercian complexes indicate these variants.

CHAPTER SEVEN
Digital Autonomy

FRIGHT, FLIGHT AND FIGHT

It is 17th March 2020, St Patrick's Day. The pubs in London are closing early. Many have already shut up shop. The Hand and Shears in Smithfield remains open to allow punters to enjoy what is normally one of the busiest and inebriated celebrations of the year. Within this ancient inn's banter-worn walls there is an air of resigned trepidation for what is to come. The Covid-19 pandemic that commenced in a distant Chinese city has brought chaos to Europe, particularly to the health services of Italy and Spain. That mayhem has now arrived in the UK and by the end of the week, the country will have entered its first ever nationally-imposed lockdown.

The talk in the Hand and Shears that night centred on how we would fare in isolation and how long the lockdown might last. Our practice was better prepared than most for the move to home working. Three years previously, PRP had opened a studio

ABOVE The Hand and Shears, Smithfield, London.
FACING PAGE The Madison, Wembley Park, Wembley, London.

in Wroclaw, Western Poland, ostensibly to bring commercial competitiveness to our UK operation. But this was not an out-sourcing operation where packages of information were produced remotely, robot-like, with only high-level communication between team heads in respective countries. Instead, this was to be a fully integrated collaborative, creative function, as if the Polish team was in our presence. We used Microsoft Teams to facilitate communication, made easier as most Polish architects have a good command of English. This meant that the move to working from home was seamless for the organisation. We were up and running within hours, at our home-based workstations, preparing for the fight to survive as a business and as human beings.

Lockdown would see an explosion in the application of hi-tech communications systems and streaming services to keep the cramped, huddled masses in work during the day and entertained in the evenings and weekends. A scramble for hardware to facilitate these systems ensued. The supply chain for the world was severely tested for the first time since the Second World War, a test which would continue after the lockdowns ended.

Fast forward to today and the scramble for communications systems has passed. Voracious competition amongst streaming companies has severely dampened the expansion plans of the previously unassailable mega-producers, as new subscribers become scattered and flighty. The rise of Zoom has been followed by a startling decline in the fortunes of the communication company, as demand for video conferencing abated.

DATA, STUPID

One aspect of information technology that has grown in importance is the world of digital storage of information in the Cloud and the hardware behind compilation of the information that is sent there. To paraphrase Bill Clinton, it's about the data, stupid. In the UK's South-East, the price of land for data centres in numerous locations in late 2022 was for the first time out-stripping that of residential.

BTR operators have been the amongst first to embrace the digital revolution in relation to how architects and their co-consultants design and create the construction documentation with which to build, manage, maintain and repair the buildings they are developing.

However, before looking at these advances in the sector, we should examine any potentially baleful consequences of technological improvements. In Chapter One we saw Dr Desiree Fields of the University of California at Berkeley drawing attention to the less than benign societal effects that large multi-family corporate interventions are having on particular locations in the United States. The activity of certain corporations has been greatly boosted by technology, as Dr Fields explains in a paper by Nick Keppler entitled "Robot Landlords Are Buying Up Houses".[1]

The paper describes how "automated landlords" have become "acquisition engines", using new data tools and technologies to speed transactions and bypass human operatives in order to minimise on-site costs of maintenance and repair, and even viewings, which are often unaccompanied by any agent of the rental companies. These innovative techniques commenced after the Great Recession of 2008, when certain data brokers began producing heat maps of foreclosures in the United States.

This information was supplied to the securities-backed corporations that Dr Fields is drawing attention to, who subsequently moved in to hoover up swathes of distressed residential properties.

The use of cloud computing and algorithms in the residential sector has seen a huge increase since then. The new data sources, which include local sales rates, construction costs, prevailing rents levels, information on rent arrears and maintenance costs are all used to inform investment objectives. The so-called acquisition engines use this multi-point data, which is fed into algorithms which "savour" it for neighbourhood desirability, including proximity to service and transport nodes and local employment statistics. Rental opportunities are broadcast and contractual commitments portals are set up on digital platforms, smart phones, iPads and apps, all promoting rapid and efficient "i-buying". In her research, Dr Fields has attended marketing conventions within this sub-sector, where, as she describes: "Everywhere people were kind of singing the praises of technology as the real linchpin in making this new single-family rental class as a reality."

Mr Keppler's paper points out that institutional investment companies own only 3% of the single-family rental market but they have saturated certain areas, where they may own as many as one in five rental properties and are acquiring more.

Dr Fields also points out that there are signs of technological breakwaters against what appears to be one-way commercial traffic. In New York City, an organisation called Housing Data Coalition amasses data to make the market more transparent to renters and provides information to show renters how to form residents' associations and how to act against aggressive rental companies.[2]

On the plus side of this activity, the need to physically visit to view an apartment for rent or for sale may soon become obsolete for the renter or purchaser. Advances in virtual reality are almost with us which, through the use of advanced high-resolution LED pixels, can create immersive environments within which it is difficult to discern virtual from reality.[3] Their application will soon extend beyond the confines of VR goggles for use within curved or spherical three-dimensional environments. The use of haptic gloves or vests will extend the immersive sensation even further, where you can feel a door handle as you open a door or touch the edge of a kitchen worktop. This will dramatically extend the marketing potential and geographic reach of residential sales teams. The potential for future entertainment offers within large BTR communal amenity suites is immense. As today's 40-somethings, who are renting in increasing numbers and who have been brought up in the age of video-games edge towards retirement, who is to say that they will not be spending seven hours a day gaming with their elder colleagues instead of spending endless hours on daytime TV?

Architects are grappling with what the potential of Artificial Intelligence (AI) and machine learning means for the profession. There is much talk of remaining agile and embracing new workflows whilst transition occurs, as one of the biggest disrupters within our professional lives breaks on our shores.

The data we create as individuals is a valuable commodity. AI is all around us, in the systems we use to listen to music, to purchase goods on-line or in transactions with financial organisations, continually modulating this data. AI has made its way into a few designers' workplaces, in the form of large language model-based chatbots and text-to-image capabilities which are helping with written bid submissions and in visualising our proposals with incredible images and video manipulations. Data-driven software currently exists, such as Autodesk Forma, Hypar and Delve. These tools allow designers to utilise data on local site conditions and regulations to quickly form building layout and masterplanning automation. Delve, a Google product, is specialised to deal with urban environments and can generate millions of design options and grade them against their degree of compliance in meeting a given set of priorities.[4] Martha Tsigkati leads a specialist research team at Foster and Partners, a leading UK-based architectural practice. She describes the current position in which we are already riding a wave of unprecedented exponential acceleration.[5]

AI is likely to dramatically accelerate the capability of architects in basic productivity, optimising design and delivery of large residential projects, improving collaboration and enhancing error detection. It will largely remove uncertainty from cost models using streams of localised cost databases and national economic projections. In time, it will help to remove net carbon generation from the design process altogether by sourcing more materials locally or by inventing new materials which are capable of being locally produced in regional factories or on-site 3D printing stations and which will gradually replace traditional materials. It will help us to stop pumping a tonne of carbon into our atmosphere for every tonne of concrete being specified in our buildings today. It will improve safety during the construction process and in completed, occupied buildings, enhancing the purity of the Golden Thread and it will ensure that operational carbon outputs are completely optimal because it will replace facilities managers who are prone to human error.

Key to the improving technology is data.

> *The two essential ingredients for an AI model are datasets, on which the system is trained, and processing power, through which the model detects relationships within and amongst those datasets. Those two ingredients are, to an extent, substitutes: a model can be improved either by ingesting more data or adding more processing power. The latter, however, is becoming difficult owing to a shortage of specialist AI chips, leading model-builders to be doubly focused on seeking out data.* [6]

Consider the data available within a practice such as PRP. It has existed for 60 years and started digitising its outputs almost 30 years ago. The transformation of this data into accessible workflows would give trainee architects access to information that could only be derived from a senior, seasoned professional who had done the rounds for decades. Our practice currently employs three document controllers to help issue design and construction drawings on live projects. Perhaps it will be the employment of data annotators that becomes essential in the near future. Scale this notion of data harvesting and classification up to the massive rental portfolio holders such as Clarion or Greystar that we have mentioned in this book and consider how valuable these unstructured datasets become.

THE FUTURE IS NOW

Within the construction industry, a number of BTR operators are leading the line in the digital response to the future management of their assets, commencing at initial concept design and the first sketches coming off the drawing board. All housing management organisations should follow this lead.

In the ever-evolving world of architecture and construction, staying ahead of the curve is essential. One advancement which continues to transform the industry is Building Information Modelling (BIM). Conceived originally in the 1970s, BIM gained traction in the early 2000s as a response to the challenges of design coordination and documentation, aligning advancements in technology with robust digital standards. Since the Covid-19 pandemic, BIM has become an even more powerful tool in remote working scenarios that have remained in place since lockdown.

Below, we will explore the remarkable benefits of BIM at various stages of the process, benefiting a wide spectrum of participants, and shed light on how it can shape the future of residential building projects in the UK.

UPHEAVAL AND THE RISE OF DIGITAL SOLUTIONS

We vividly recall the unprecedented chaos brought about by the Covid-19 pandemic. As lockdowns swept across the globe, the world scrambled to adapt to remote work and virtual communication. In this tumultuous landscape, BIM emerged to a new, previously more sceptical audience as a vital tool for seamless collaboration and efficient project management. Gone were printed drawings, red pens, and physical models to elaborate on initial concepts and ideas; in came screen sharing "live" designs in three dimensions (3D).

Visionary architectural practices were embracing BIM for a long time before the pandemic hit as a means to enhance competitiveness, already leveraging cloud technology to integrate diverse teams and work on building models across different geographical locations. With the shift to remote working a natural progression occurred, as the digital platforms Zoom and Microsoft Teams were embraced adding much improved communication channels. This adaptability allowed architectural firms to continue their operations seamlessly, ensuring minimal disruptions during the early days of lockdown. The techniques we had already learnt through creating isolated virtual reality (VR) 3D views for project consultations became almost the norm to facilitate a discussion around design evolution via a video call.

WHAT IS BIM?

At its core, Building Information Modelling (BIM) is a digital representation of a building's physical and functional characteristics. It enables architects, engineers, contractors and clients to collaborate through federation of discipline-specific models, usually on a common software platform (but more properly through Open Data standards), integrating various design elements and construction data into a comprehensive 3D model. BIM goes beyond traditional 2D drawings, providing a three-dimensional, data-rich environment that, if used appropriately, can enhance decision-making, streamline workflows and improve project outcomes. It is important to understand however, that BIM is not just the building model itself. A key part of BIM is digital "information management" and many of the efficiency gains and improved project outcomes we expect rely on common standards and information clarity.

This is becoming even more prevalent as we see increasing focus on the importance of data, both as a record of the construction process and as a deliverable to pass in to a building owner's Facilities Management System. We are beginning to see a number of clients embracing this methodology to inform and evolve their project briefs.

FEASIBILITY: INITIAL CONCEPTS AND OPTIMISING BUILDING PERFORMANCE

The feasibility stage sets the foundation for a successful project. BIM empowers architects and contractors to conduct more dynamic appraisals, generating accurate massing studies and refining the business case in terms of cost per square metre against various revenue models generated through different dwelling mix option studies. By working closely with clients, BIM assists in refining project briefs, ensuring alignment with design objectives and budgetary considerations.

BIM takes early design to new heights by enabling detailed massing studies, assessing crucial factors such as sun path, daylighting and wind studies, enabling dynamic feedback to become possible. Software packages such as Autodesk Forma help design teams with conceptual design capabilities, predictive analytics and automations to make solid project parameters using data-driven inputs.[7] With such data-driven approaches, BIM can facilitate streamlined workflows for analysis of potential environmental issues, allowing architects to optimise the often-conflicting building performance criteria of maximising daylight and minimising overheating while creating energy-efficient designs. Such insights empower design teams to make more informed decisions that positively impact both the environmental and running costs as well as the residents' experiences of the spaces, we create. These techniques were employed on Wembley Park and Coppermaker Square, two of the case studies in this book.

DESIGN OPTION APPRAISALS: HARNESSING TECHNOLOGY'S POTENTIAL

As we begin to see the shift in mentality away from sales targets towards designing for longevity within the BTR sector, the dial is also shifting, with project briefs beginning to focus on the quality of the experience for a longer-term tenancy, building a community, creating a buzz and building a sense of place in and around a neighbourhood that residents are proud to call home.

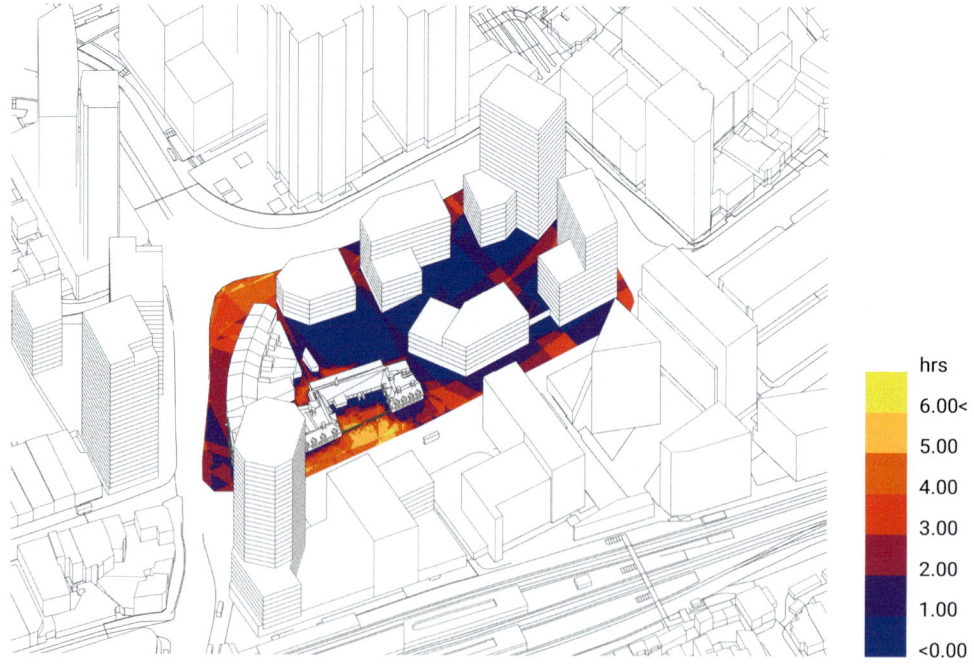

Early BIM massing study used to assess impact of adjacent site proposals on "average sunlight hours" for areas of public realm.

More emphasis is being placed on the communal amenity spaces that can differentiate a place to live for the renter when compared with the private landlord offer. On our BTR schemes we've seen everything from the more common cinema room for group viewings to larger rentable kitchen and dinner party hosting facilities for those renting smaller homes but not wanting to downsize on their social options. We've even explored poodle parlours for the pet-friendly developments – nothing enhances an Instagram post of your attractive apartment more than including your freshly groomed four-legged friend. With legislation currently going through Parliament covering the rights of tenants to keep pets in rented accommodation, this is likely to be a line item in future project briefs.

BIM's integration with advanced visualisation tools revolutionises design option appraisals. Stakeholder and local community engagement are enhanced through realistic computer-generated imagery, interactive walkthroughs and immersive VR experiences. Architects can leverage software like Enscape and Twinmotion to bring designs to life, ensuring clients have a clear understanding of the project's vision, "experience" the spaces and public realm in a digital context, and allowing them to make informed decisions with more confidence.

DESIGN COORDINATION: STREAMLINING COLLABORATION AND EFFICIENCY

In a complex construction project, design coordination is crucial to ensure seamless integration of various systems and components. With the right forward planning, BIM allows for a standardised kit of parts that can be utilised across multiple buildings and within a single structure, promoting efficiency and consistency. Efficient layouts and ease of maintenance are key considerations in the design coordination phase, and BIM excels in these areas. By creating virtual models that accurately

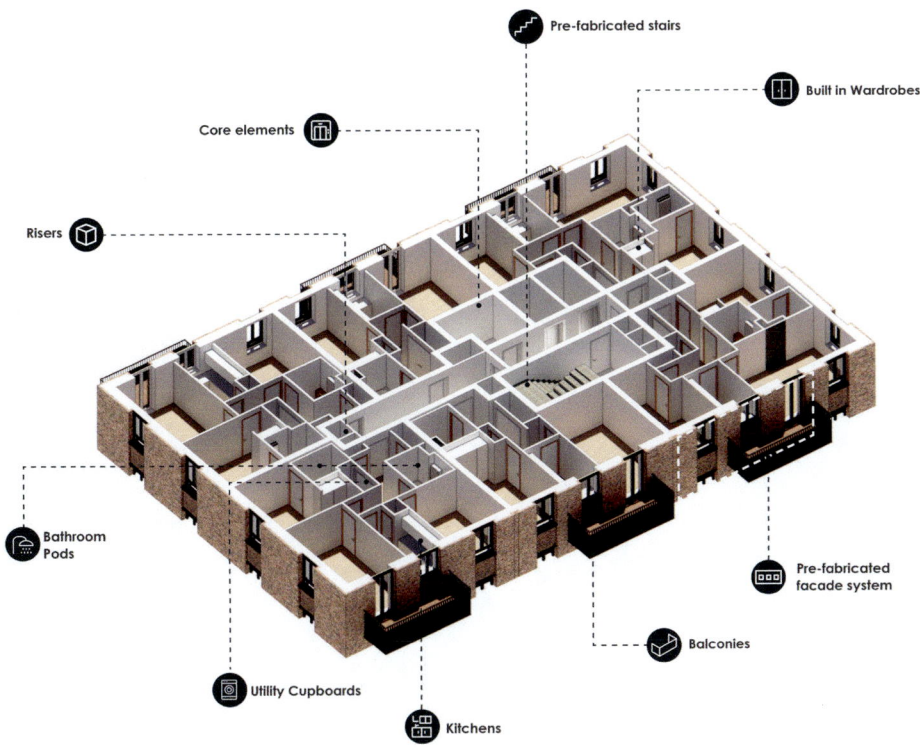

Approach to a BIM "kit of parts".

represent the building's components, architects can optimise layouts to maximise space utilisation, identify potential clashes or conflicts early on, and ensure smooth construction processes.

Moreover, cloud-based "viewing" platforms empower clients by enabling them to interact with the models on their terms. This level of involvement fosters a deeper understanding of the design intent and enables clients to provide valuable feedback, ensuring that the final product aligns with their vision and requirements. By controlling the data and selectively sharing information, BIM allows stakeholders to focus on the right information at the right time, eliminating confusion and enhancing project coordination.

CONSTRUCTION: ENHANCING EFFICIENCY AND QUALITY

The holy grail of construction systems in the UK is off-site and factory assembled modules and components in order to increase build efficiency, to speed construction and to reduce waste. Over the years, the industry has been continually compared to the car industry in an effort to compel it to modernise and upgrade what remains a very traditional industry heavily reliant on bricklayers, carpenters and poured concrete. The Elon Musk of construction has yet to appear.

Volumetric construction has become the Rubicon for new delivery techniques. It has all but collapsed in the UK, such is the investment required to make it happen and the design planning that needs to be integrated in order to optimise assembly and delivery. Berkeley Homes, Legal & General and Ilke Homes have all struggled and the latter, a volumetric specialist, went into administration in mid-2023. Swan, a housing association, invested massively in two modular factories. The organisation no longer exists, having been subsumed in 2023 by Sanctuary, another housing association. It is clear that the idea of efficient delivery of factory produced homes does not square with the sales rates that the volume housebuilders envisage or the development programmes of the providers of affordable homes.

And yet significant factory assembled components, designed in a BIM environment, have been utilised on all three plots of the Wembley Park masterplan, one of this book's case studies. The contractor has deployed factory assembled elements in a

Bathroom pods from CGI concept, to suppliers 3D production model before rolling off the production line.

DSC used on E03 - E05

QR code applied to the panel

Off-site and on-site SISK QA check

QR Codes

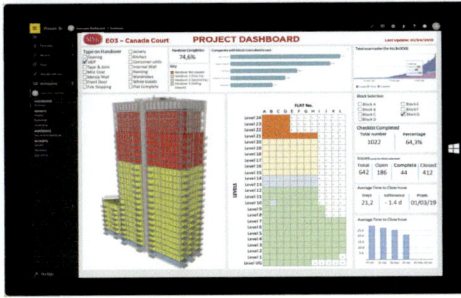
Live dashboard

QR codes used for production quality control audits, through to delivery and installation tracking against programme targets.

number of areas at Wembley including bathroom pods from Italy across each of the Wembley Park plots, factory assembled balconies and pre-cast façades panels from Lincolnshire used to clad The Robinson. Each instance was reliant on accurate BIM-driven deliverables and data to ensure an optimal, factory processed output. This has brought significant savings and programme efficiencies to Sisk, the contactor for two of three case study plots at Wembley Park.

When it comes to the construction process itself, BIM continues to shine. It simplifies record-keeping, ensuring accurate documentation of crucial elements such as completed installations and commissioning – essential data for any records related to fire safety measures. At Wembley Park, Sisk used components labelled with QR codes to facilitate quick updates to a central database and to feed into a QA monitoring platform for the duration of the build, logging key data on construction milestones and presenting clear visual updates on progress against construction programmes.

Additionally, BIM facilitates improved defect resolution by providing a comprehensive database of information that contractors could access and utilise both before and during construction and beyond. Sisk's use of BIM360, an Autodesk cloud-based solution that allows project teams to effectively work in a collaborative environment, to proactively manage coordination ahead of construction on site, also flowed through into progress QA checks. This resulted in a 30% increase in efficiency on staff time associated with this task when compared to "paper" processes and the conventional task of marking up drawings back in the office.

EMBRACING TECHNOLOGICAL ADVANCEMENTS: DIGITAL RECORDS

With the UK Government committed to implementing Dame Judith Hackitt's Golden Thread recommendations, the use of digital tools and systems will be an integral component of the wider building safety programme.

As technology advances, the applications of BIM become increasingly exciting. Innovations like Openspace and Oculo bring a new dimension to the industry, allowing stakeholders to experience virtual walkthroughs and immersive "streetview" style environments throughout the construction phase. This allows for a much wider capture of the progressive build, layer by layer, and not just those isolated elements that are selected for review. These cutting-edge tools empower clients to explore, track and record their build phase.

Our practice is a founding member of BIM4Housing, an informal research group populated by a number of London-based architectural practices, and we continue to engage with this group by hosting seminars and leading open discussions around BIM and digital working. There is an increasing focus on addressing the quality, cost, programme and safety challenges facing the industry, and how the Information element of BIM can improve outcomes.

With regard to the Information Management functions, it is essential to ensure that the client's requirements for the Golden Thread and Digital Record data provision are fully met. The Digital Record requires data to be collected and stored regarding the structural and fire safety elements of a building, and it is essential to ensure that a process is in place to collect the required data at each of the formal project gateways. This can also be linked back to the BIM model and presentable to the client and third parties in a standard industry recognised "Open" data format where required. The collected data can then inform the Safety Case for new buildings, a legal requirement arising from the Building Safety Act 1922, along with client organisation safety and incident response protocols and processes.

EFFECTIVE MANAGEMENT:
STREAMLINED FACILITIES AND CUSTOMER SATISFACTION

BIM's benefits extend beyond the design and construction phases. In the realm of facilities management, BIM offers efficient data management and comprehensive insights. The integration of COBie data (Construction Operations Building Information Exchange) ensures that facility managers have access to accurate information about equipment, maintenance schedules and asset management right down to when a light bulb needs to be replaced. This streamlines facility operations, reduces downtime and enables fast response times, resulting in enhanced customer satisfaction.

Furthermore, BIM enables the collection and analysis of data to provide valuable feedback on facility performance. By leveraging this information, property managers can optimise energy usage, identify maintenance needs and make data-driven decisions to continuously improve the quality of service provided to occupants.

Take Wembley Park as an example. Through their in-house development of data reporting tools, the Quintain Living team are able to identify abnormalities and areas of concern around patterns of energy or utilities use. This could range from identifying lights left on in vacant properties, incorrect settings on heating, even excess water usage through toilet cisterns continually flushing. In turn, the management team can feed this back to residents or identify any training needs on systems.[8] With sustainable living moving ever higher up the agenda, combined with a cost of living crisis, who doesn't want to reduce carbon and save money on utility bills right now?

CHAPTER EIGHT – CASE STUDIES

1 Moda, The Lexington
2 The Mercian
3 Coppermaker Square
4 Lewisham Gateway II
5 Wembley Park

FACING PAGE The Robinson, Wembley Park, Wembley, London.

CASE STUDY 1
Moda, The Lexington

- **CLIENT** Moda Living
- **ARCHITECT** Falconer Chester Hall
- **BTR OPERATOR** Moda Living
- **MAIN CONTRACTOR** BCEGI
- **LOCATION** Liverpool Waters, Liverpool
- **START ON SITE** July 2018
- **COMPLETION** August 2021
- **GROSS INTERNAL FLOOR AREA** 27,270 m²
- **CONSTRUCTION COST** £64 million
- **CONSTRUCTION COST PER M²** £2,346

Post-construction site plan.

Post-construction axonometric view.

BACKGROUND

Moda Living's Moda, The Lexington is a key component of the Liverpool Waters project, a 30-year vision to completely transform the city's northern docks. The development is a 34 storey, 325-state-of-the-art Build To Rent scheme. It is the essence of an elegant tall building positioned within one of the most important urban riverscapes in the UK.

Moda's brief was to provide a building that would establish its brand in Liverpool, with efficiency of cost, construction and building management being a pre requisite, whilst optimising the living experience through the communal spaces enabling a sense of community to develop. The design intent was to deliver a commercially-viable tall building for the BTR sector that told a story of the relationships between the Liverpool and New York skylines and international trade.

CONSTRAINTS AND DESIGN RESOLUTION

The site is located on Liverpool's northern docks. This is a complex system of quays and wharves which saw their greatest use at the height of the British Empire and which have been very well preserved so that much of the system remains in working order. The development sits in close proximity to the listed Dock Wall, part of Liverpool's proud industrial heritage. This historic artefact, which dates back to the 1800s, had to be kept intact, meaning the foundation solution for the building needed to respect this statutorily listed structure.

The design team were mindful throughout the design process of the maritime location and the former designation of Pier Head, Liverpool's famous frontispiece overlooking the River Mersey, as a World Heritage Site. This part of Liverpool has an extraordinary history of relationships with foreign lands, especially New York and the Anglo-American relationship that has influenced historic buildings in Liverpool, not least in the architectural form of the nearby Liver Building. The design of Moda, The Lexington pays homage to the slim, stylish skyscrapers of New York, especially pioneering modernist masterpieces such as the Empire State Building and the Rockefeller Centre. The building's massing is extruded from a simple rectangular footprint in the shape of two side wings and an indented centre shrouded in a select palette of materials with a fenestration which tapers and dissolves as it reaches the skyline.

FACING PAGE View from the north-west with the Liver Building in the background.

Entrance portico.

Car park and amenity terrace.

The link to Manhattan is reinforced through elements of Art Deco styling and an image of the RMS Aquitania, the Cunard ocean liner whose maiden voyage took place in 1913 between Liverpool and New York, which is engraved within the façade of the car park.

Several consultations were undertaken, including the formal pre-application consultation. Prior to this, the team participated in a series of Developer Forums, instigated by Peel Holdings, which brought together all parties that had an emerging interest in the Princes Dock neighbourhood.

The third stage involved engagement with the wider community. This took the form of an exhibition over two days in April 2016. Feedback was assimilated into the Statement of Community Involvement. The final stage was a meeting with Places Matter, an independent design review panel hosted by RIBA, to provide impartial advice.

Due to the maritime environment, the building is largely unsheltered and the exposure to strong winds along the Liverpool waterfront is well known. Wind tunnel studies were conducted to investigate the effects of current and likely future surroundings at a facility in Milton Keynes. This informed the Moda design and the materials used in the project.

CONSTRUCTION SYSTEMS

The constricted nature of the site, constrained further by large sandstone boulders and other relic foundations, meant that the foundation solution chosen was a piled raft system. The structural design above is efficient with a centralised core. This optimises the concrete structural frame and column sizes, improving the scheme's embodied carbon credentials by using less concrete within the frame. The central core also optimises daylight and solar gain, whilst maximising views across the city and waterfront and achieving dual aspect apartments on all four corners of the building.

The project utilised MEVA's automatic climbing jump formwork and screen system for the construction of the reinforced concrete core. Whilst the system had been used before the construction of Moda, The Lexington, it is comparatively new.

View from the north-east towards Pier Head.

Façade detail.

Communal lounge.

CHAPTER EIGHT – CASE STUDY 1 – MODA, THE LEXINGTON 117

The MEVA system was selected due to the exposed location of the site and the prevalence of high winds. The self-raising nature of the system negates the need for crane "hook time" reducing the probability of progress being affected as a result of the crane being "winded off". The enclosed self-rising screens provided safer working conditions for the construction team and improved the quality of the core through shielding the team and works from the worst of the inclement weather.

A Computer Fluid Dynamics model was created to predict the structural wind behaviour and maximum accelerations for occupancy comfort. This alternative method was used to save cost and time, opposed to the traditional laboratory wind testing regime. Vent terminal covers on the external façade were carefully designed to prevent whistling in high winds.

Traditionally, floor plates of this nature are formed from reinforced concrete alone but in order to achieve the spans necessary in Moda, The Lexington, this would have meant thick heavy floor slabs resulting in a costly approach with a heavier foundation solution. By utilising post tension, the structural engineer's team was able to reduce the weight of concrete and in turn reduce the amount of embodied carbon within the building. The thin post-tensioned floor slabs fully adhered to tight deflection constraints for the unitised façade. The design team worked closely with the façade manufacturers to predict and tweak deflections to suit their requirements.

BTR AMENITIES

The 17th floor on the building is dedicated to communal spaces and has a higher ceiling height to create a "waist band" to the elevation externally and a differentiator for the internal space. Moda had a clear focus of providing outstanding communal facilities to allow the residents to create a Moda community which at the time of the design concept was not a common feature. In addition to the 17th floor, the second floor includes an outside terrace with seating and landscaped areas including outdoor cooking facilities and a gym. Below this terrace abutting the main tower is the building's car park.

BTR amenities comprise a sky lounge, gym, community kitchen and cinema room. The upper roof level includes viewing platforms from a rooftop garden providing unrivalled 360-degree views of the city and river, a view which is also available from the cinema room when the black-out curtains are not drawn.

The interior design for the amenity areas has been conceived by Naomi Cleaver, incorporating strong Art Deco themes exemplified by the ground floor corridor leading from the double height reception which incorporates a dramatically lit, segmented arched ceiling.

ENVIRONMENTAL SUSTAINABILITY ASPECTS

The focus of the project brief was on adaptability and flexibility, which ensured a sustainable design from the outset which adheres to Moda's core brand priorities of outstanding ESG performance, leading technology and best-in-class health, wellbeing and service offer.

Moda, The Lexington achieved a 2-star FitWel rating, which guarantees the neighbourhood improves the overall health of its occupants, from encouraging exercise, to outstanding outdoor spaces and internal environmental control, acoustics and daylighting.

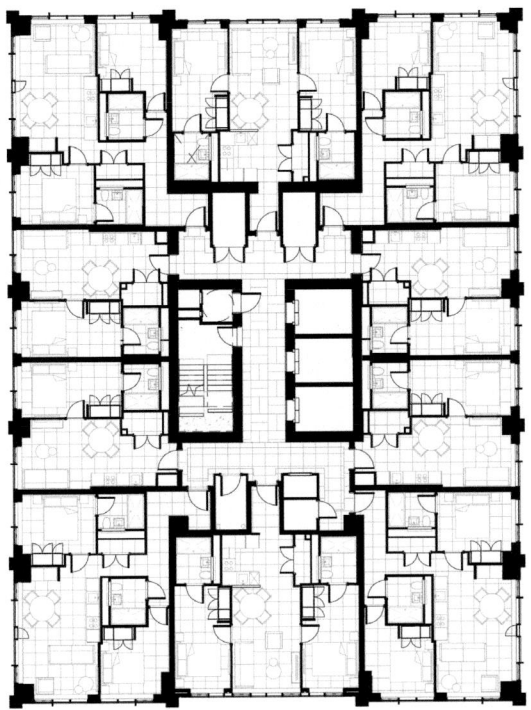

Level 14–16 plan.

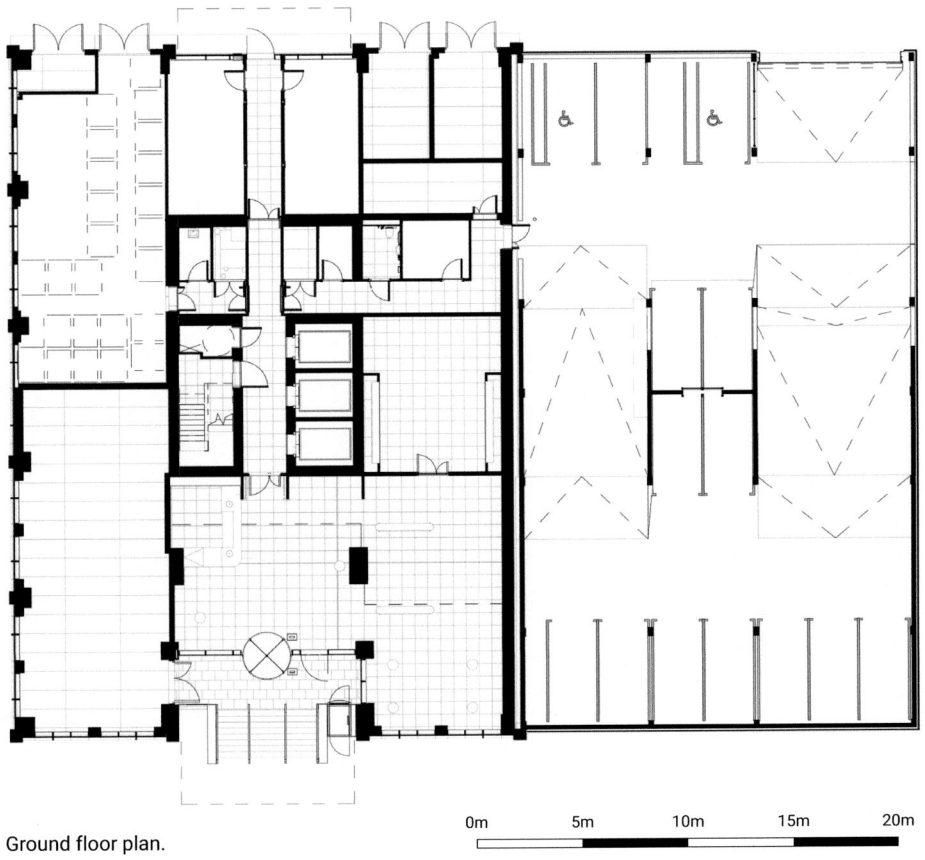

Ground floor plan.

CHAPTER EIGHT – CASE STUDY 1 – MODA, THE LEXINGTON

Internally, the apartments benefit from MVHR (Mechanical Ventilation and Heat Recovery), openable windows for resident comfort/control, and 95% dim-out curtains which help reduce solar gain in summer months on south-facing façades.

Moda, The Lexington's performance is made even more efficient through Moda Living's work with technology provider Utopi to build a complete digital infrastructure and optimise smart building technology across the Moda portfolio. Utopi's platform uses IoT for automated building management to reduce energy usage, and sensors throughout the buildings to monitor the internal environment and provide a wellness score for each community.

Moda, The Lexington is modern, efficient and energy-conscious building which encompasses a number of low-carbon energy efficient technologies, despite Liverpool Council's minimal sustainability requirements. The high-performing envelope works seamlessly with the building services systems ensuring the internal spaces are comfortable, maximise natural light whilst reducing solar gain and allowing fresh air via a mixture of passive ventilation and mechanical heat recovery units. The resultant U-values are 0.15 W/m²k for the external walls, 0.13 W/m²k for the floor and 1.48 W/m²k for the windows.

Artificial lighting is achieved via low energy LED lamps with simple controls to minimise energy wastage. Heating of the apartments is achieved via a central energy centre with high-efficiency gas condensing boilers, with a distributed low-temperature hot water network serving high-efficiency heat interface units within each apartment. Enhanced insulation of the heat network reduces heat losses and increases the efficiency of the network.

Front elevation roofscape.

Car-park rooftop amenity terrace.

View from the South-West.

CASE STUDY 2
The Mercian

- **CLIENT** Moda Living
- **ARCHITECT** Howells
- **BTR OPERATOR** Moda Living
- **MAIN CONTRACTOR** John Sisk & Son
- **LOCATION** Birmingham
- **START ON SITE** March 2019
- **COMPLETION** June 2022
- **GROSS INTERNAL FLOOR AREA** 45,300 m²
- **CONSTRUCTION COST** £110,000,000
- **CONSTRUCTION COST PER M²** £2,400

Pre-construction figure-ground plan.

Post-construction figure-ground plan.

BACKGROUND

Cities are built on people and talent, and this residential development in the Broad Street district of central Birmingham attracts people to the very heart of a city in the throes of a remarkable renaissance. Moda Living's The Mercian rises to 42 storeys and provides 481 homes for rent in Birmingham's tallest inhabited building, acting as a launch pad into the city for knowledge workers at newly arrived companies including Goldman Sachs and PwC, as well as the city's burgeoning tech and digital sectors.

Delivered on the Build To Rent model, The Mercian will help to ensure that Birmingham has the next generation of a residential offer to attract and retain the changing demographic of people working in the city. Not only tapping into rejuvenated city infrastructure, but the building also stands to tap into the social infrastructure of a better-connected, healthier and greener city.

CONSTRAINTS AND DESIGN RESOLUTION

Positioned on a constrained city-centre plot, the building's façade rises directly from the pavement's edge with the principal entrance welcoming residents directly from a bustling Broad Street.

Located just outside the infamous 'concrete collar' of Birmingham's post-war Inner Ring Road, The Mercian is integral to the regeneration of a district caught up in one of the greatest planning blunders of the 20th century. Today, the City Council's efforts to undo the strangulating effect of the ring road system are creating a 21st century city made for people rather than cars.

The Mercian is a marker of the new Birmingham, an elegantly orthogonal tower signalling the city's resolute rebirth. Just as the Chicago School architects pioneered the skyscraper at the turn of the twentieth century – and redefined it in the post-war years – at The Mercian, we set out to define an architecture that epitomises a new era for Birmingham.

FACING PAGE The Mercian standing tall on the Birmingham skyline.

The Mercian with unitised façade.

CONSTRUCTION SYSTEMS

Responding to an urban grain of horizontal podiums and vertical slab blocks formed from a concrete frame structure, the slender, subtly burnished tower rises from a monumental precast clad-plinth engaging Broad Street with three levels of dynamic frontage. A reference to Birmingham's brass foundries and the Timmins Brassworks once located on the site, the façade's defining rhythm of bronze fins was constructed as a prefabricated unitised system to maximise build quality and speed with minimal waste. Façade compositions are based on a "double order" of architectural articulation—emphasising verticality and elegance and culminating in a "crown" of finely elongated proportions.

Residents' amenity spaces and arrival atrium.

Apartment interior.

Residents' podium garden.

CHAPTER EIGHT – CASE STUDY 2 – THE MERCIAN

Broad Street podium active frontage with retail units.

Bronze unitised façade "veil".

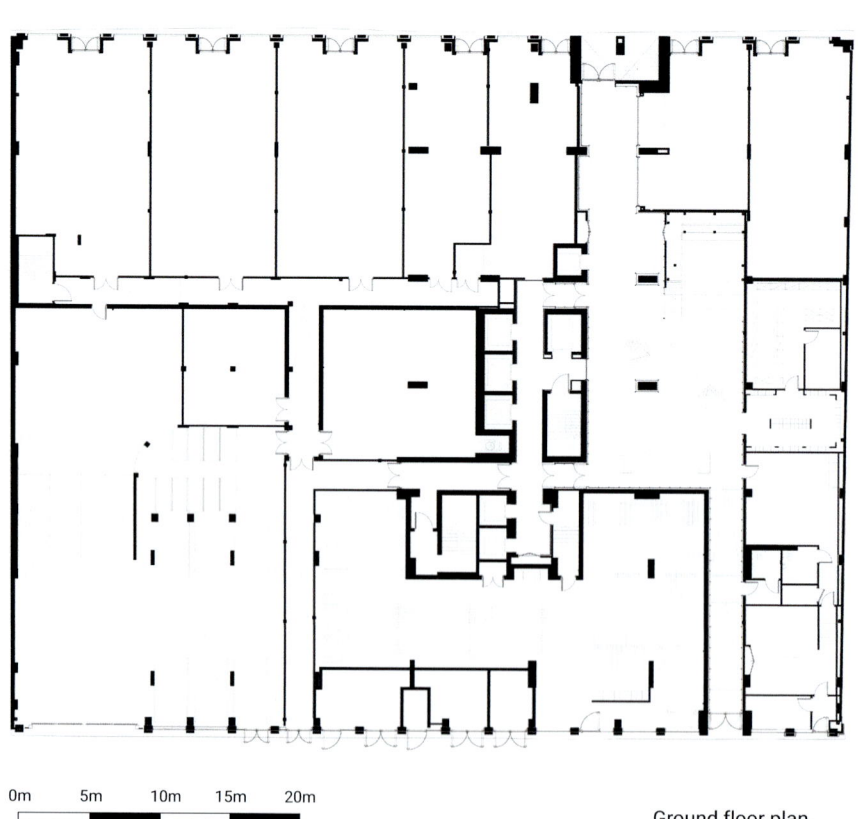
Ground floor plan.

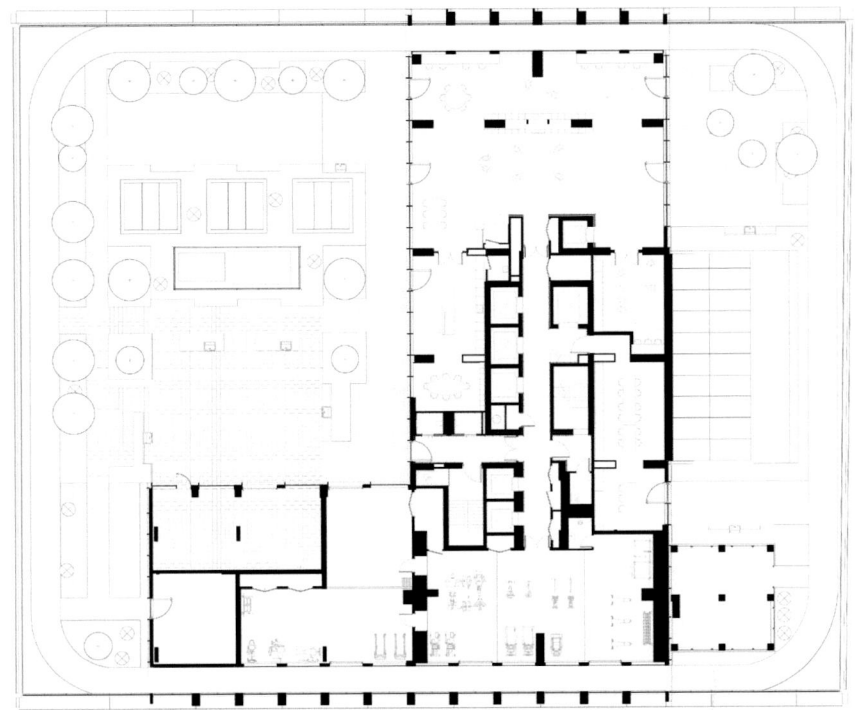

Third floor plan with podium.

Typical lower and upper residential plan.

CHAPTER EIGHT – CASE STUDY 2 – THE MERCIAN

BTR AMENITIES

The Mercian establishes new frontiers in Birmingham's rental market, offering superior quality homes with an enhanced service offer and extended amenities. Residents of 481 studios, one-beds and two-or three-bedroom family apartments have access to entertainment facilities, a cinema, a 24-hour gym and wellbeing support on tap.

Most of the amenities are clustered at podium level with the top of the building reserved for penthouse-style apartments. A unique feature is a running track which loops around the development's 1,400 sq m podium terrace while the building's technology allows residents to fine-tune their apartment environments through their phones. A multi-purpose entertainment room has the capability of opening up to the podium deck to enable all-season functionality.

Finished in crisply-detailed, fair-faced concrete, The Mercian's podium houses a triple-height residential reception, single and double-height retail units, residents' amenities and on-site management team alongside a floor of flexible workspaces for use by tenants and citizens.

200m residents' running track.

Residents' podium roof garden.

Façade crown to the top of the building.

ENVIRONMENTAL SUSTAINABILITY ASPECTS

Moda is committed to delivering exemplar sustainable residential neighbourhoods and puts environmental performance, health and wellbeing at the forefront of everything it does across its portfolio of rental brands and developments.

Designed as a 21st century smart building, data on thermal comfort levels, CO_2 and lighting conditions is automatically tracked in real-time through the residents' app and can be adjusted to meet wellbeing standards and environmental performance. The technology also allows residents to monitor their energy usage and costs in real-time, encouraging them to minimise these. The building operates 100% on renewable energy from wind, tidal and solar sources. As a long-term operator, Moda Living bulk buys renewable energy for 12 months at a time, passing the cost savings onto its residents.

CASE STUDY 3
Coppermaker Square

- **CLIENT** Unibail-Rodamco-Westfield (URW)
- **ARCHITECT** PRP
- **BTR OPERATOR** Greystar
- **MAIN CONTRACTOR** URW
- **LOCATION** Stratford, London
- **START ON SITE** February 2018
- **COMPLETION** Due December 2024
- **GROSS INTERNAL FLOOR AREA** 145,244.1m²
- **CONSTRUCTION COST** £750 million+
- **CONSTRUCTION COST PER M²** £5,163.72

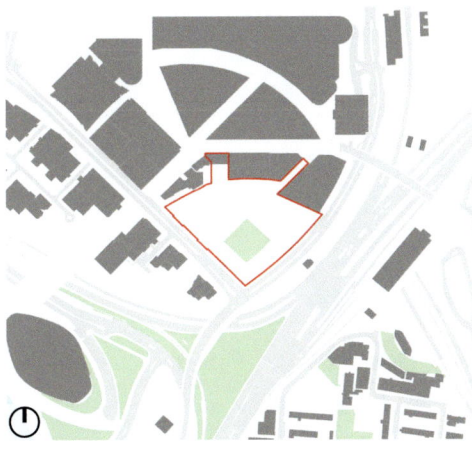
Pre-construction figure-ground plan.

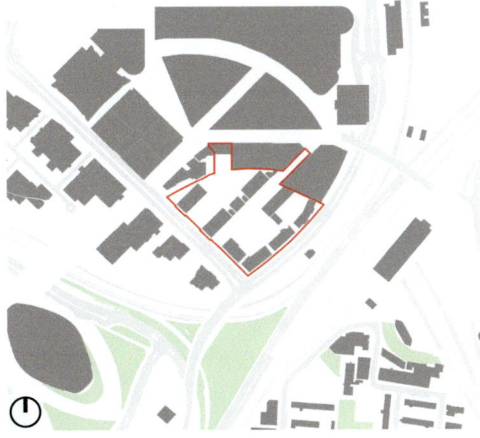
Post-construction figure-ground plan.

BACKGROUND

Coppermaker Square is a landmark Build To Rent development of sector-leading accommodation and associated amenities. The project has been developed by Unibail-Rodamco-Westfield (URW) adjacent to Westfield Stratford City, one of the busiest shopping destinations in Europe. The location could hardly be more ideal for a BTR development given that Stratford station is one of the most connected in London, existing retail provision and significant public amenity on the doorstep in the form of the Queen Elizabeth Olympic Park. URW has appointed Greystar as the managing and operating company for the facility.

PRP, fresh from designing the major BTR development next to Wembley Stadium (see Wembley Park Case Study) were commissioned as design and delivery Architect having picked up a high-level outline planning consent achieved by Glen Howells Architects (GHA). GHA remained involved as Design Guardian and represented URW in discussions with the London Legacy Development Corporation (LLDC), the planning authority. PRP led the design team to prepare planning applications for Reserved Matters and associated Non-Material Amendments. Planning permission was granted in February 2018. Construction commenced in 2019 with a budget of over £750m and it is being constructed in a single phase, with sectional completion of each residential building and associated amenity spaces. It is the largest single-phase construction project in PRP's 60-year history.

The development provides 1,225 BTR dwellings with a mix of studio, 1, 2, 3 & 4 bedroom duplexes and apartments. A high degree of repetition has been designed into the scheme; for efficiency there are only 74 dwelling types. 10% of plots across different sizes are to an adaptable standard under Approved Document M. Also provided are a pair of leisure units at over 8,000m² and a service yard to the existing facility, an amenity hub with wellness spa and a two-storey, glass-roofed office space at 8,160m². Storey heights range from 4 to 39 storeys across 12 distinct buildings set within a landscaping podium over a two-storey basement.

CONSTRAINTS AND DESIGN RESOLUTION

Site constraints include existing roads Westfield Avenue to the south-west and Montfitchet Road to the south-east. A Docklands Light Railway tunnel is immediately adjacent to the site, as is Westfield shopping centre and car park to the north-west

FACING PAGE View from Westfield Avenue towards the towers, with the mansion blocks in the distance.

Illustrative site plan.

and north-east. Added to this mix is the mainline railway and tube lines across the road to the south-east, a recent addition to which is the Elizabeth Line. A Marks & Spencer (M&S) department store forms part of the northern boundary, a windowless nine-story edifice.

From a security perspective, being close to the retail destination and Olympic legacy local sports arenas, including the West Ham United FC home ground at the Olympic Stadium, meant that site lockdown, access control and upgraded glazing performance have needed to be incorporated. Football fans passing the development in their thousands on match day was a particular concern. Strict performance criteria for the façade influenced the narrow, full-height vent windows with fins as well as the resolution of private amenity requirements for each flat by providing external balcony space within the apartments of the tower buildings. This solved the issue of providing protection from strong winds to projecting balconies and simplified the external envelope of the towers.

Within the pre-existing site boundary was a coach park built on a raised podium from the time of the Olympic Park creation, with grassed banks sloping down from road level towards Westfield shopping centre car park and existing structures adjacent to

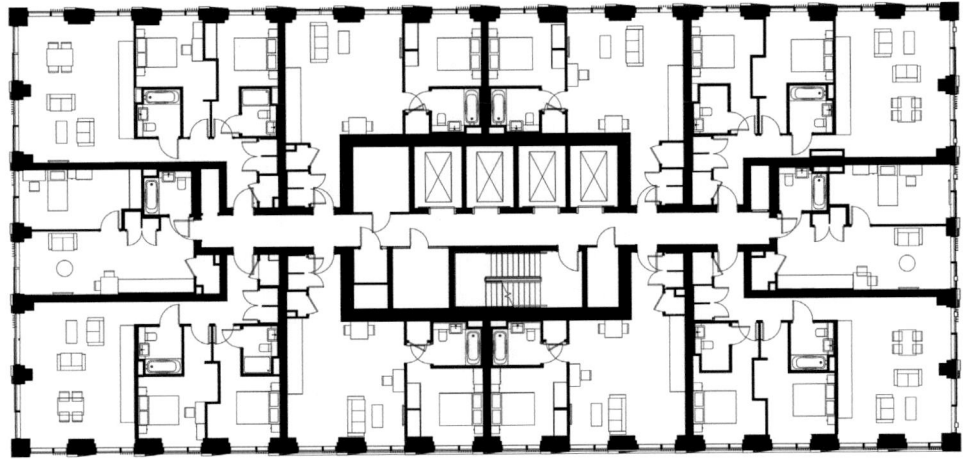

Block A1, typical floor plan.

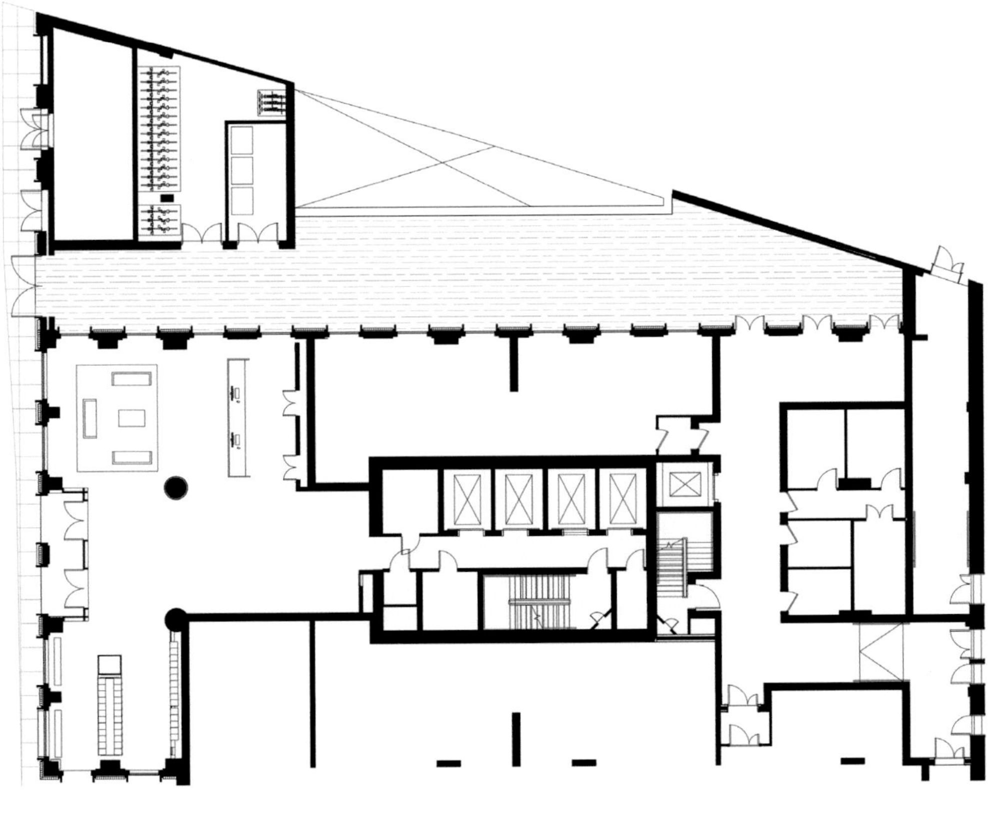

Block A1, ground floor plan.

CHAPTER EIGHT – CASE STUDY 3 – COPPERMAKER SQUARE

the north-west, including the M&S store, and north-east. Over several months this fill was removed truck by truck to reveal an edge boundary condition 8 metres in depth. The retaining structure was formed steel and concrete piling with a capping beam.

Adjacent to the existing M&S building is an intricate junction framed by a concrete slab structure on columns presenting the entrance portal to the shopping centre car park. Vehicles drive under this structure, via a series of ramps to the car park. Servicing lorries also access this space to serve the M&S store. The near constant access requirement for this servicing meant the site logistics around this existing structure and entrance were incredibly complex as the construction of Coppermaker Square could not disrupt the retail servicing or car park use for shoppers. Added to this was the structural gymnastics of providing a steel frame capable of carrying the loads of the 12-storey mansion block above the existing car park entrance slab, which was insufficient to do so without structural assistance. The resultant solution comprises a full-storey structural steel transfer zone and additional concrete slab and encasement which pushed the building up by 1.5m beyond what had been allowed for at outline design stage. This zone included 25m long steel beams to transfer new building loads down through the grid of the existing columns below to the foundations, which in turn had to be increased in capacity. The delivery to site and installation of these steels included huge transport vehicles and cranage that needed careful managing on site to maintain the construction programme. Similarly, an existing partial bridge link structure from the shopping centre was incorporated into the design. Large supporting columns are on show within the wellness spa gym and structural and finish movement joints allow for the new and existing structures to co-exist.

The project also had to negotiate one of the most challenging planning jurisdictions within the UK. The LLDC was set up as a special corporation to deliver a successful post-Olympic environment and this included its own municipal planning authority. The LLDC has had the delivery of quality in design and construction as one of its chief drivers and this created a comparatively rarefied planning regime for obtaining consents and approvals.

The façade concept is based on two distinct strategies. Firstly, the tower buildings are to express their innate verticality. Secondly, the lower height mansion buildings are to follow a horizontal theme, accentuated by the balcony guarding design. Both sets of buildings have a ribbed and textured base of robust GRC cladding to the lower storeys.

The upper façades of all buildings use aluminium cladding with a textured and grained PPC finish for longevity, ease of maintenance and the ability to form the sawtooth profiled panels on the towers that give shadow and depth to the façade. For the towers, the sawtooth pattern to the inner, chamfered, facets of cladding continues the subtle, visual texture across the large repetitive façades.

Vertical fins in bronze-coloured metal cladding provide barrier protection to opening vents on the towers and in certain locations on the mansion buildings. Following discussions with the municipal planning team during the construction drawings phase, a more distinct design feature was required to separate the mansion buildings from the towers but remain within the spirit of the design concept. This resulted in a change to a light-coloured brick slip system to the horizontal bandings. This system was required to be included in the premanufactured unitised façade panels and the

View from the corner of Westfield Avenue and Montfitchet Road with the "Hows" building corner balconies in the foreground.

Amenity hub "Foundry" building private dining and bar area with exposed services aesthetic.

Amenity hub "Foundry" building co-working space private booths area with space for quiet personal working.

CHAPTER EIGHT – CASE STUDY 3 – COPPERMAKER SQUARE

The "Xavier" tower entrance lobby with co-working area.

Amenity hub "Foundry" building seating terrace, overlooking the landscaped Coppermaker Square.

prefabricated balconies. Specific detail was paid to coordinating the brick detailing at the soffits and banding junctions, which has proven successful.

Guarding to sliding glazing, terraces, patios and balconies is formed of light and dark bronze PPC metal railings, with vertical fins to the vent panes on all buildings. Metalwork details, including window and door frames, are a carefully chosen palette of light and dark bronze colours to complement the lighter cladding elements.

CONSTRUCTION SYSTEMS

Concrete frame is the principal construction system backed by a strong focus on offsite manufacture and prefabrication to drive efficiency, including the façade as unitised and stick façade systems as well as the provision of balconies, bathroom pods and prefabricated utility cupboards. Internal components have been driven by two interior design colour schemes with a light and dark colour palette to suit varying tastes. Other components have been extensively categorised into types such as kitchens, doors and wardrobes. Design decisions made early in the process ensured for a quality outcome, such as having columns coordinated and buried within the depth of party walls following rationalisation of the structure to avoid projections to the internal finishes.

There has been a close relationship between the digital design information and the reality of the site construction work. Working in a BIM Level 2 environment has meant a high degree of coordination between consultants and also with contractors, with the 3D scenario used to tackle complex areas of coordination. In particular, builderswork requirements through structure for the services design were tracked in detail. This is an on-line portal which is uploaded with construction drawings, which is used to navigate works on site in order to sign-off sub-contractor installations and to streamline snagging. It also allows for remote approvals of remedial works thanks to the main contractor's integrated use of photographic evidence and tracking of observed issues.

BTR AMENITIES

The amenity provision includes a wellness spa in the basement, private dining and flexible work spaces within the central hub, known as the Coppermaker Club and associated basement spaces providing support facilities.

The wellness spa includes a 25m swimming pool incorporating drown detection and alarm technology. It includes a vitality pool with luxurious showers adjacent, a steam room and a sauna. A range of changing facilities incorporates accessible and family provision. A fully fitted out gym has a glass wall overlooking the pool hall and has studio spinning space complete with energetic lighting layout and mirror wall, sprung floors, multi-use yoga and dance space. Beyond this are the staff facilities including changing, office, break-out and storage facilities.

Also within the basement is fully accessible car parking, cycle parking and plant spaces, plus a series of resident ancillary spaces which can be used for storage. This enables bulkier personal items (such as skis, golf clubs etc.) to be stored securely outside the dwellings, leaving vital storage space for the more day-to-day items within the dwellings themselves.

Entrance lobbies have been designed as welcoming, high, well-lit and comfortable spaces as an extension to amenity spaces with meanwhile working and relaxation zones included. Post-box, metalwork and signage design and finishes incorporate a copper-coloured theme for the branding design.

A luxuriously fitted out media space within the mansion buildings offers another amenity space to be booked for resident use, including a kitchenette and specialist designed cinema and presentation space complete with tiered seating and acoustic wall finishes.

A key aspect of the scheme is the quality of the central landscape amenity. The prime space is a new public square which is overlooked by most of the new buildings. This forms the green heart of the scheme, and has been designed to be an oasis of calm

Wellness spa view through to the pool hall from the picture window of the gym.

and tranquillity consisting of a central, open area of lawn with smaller intimate spaces incorporating ornamental planting, hedges and seating. Screen planting is provided along the edges of all private amenity terraces at the base of each building, providing privacy for residents and further greening the public realm. The space is intended to be publicly accessible, open during daylight hours, It also provides connection with the wider shopping centre thoroughfare. An array of high-quality external amenity facilities includes a roof garden which is accessible to all residents via the Residents' Amenity Hub. It breaks up into a series of sub-spaces, including various amenities such as barbecues and an outdoor spill-out space for the Hub.

The approach to play is to integrate varied facilities throughout all spaces, creating different opportunities for young children age and different abilities to interact with each other and the landscape, and encourages physical activity for the children from an early age. Play clusters and landscape trails are integral.

ENVIRONMENTAL SUSTAINABILITY ASPECTS

Connection to the local district heating and cooling network, high-performance fabric efficiency measures and major transport and shopping destinations on its doorstep (resulting in a healthy PTAL rating) means the development is highly sustainable. This is supported by the use of prefabricated elements brought to site to reduce waste and speed up installation.

Amenity hub "Foundry" tower kitchen with vertical aesthetic light colour palette including bespoke lighting and integrated appliances.

"Harrison" tower entrance lobby with feature lighting, joinery and post boxes.

Passive features

The window design in all of the dwellings allows the rooms to have good amounts of daylight throughout the year, minimising the use of artificial lighting and having a positive impact on the wellbeing of the users. Additionally, the glazing ratios help the ingress of solar gains, allowing for passive solar heating which limits the need for mechanical space heating in winter. The window design has also aimed to limit summertime solar gains to reduce space-cooling demands. This reduces the likelihood of high internal temperatures, creating a comfortable environment for the occupants.

The design proposes a very efficient thermal envelope and façade to mitigate against the effects of climate change. Improved airtightness and high levels of insulation have been incorporated, including double glazing and low g-values to reduce the risk of overheating. Despite the low g-value applied, it is intended to keep the window light transmittance higher than 70% to provide adequate daylighting and reduce the reliance on artificial lighting.

Heat losses through the building fabric have been minimised with thermal insulation. The design of an efficient thermal envelope allows for reduced demand for space heating during the cold months of the year. The resultant U-values have been 0.12 W/m2k for the roof, 0.15 W/m2k for the external walls, and 1.40 W/m2k for the windows.

The design has considered natural ventilation for the dwellings by incorporating openable windows that provide the potential for very effective daytime and night-time natural ventilation, with high levels of occupant air flow control. To minimise the potential overheating risk, passive design measures such as increased opening sizes, blinds, and ventilation panels, among other features, were included.

The absence of projecting balconies to the towers significantly increases the Average Daylight Factor (ADF) levels achieved for homes in the towers. This is due to the ability to locate glazing directly to the external wall line with no obstructions above in the form of winter gardens or balconies.

Systems

Mechanical Ventilation with Heat Recovery is incorporated throughout the development. The system is used for background ventilation year-round, with a summer by-pass function to provide mechanical ventilation during summer. Where ambient conditions allow, residential units will mostly use natural ventilation during summer to purge excess heat, while the MVHR system will extract stagnant stale air and provide fresh background air. Comfort cooling has been provided in the residential tower buildings.

Circularity

In this case study too, the use of modular materials and the concept of building in layers will make it easier to repair the different building components if and when needed, or to replace them when they reach their end-of-life. This will result in a significant reduction in material waste. The use of prefabricated elements further contributes to the circular economy strategy of the scheme, with faster construction, cost savings and waste reduction.

View from the landscaped podium adjacent the "Harrison" tower looking towards the "Bussell" and "Xavier" towers.

Water efficient fittings and appliances have been selected, as they use significantly less water than their traditional counterparts by limiting water flow through pipes and fittings and by changing conventional design to more ergonomic. The water conservation strategy proposed for the scheme incorporates flexibility in the specification of water fittings and appliances.

Preference has been given to the selection of sustainable materials with a low environmental impact over their life cycle. Their selection has been focused on materials that are sourced in a responsible way and have a low embodied carbon impact during their extraction, processing, manufacturing and recycling.

Energy

The project is within the vicinity of an existing energy centre and therefore will be connected to the existing district heating network. Access to district heating provides opportunity to benefit from low-carbon heating and cooling energy. The centre has been designed to be served by a gas fired CHP but the operator is developing plans to decarbonise the energy centre.

As lighting represents a high demand in energy usage, it is important to consider efficient solutions for its consumption. With this in mind, the scheme has aimed to install 100% energy efficient lighting to serve all the domestic areas.

The wellness spa pool hall looking towards the steam and sauna rooms and vitality pool and experience showers.

CASE STUDY 4
Lewisham Gateway II

- **CLIENT** Muse
- **ARCHITECT** UNStudio/PRP
- **BTR OPERATOR** Get Living
- **MAIN CONTRACTOR** Balfour Beatty
- **LOCATION** Lewisham, London
- **START ON SITE** July 2020
- **COMPLETION** forecast May 2024
- **GROSS INTERNAL FLOOR AREA** 57,580.9m²
- **CONSTRUCTION COST** circa 200 million
- **CONSTRUCTION COST PER M²** circa £3,470

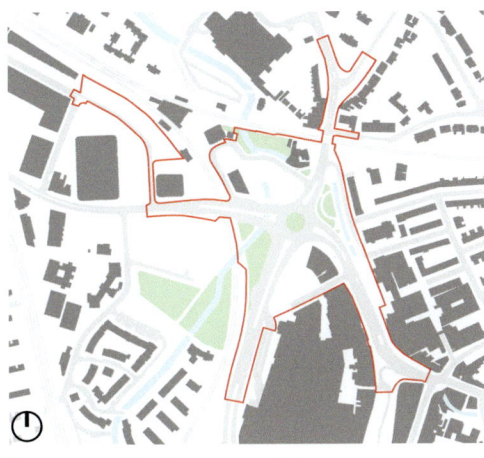
Pre-construction figure-ground plan.

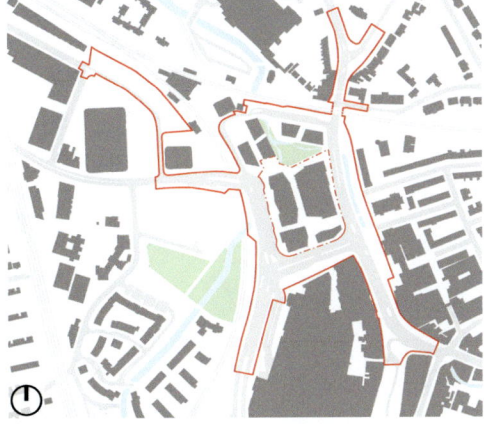
Post-construction figure-ground plan.

BACKGROUND

Lewisham Gateway is a design-led, high-density, mixed-use development set in the heart of Lewisham Town Centre, delivered for a JV (Lewisham Gateway Developments Limited – LGDL) between the London Borough of Lewisham, GLA, TFL, London Bus Services and MUSE, with later involvement from Get Living London and Fizzy Living. It forms the centrepiece of the town centre's revitalisation, comprising retail, leisure, office and multi-tenure residential accommodation. The development substantially reconfigures the road layouts and two rivers running beneath the site to create two new publicly accessible spaces. Underpinning the whole scheme is the residential component, which principally consists of BTR with some Co-living and open market sale.

The brief from LGDL was to create an exemplar high-density, mixed-use scheme that would regenerate the town centre, providing impetus for wider investment from the private sector, and reconnect the fragmented public realm and connectivity.

The scheme was originally granted Outline Planning consent in 2009 and is due to be completed in 2024. The outline consent came with parameters and a design code, all of which were substantially updated over the years to reflect current market conditions and changing regulations. PRP were instrumental in shepherding through planning this complex project, through multiple submissions and amendments, with multiple clients and stakeholders, on a highly constrained, technically challenging site.

CONSTRAINTS AND DESIGN RESOLUTION

The site was extremely constrained with significant challenges and considerations. The roundabout in the heart of the site was well known as one of London's most dangerous, especially for cyclists and pedestrians trying to navigate from the overground station and DLR station to the town centre. The proposals sought to address this by removing the roundabout, forming a revised road network that created a new and significant development parcel. This in turn enabled the de-culverting of the two local rivers – the Quaggy and the Ravensbourne – bringing them both together on the edge of a new public park. The new parcels contributed to new public realm with safe walking and cycling routes and a rationalised road crossing strategy to improve interconnectivity and safety of local pedestrians moving from the town centre to the stations.

FACING PAGE View from Confluence Place.

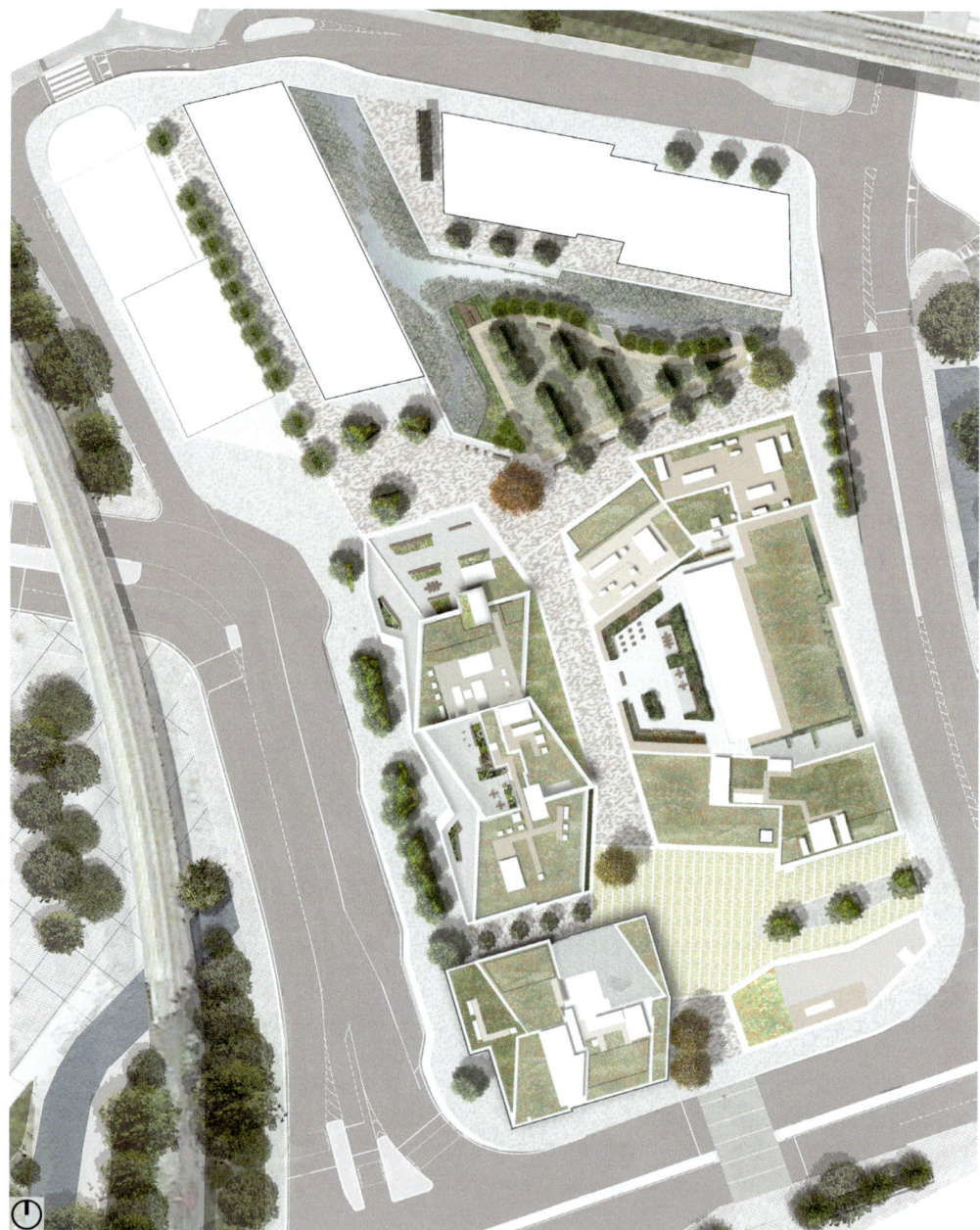

Illustrative site plan.

Topographically, the site sits in a small valley with much of the surrounding context low in scale and nestled within trees. A small number of taller, denser developments within the town centre, such as the Barratt Homes Renaissance project, Lewisham Shopping Centre and Citibank Tower contrasted heavily with the two-storey Victorian housing sitting within conservation areas and the listed St Stephens Church, which is adjacent to the site. Regeneration often requires a step change in scale, and Lewisham Gateway is no exception. The design worked hard to successfully mediate between the higher density town centre context and the lower density surrounding and heritage assets.

The design developed along a fairly linear process, with significant public and stakeholder engagement from day one. The overall vision for the masterplan, and original outline consent, was achieved by Arup, with significant engagement. Post the aftermath of the financial crash of 2009, which impacted viability and therefore progress, LGDL took the scheme forward with PRP through a series of successful phased Reserved Matters Applications. The first phase delivered much needed public space of Confluence Place – so named as it became the place of convergence of the Quaggy and Ravensbourne – and two blocks consisting of traditional for sale homes and a small amount of BTR for Fizzy Living. At this point BTR was in its infancy in the UK, and the now commonplace proportions of amenity and support spaces had not become ossified. PRP, now collaborating with UNStudio of the Netherlands, delivered Phase Two with all the 649 homes as BTR, now containing all the traditional support and amenity spaces expected of a BTR development, plus incorporating Get Living London's first Co-living offer.

One of the biggest challenges of Lewisham Gateway, and one that the design successfully navigates, is the complex interplay of uses. Town centre sites require 24-hour activity and vibrancy, but with that comes the natural conflicts and compromises between differing commercial uses and residential. The ground floor has been designed to deliver an active, engaged and diverse mix of uses such as food and beverage, co-working, retail and a cinema, along with all the residential entrances and lobbies to serve the different tenures. A new retail street has also been created for the project through the centre leading from Confluence Place to St Stephens Square, creating a new civic space at the heart of the southern part of the site. Servicing, plant and other ancillary uses, so often the killers of street-side activity, have been carefully embedded within the urban blocks and out of sight.

Residential uses sit above one and, in some instances, two different commercial uses, with the technical challenges of achieving a fit-for-purpose environment for legibly accessing communal entrances to homes and complex and non-residential servicing requirements.

Axonometric.

Cinema/Block C.

BTR AMENITIES

Although the first phase, due to its pioneering nature, did not contain any of the traditional amenities now expected of BTR, the second phase of development made up for this with a well-rounded offer.

What was most compelling about the design was the exo-amenity, or external amenities to the buildings, complementing the internal offer. Residents had access to the gym, co-working spaces, all the usual town centre uses and public realm, plus the deep and varied facilities that Lewisham town centre had to offer.

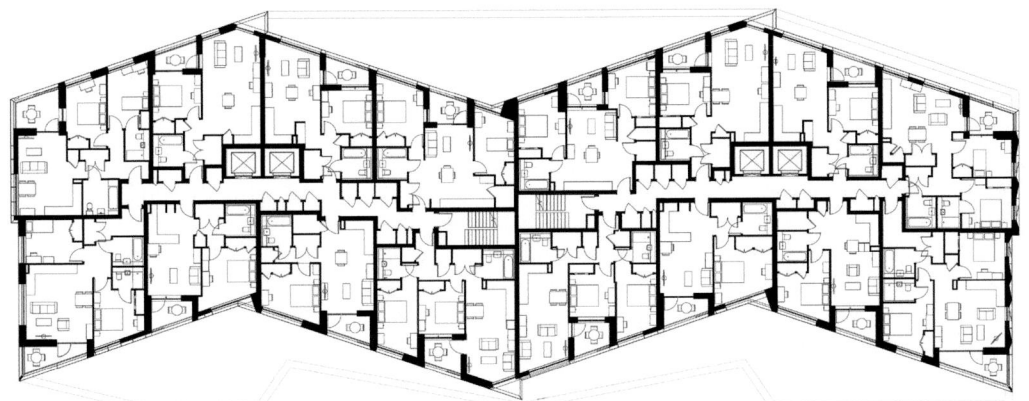

Block D1, fourth floor.

Block D1, third floor.

CHAPTER EIGHT – CASE STUDY 4 – LEWISHAM GATEWAY II

This highly complex scheme contained all the elements of a vibrant town centre on a postage stamp site – cinemas, retail, restaurants, co-working spaces, a gym and a variety of programmable civic and public spaces.

Outdoor amenity spaces are provided for the residents. At podium level, located in building C1, the design includes paved areas with seating, tables and chairs, set between raised planters. The terraces are organised to provide areas to congregate and enjoy the views out over Lewisham, as well as more intimate areas for sitting or dining out.

CONSTRUCTION SYSTEMS

The site is incredibly restricted and the logistics of building such a high-density project were detailed and involved. Construction methodology and phasing was as much part of the design process as aesthetics and placemaking. Phase 2 especially required detailed consideration about site set-up and compound, as little space was available. Workers facilities and site accommodation were raised on specially-fabricated steel stilts within gaps between blocks to allow construction traffic to pass underneath. Limited set-down space and storage meant a just-in-time programme of deliveries, heavily managed to ensure programme progress and reduction of impact to local traffic flows.

The structure is a mix of traditional reinforced concrete and post tensioned (PT) concrete slabs. The use of PT reduced the overall building height, used less concrete and achieved a carbon saving for the structural frame materials. Due to the lack of space on site and the requirement for the highest quality, many elements of the rest of the building were fabricated off-site. Façades are unitised and craned up to the required level and fixed, speeding up closing-up of the building and allowing for internal fit-out to be completed swiftly.

The project includes four blocks; Block C, D1, D2 and Block E. Block C comprises two elements connected by a three-storey high podium. The northern part of the building will comprise ten storeys, whereas the southern part of the building will be 12 storeys high. In total, Block C will provide 67 apartments, 119 Co-living studios, associated communal spaces, a cinema, retail, associated back of house facilities and a service

View from Molesworth Street.

Street view.

St. Stephen's Square.

yard. Block D1 comprises a rising concertinaing form with a small two-storey high podium element. The northern part of the building starts at 16 storeys and the southern part rises up to 19 storeys. In total, Block D1 will provide 243 apartments, a gym, retail, a ticket office and associated back of house facilities. Block D2 is comprised of a tall building of 30 storeys with a small two-storey podium element. In total, Block D2 will provide 220 apartments, retail and associated back of house facilities.

ENVIRONMENTAL SUSTAINABILITY ASPECTS

The project embraces a number of features and strategies that have positively contributed to the delivery of a highly sustainable scheme.

PASSIVE FEATURES

Dual aspect ventilation has been incorporated to provide natural ventilation and good indoor air quality, as well as to use passive cooling techniques during the warmer months.

The design of the glazing proportions was driven by the desire to provide good daylight quality for all dwellings, whilst avoiding summertime overheating; this was achieved by proposing different glazing proportions based on orientation. The generous window-to-wall ratios in most of the rooms allow good amounts of daylight throughout the year, minimising the need for artificial lighting and having a positive impact on the wellbeing of the users. Additionally, the glazing ratios help the ingress of passive solar heating, which limits the need for space heating in winter, limits summertime solar gains to reduce space cooling demands and limits the likelihood of high internal temperatures.

The need for space heating during the colder months has been reduced through the provision of an effective thermal envelope. The thermal transmittances of the elements constituting the building envelope have been minimised, with the different elements achieving U-values of 0.11–0.16 W/m²k for the roof, 0.20 W/m²k for the external walls, 0.13–0.16 W/m²k for the floor and 1.40 W/m²k for the windows.

View from Molesworth Street.

Taking into consideration that the sustainability strategy was made in 2016, the values might not exceed the ones suggested by LETI. Nevertheless, they are exceeding the Building Regulations Part L1A (2013).

The design of the elevation also contributes to the climate-responsive approach proposed by the scheme, with the integration of perforated aluminium panels, a feature which provides sun protection during the summer months, in addition to providing privacy for the residents. The screen allows daylight to pass while preventing overheating in summer.

SYSTEMS

Mechanical Ventilation with Heat Recovery has been implemented in the development. The system will be used for background ventilation year-round, with a "summer bypass" function to provide mechanical ventilation during summer. Where ambient conditions allow, residential units will mostly use natural ventilation to purge heat from the units, whilst MVHR will extract stagnant stale air and provide fresh background air.

CIRCULARITY

Pre-fabricated elements have been used, as part of a circular economy strategy which allows materials to be easily replaced and therefore helping reduce material waste. These elements also allow a faster construction process, cost savings and waste reduction.

Water consumption in the development is minimised through the specification of highly-efficient water installations. This limits water consumption in apartments to 105 litres per person per day. This is in line with the previous Code Level 4 requirement and equivalent to the requirement set out in GLA Guidance. Commercial areas will target a 40% reduction in water consumption by implementing water efficient fittings such as low flow showers and taps, dual flush WCs, and water efficient white goods. Hot water will be provided by the centralised Combined Heat and Power plant and gas boilers.

ENERGY AND FABRIC

The masterplan has been designed to accommodate two energy centres and enable the implementation of a district heating energy network. Once Phase 2 is completed, the two energy centres will be connected through a common district energy network that will serve the entire Lewisham Gateway scheme. It is anticipated that due to the implementation of Combined Heat and Power (CHP), a reduction in regulated CO_2 emissions of 20–25% is targeted. The two energy centres will be designed to facilitate the potential future connection of the site-wide energy network into an area-wide district heating network.

In line with planning policy targets, the development will be provided with an on-site PV array of 9 kWp which, based on solar irradiance data for London, would generate 9,700 kWh of renewable electricity per annum (based on annual PV performance of 150 kWh/m²/yr), reducing CO_2 emissions by 5 tonnes per annum.

The approach to sizing the CHP has been undertaken based upon providing 100% of the hot water for the main water-consuming areas and up to 50% of the space heating demands for the residential units, cinema and library areas. Based on the space heating and hot water parameters, it is anticipated that a further reduction in regulated CO_2 emissions of 420 tonnes could be achieved. This results in an overall CO_2 emission reduction of 24%.

View of the high street.

CASE STUDY 5
Wembley Park

- **CLIENT** Quintain
- **ARCHITECT** PRP
- **BTR OPERATOR** Quintain Living
- **MAIN CONTRACTOR** Sisk/Wates
- **LOCATION** Wembley, London
- **START ON SITE** January 2017
- **COMPLETION** June 2021
- **GROSS INTERNAL FLOOR AREA** 179,153.4 m²
- **CONSTRUCTION COST** £601.2m
- **CONSTRUCTION COST PER M²** circa £3,356

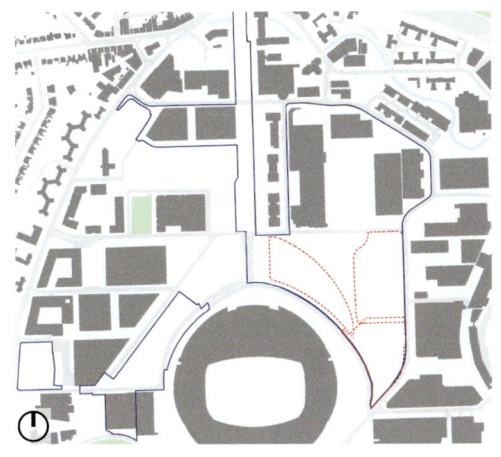
Pre-construction figure-ground plan.

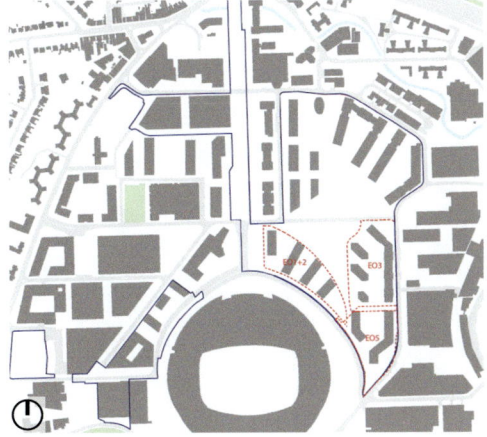
Post-construction figure-ground plan.

BACKGROUND

The Wembley Park development depicted within this case study is three projects in one, providing 1,834 dwellings as part of Quintain's wider transformation of the land around Wembley Stadium. In addition to the new homes, the three projects which are part of the wider 85-acre site provide ten ground floor retail units, a 29,000 sq ft gym, 3,000 sq ft crèche, office space, a public Multi Use Games Area and the first phase of a new seven-acre park.

The three adjoining projects – Canada Gardens, The Robinson and Madison, Lexington and Bowery – are situated immediately to the north-east of Wembley Stadium and were built more or less concurrently by two contractors, Sisk and Wates, in three separate building contracts. Each of the developments is aimed at a slightly different customer base, which is expressed through the types of homes available to rent and through the design of landscape, interiors and amenities. The boutique design agency, Fossey Arora, conceptualised the interiors along three distinctly evocative themes and contributed hugely and collaboratively to the podium and rooftop terrace environments.

With 743 Build To Rent homes across seven buildings, Canada Gardens is the largest development at Wembley Park. 303 of these homes are classed as Discount Market Rent. These homes are pepper-potted throughout the development to ensure they are tenure blind and 80 wheelchair adaptable homes are also provided. The tallest of the buildings is 26 storeys high.

Immediately south of Canada Gardens, The Robinson development comprises 458 homes and forms the southern gateway to Wembley Park. The tallest building is 23 storeys high. It is aimed at graduate living and sharers and includes larger four-bedroom homes which are provided with a range of playful, unique amenities.

Madison, Lexington and Bowery comprises 633 homes within four buildings splayed radially, providing three distinct landscaped gardens between. The tallest buildings are 15 storeys high. Retail, office, community and leisure floorspace are also provided. The development, which overlooks the iconic Olympic Way and the new Olympic Steps, includes a landscaped podium with views to the neighbouring

FACING PAGE Canada Gardens.

Wembley Park illustrative site plan.

National Stadium. Two buildings adjoining Madison, Lexington and Bowery have been sold to Brent Council's affordable housing subsidiary for key workers and to Legal & General for provision of affordable homes.

The three sites have seamlessly integrated a challenging mix of distinct parking requirements. This includes over 160 event day spaces for coaches at grade within a large structure below the podium gardens, over 200 accessible parking spaces linked via a pedestrian bridge to the stadium concourse and 330 residential car parking spaces below ground, via a linked basement car park across plots and undulating site levels. 1,000 bicycle spaces are provided in a range of locations to facilitate short stay (daily access) and long stay that can be flexed with resident storage cages.

Landscape is a key theme across the three developments and the scale of development that has been realised allows vistas to be created within the necklace of 14 buildings which are truly impressive.

CONSTRAINTS AND DESIGN RESOLUTION

Delivery of the three plots amongst an already active residential neighbourhood and an adjacent, frequently used National Stadium, took exceptional logistical management and collaboration, with peak construction activity requiring over 1,500 construction workers on site at the same time.

Canada Gardens

The design intent for Canada Gardens was to integrate with the emerging "Eastern Lands" portion of Wembley Park, orientating the buildings so as to create connectivity with the surrounding public realm including the new park (Union Park) and the neighbouring buildings.

A significant challenge to the design was the need to incorporate the event-day coach parking and a huge energy centre, which required the installation of two 9-metre-tall buffer vessels, whilst activating the ground plane and creating a recognisable residential address.

The resolution created a ground level series of commercial and community spaces, interspersed with individual secondary building lobbies and coach accesses and escape routes addressing both the park and the existing First Way road to the East.

The tallest building, at 26 stories, forms the gateway to the park and draws people towards the super lobby – the principal entrance for residents – located at its base and giving a welcoming openness upon arrival. Angled lozenge-shaped blocks then federate the scale towards the stadium, opening up views to Union Park and from within, maximising valuable long-range views for a greater number of residents through to the bustling 85-acre estate.

Grand lobby entrance, Canada Gardens.

The unique challenge to the development was how it would successfully link all the buildings and resident experience via a single communal lobby. Residents arrive at the grand lobby, collect their post and parcels, interact with staff and neighbours, then move up to podium level via the exposed brick staircase past the clubhouse and meander through the tranquil gardens to their given building.

Dividing the building's western urban block has offered residents the benefit of colourful views and a sense of connection between their home and this new neighbourhood for London. Furthermore, it allows sunlight to perforate the buildings, optimising the development's access to natural daylight. The high glazing ratio of 33% and floor-to-ceiling windows further enables this provision of good natural lighting.

Canada Gardens grand lobby entrance.

Reception area, Canada Gardens.

Coach parking, Canada Gardens.

Canada Gardens third floor plan.

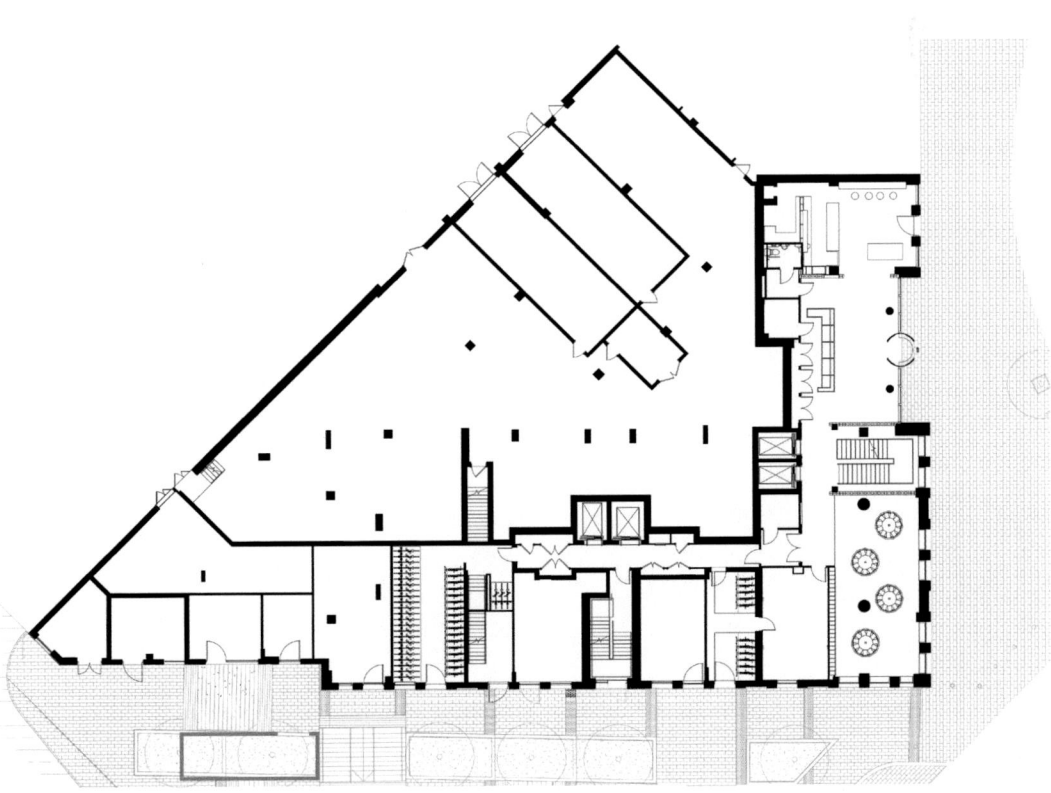

Canada Gardens ground floor plan.

CHAPTER EIGHT – CASE STUDY 5 – WEMBLEY PARK

The Robinson

The site was originally intended to be a multi-storey event-day car park with coach parking at its base, but this has had its potential re-imagined by wrapping the required parking with residential accommodation and embracing the location as a destination for living at the corner of Union Park. The Robinson achieves a significant increase in scale from that envisaged for the original car park proposals, by carefully placing massing to preserve key views across the borough and the iconic stadium whilst marking the arrival by vehicle from the east, an important nodal point that would have otherwise been ignored.

The resulting development responds appropriately to the movement infrastructure of the wider masterplan and anticipates the potential development of the extended Wembley Opportunity Area, creating a critical link to the east, and the future integration of the industrial estate in this location.

The architecture responds to the built form of the stadium, addressing its operational challenges as well as its local surroundings. Each apartment has been designed to maximise views either to the stadium, Union Park or the City of London to the south. The development incorporates ground floor retail, coach and car-parking to serve residents and 80% of the stadium's events. A second-floor footbridge connects blue badge parking to the stadium's concourse.

The site's corner location and neighbouring construction activity meant there was minimal space for construction logistics. The design embraced the challenge, including the need for precast concrete façades by articulating the façade brickwork and panelisation of façade elements so as to hide the joints and retain the brick vernacular characteristic of the Eastern Lands.

The Robinson.

The Robinson at night.

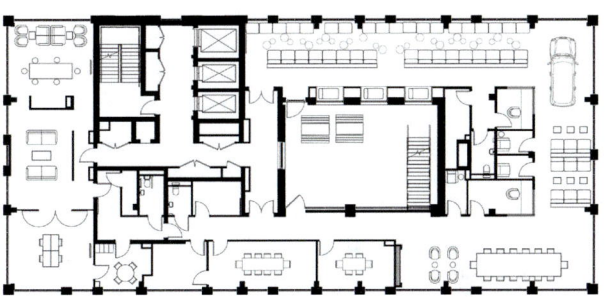

The Robinson sixteenth floor plan.

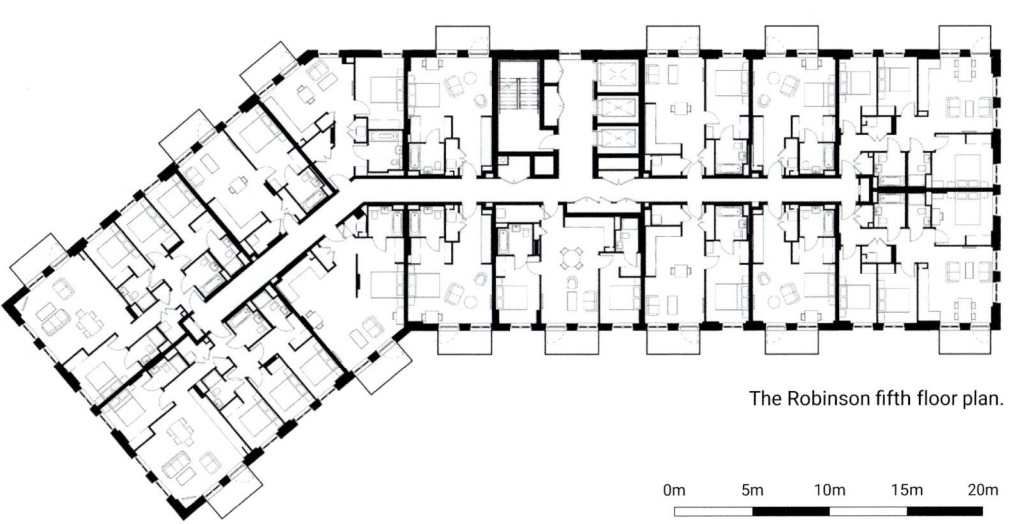

The Robinson fifth floor plan.

0m 5m 10m 15m 20m

CHAPTER EIGHT – CASE STUDY 5 – WEMBLEY PARK

Madison, Lexington and Bowery.

Madison, Lexington and Bowery

The Madison's location holds a strategic position within the Wembley Park masterplan. Situated at the southern end of Olympic Way, the design needed to reflect the scale, massing and appearance of the Plot W03 development opposite, as together they form a striking pair of landmark buildings which effectively mark a southern gateway to Wembley Stadium and provide a nod to the original iconic Wembley stadium twin towers, long since demolished. The previously approved outline planning permission set the parameters for height and massing. The angled edge to three of the blocks allows these buildings to benefit from an eastern facing aspect, allowing greater daylight into homes. This design approach optimises views and legibility, giving many residents views of the park.

Previously an open car park, the existing physical form of the site was flat, with no distinct features, although the brief presented a challenge in managing site levels within the proposed development. The site was dissected by a number of key utilities which were re-routed pre-construction. These included an existing water main, a gas main and a Thames Water foul-water sewer. The site location also required a careful articulation of the urban grain to ensure that the new development would not turn its back on the stadium and instead respond to both Union Park, the elevated stadium concourse and Atlantic Crescent, the only road serving the site.

The development's base storey provides 3,376 sqm of commercial floorspace on its northern, western and southern façades, animating the buildings' key frontages onto the Park, Olympic Circus and Perimeter Way, adding to the life and vibrancy of the streetscape.

A basement is located below the residential courtyard providing 10 wheelchair parking bays and 20% active and 20% passive Electrical Vehicle charging points. A total of 934 cycle parking spaces are provided at the upper ground level of each block to serve the residents.

A specific design constraint for the BTR buildings was how to link circulation from the separated finger buildings whilst managing access and level limitations. The resolution is via a subterranean corridor from the super lobby, which is afforded natural light via a sunken courtyard within the podium garden above, which doubles up with the gym to visually connect activities and residents within.

A notable challenge and success in resolution is the way the development seamlessly combines three differing tenures without visual distinction to create a homogeneous and integrated community. The requirement for tenure ownership of gardens and communal entrance areas for management and acquisition is hidden by subtle separation of boundaries and shared overlooking of spaces. This has been achieved by embracing level changes across the site to provide natural steps to boundaries within the podium gardens. The architecture and materiality of the buildings is consistent for each block.

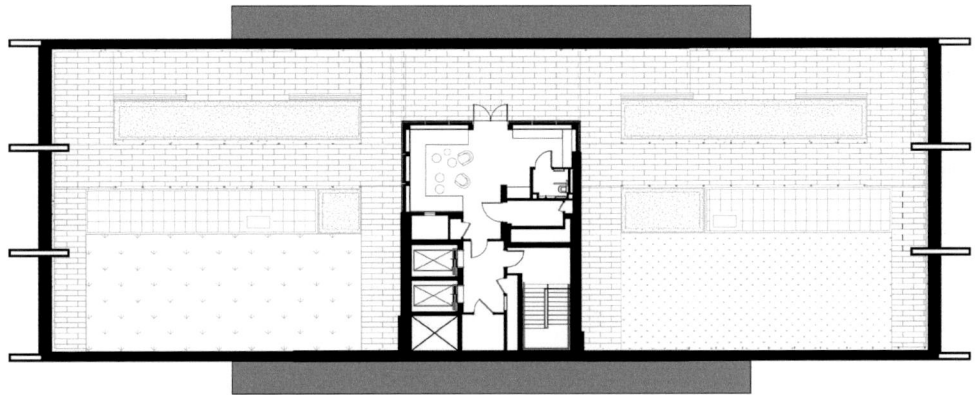

Madison sixteenth floor plan.

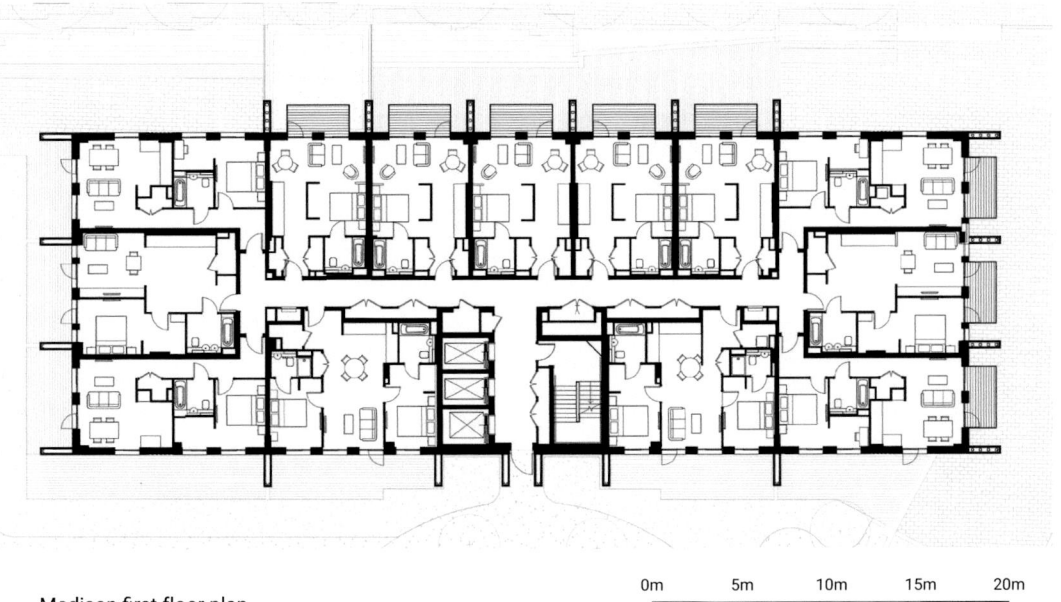

Madison first floor plan.

ENVIRONMENTAL SUSTAINABILITY ASPECTS

Sustainability was a key aspect of the development. The Canada Gardens houses an energy centre operating a sitewide district heating network to serve the three plots and the wider Wembley Park homes and commercial units. All three sites have Envac integrated, an innovative, streamed waste fractions system that sucks waste and recycling down underground tunnels at 70kph to a collection centre at the edge of Wembley Park, minimising the use of refuse lorries and negating the use of ground-floor bin storage facilities for residents. Envac has been incorporated within Quintain developments since they first started regenerating the neighbourhood.

A number of innovations were tested throughout construction. On Canada Gardens, 91.7% of total construction waste from the site was recycled. A smart waste system was used which utilises an environmental site monitoring and reporting tool for all waste. The concrete frame utilised the same ply for all shuttering, as it was not replaced every fourth floor typically, as there were no exposed concrete finishes internally. This resulted in a 70% saving of ply during the frame construction. QR codes were used to track quality process across the site, which produced automatic updates for the programme. This resulted in a 25% time saving on the QA process versus traditional paper methods; a 10% increase in production efficiency; and a 74% reduction of printed drawings. Cloud technology reduced waste and re-work on site. Additionally, the construction operation typically employed 40% local labour, including opportunities for local long-term unemployed and apprentices.

The development is served by an innovative district heating system, anticipating a 42% reduction in carbon emissions beyond the original masterplan's 2013 Building Regulations. The total building NOx emissions are 74% lower than the Building Emissions Benchmark for energy, and 81% lower for transport.

Coach parking ventilation is facilitated largely by natural means across the plot, minimising the need for mechanical extract and ensuring that noise from plant would not be a factor on the podium gardens above.

Overheating analysis and modelling were carried out throughout the design development to ensure mitigation and passive measure were optimised. All homes have natural ventilation, with a small number requiring MVHR due to proximity to noise pollution. Communal corridors were assessed against CIBSE TM52 to

Community gardens, Canada Gardens.

Relaxing water feature, Canada Gardens.

determine potential solutions for overheating. As the communal corridors have a push/pull smoke extract system, this was combined with ventilation systems linked to temperature sensors, with additional adiabatic cooling available for extreme summer peaks.

All buildings have a range of water attenuation systems, with a top-down strategy from communal rooftop amenity terraces, biodiverse roofs, blue roofs, communal amenity gardens including allotments and fruit trees to the new neighbouring park sustainable drainage system. The pond system allows water to rise for 1 in 30 yr. events whilst the surrounding lawns and parks accommodate 1 in 100 yr. events.

Biodiversity Gain and Urban Greening factor exceed legislative and planning requirements.

The contractor, Sisk, developed a close relationship with local foodbank Sufra throughout the duration of the project. This has included Sisk providing the charity with a new professional catering kitchen, allowing the organisation to support more people with emergency food aid. The teams have also spent time volunteering in Sufra's allotment-style community garden, including using up-cycled timber pallets from the construction site to make seating and planters.

CONSTRUCTION SYSTEMS

The principal construction system employed on all three plots at Wembley Park is reinforced concrete frame with concrete slabs on concrete pile foundations. Sisk, used slip form concrete which involves concrete, being poured into a continuously moving form, allowing the contractor to build vertically on two concrete cores, one of which was 22 stories high. Whilst there was no consideration of volumetric construction, considerable design planning and execution has gone into the use of factory assembled components on all three plots of this case study, particularly on Canada Gardens and The Robinson. This hybrid approach to off-site manufacture is a highly optimal method of building, particularly given the recent collapse of several volumetric initiatives.

Factory assembled elements include bathroom pods from Italy, factory assembled balconies and pre-cast façade panels from Lincolnshire used to clad The Robinson. Each instance was reliant on accurate BIM-driven deliverables and data to ensure an optimal, factory processed output. The Robinson development was the first plot

Pre-cast façades being craned into place, the Robinson.

Factory assembled balconies, Canada Gardens.

in Europe to use robotics for construction to increase block-laying productivity, whilst the precast façades reduced the time spent on site, removing the need for scaffolding, which in turn reduced site compound size, noise and disruption to residents nearby. This has brought significant savings and programme efficiencies. The Robinson also has exposed concrete ceilings to each of the apartments, requiring careful coordination of services but dispensing with the installation of conventional ceiling systems. This also maximises the ceiling height within dwellings and exposed thermal mass – both factors in optimising residents' wellbeing.

Canada Gardens and The Robinson used components labelled with QR codes to facilitate quick updates to a central database and to feed into a QA monitoring platform during construction, logging key data on construction milestones and presenting clear visual updates on progress against programmes. Also on these plots, BIM-facilitated defect resolution provided a comprehensive database of information that could be accessed both before and during construction and beyond. The contractor used software that allowed the project teams to collaboratively manage coordination ahead of construction and this flowed through into on-site quality checks. This resulted in a 30% increase in efficiency on staff time associated with this task when compared to the conventional task of marking up sub-contractor drawings.

BTR AMENITIES
Canada Gardens

This is the first family-focussed development by Quintain at Wembley Park, with a large number of three-bedroom homes.

Seven buildings, incorporating 743 homes, overlook an acre of landscaped podium gardens and with views over Union Park. These are components of Fossey Arora's aim to provide a landscape-led harmonious way of living, with greenery pervading everything. Canada Gardens is flooded with nature, with an extensive selection of flowers, bushes and trees, as well as grassed areas, a greenhouse and allotment beds for the residents to grow their own fruit and vegetables. The gardens are dotted with dining areas, outdoor kitchens and BBQs, as an extension of residents' private living space, creating a flow between indoors and out. For children there is a pirate ship play park and water feature and a dog run to ensure the outdoor areas cater to both the human and animal family. Designer work-from-home timber sheds are provided for those wanting to work with nature all around and for relaxation and entertaining there is an impressive Canadian-themed residents' clubhouse served by an F&B retail unit below.

An expansive rooftop terrace and sky-lounge on the 26th floor has views across London and provides a versatile space, with zones to sit and relax, giant Jenga and lovely grassy areas that are ideal for yoga practice as the sun rises.

The super lobby continues the theme of greenery, with indoor trees and a hanging garden from the library balcony above. Diffusers add the scent of orange, bergamot and lavender, bringing an essence of summer sunshine inside the principal entrance area.

Lawn area surrounded by diverse planting, Canada Gardens.

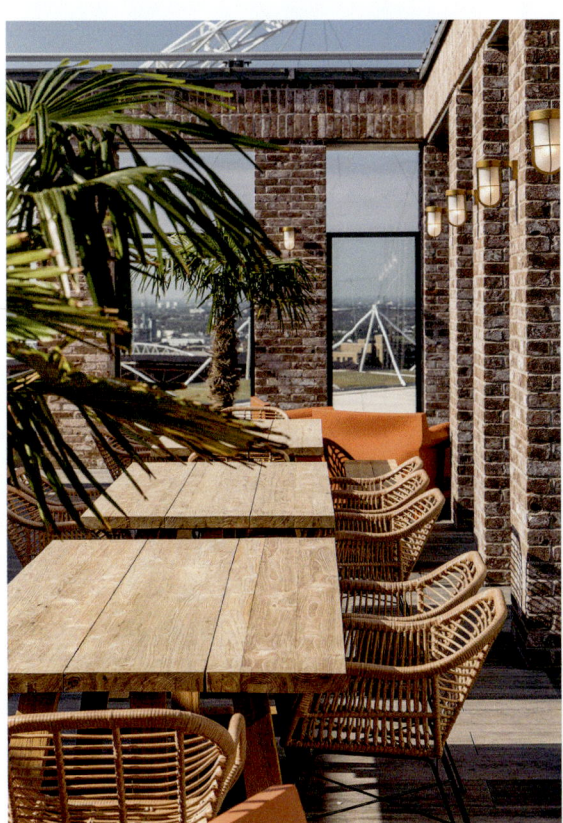
Rooftop terrace with views across London.

Canada Gardens gateway building.

CHAPTER EIGHT – CASE STUDY 5 – WEMBLEY PARK

Stairwell, Canada Gardens.

Brick and balcony detail, Canada Gardens.

Outdoor kitchen area.

Pirate ship play area and water feature.

Work-from-home sheds set within peaceful locations surrounded by plant beds and trees.

The gardens and play areas at Canada Gardens.

Canada Lane, used for coach parking, with footbridge linking Canada Gardens and The Robinson

Shared library space.

168 THE RISE OF BUILD TO RENT IN THE UK

Interior of the Canadian-themed clubhouse.

Relaxed seating in the shared rooftop terrace.

The Robinson

Recent graduates are the target age group for this part of Wembley Park, with Fossey Arora-driven themes of fun, irony, satire, sarcasm and British eccentricity and wit defining many elements of the building.

This starts with the deliberately over-sized, metal front doors to the super lobby, with multiple door knockers peppering the inside, suggesting a portal to a type of Wonderland. Adjacent is an eye-blinding baby pink post room which has Paul Smith-style striped post boxes with Dr Martens feet. Floating chairs and a giant mirror-ball serve to contradict and challenge the senses on arrival.

The residents' lounge has an arrival hall which includes a multi-layered art wall, along with a super-long bank of brightly coloured seats, with portholes overlooking a mini courtyard. Designed for working and socialising, the residents' lounge features a Damien Hirst-inspired taxi coffee machine. The space brims with unexpected elements such as this and a glass-backed fireplace framing an incredible view of London. A 19th century Rococo-style, giltwood wall mirror sits above competing with the viewer on where to look.

A dining room sits within the residents' lounge, as well as a kitchen for getting together to cook. Work pods and private booths for phone calls allow residents to use the space for work. The courtyard space beyond has a big slide to get quickly from one level down to the next

Outdoors, a UK festival feel is embraced. A John Lennon-inspired peace garden provides for moments of quiet reflection, with a circular seating area surrounded by dense foliage and swings for lighter-hearted moments. A dog park is located next to a wooden playground for children and a lawn area, scattered with deckchairs, that is ideal for picnics or movie screenings on summer evenings. Continuing the spirit of fun and adventure is the Mad Hatter's Tea Party Garden for socialising. A wooden framework with retractable roof has imitation crystal chandeliers. Brightly coloured giant flowerpots and wooden panels hide a bright pink kitchenette and an oil drum BBQ.

A path winding through the podium garden brings all of these areas together, creating a journey with incidents and interest, including a camper van planter packed with flowers as a resting spot.

At roof level within a 360-degree sky-lounge is a juice bar in the shape of an orange. Outside is an out-sized bank of coloured recliners, the longest sun lounger in London with plants dotted around in brightly painted oil drums and with access to the slide to get down to the mini courtyard below.

The Robinson's other shared rooftop has three bespoke, colourful custom-built, work-from-home camper vans sitting nonchalantly within their own, dedicated rooftop space with nearby picnic tables and deckchairs. These installations, both pragmatic and playful, define the character of what has been created within this funscape at The Robinson.

The Robinson.

Outdoor amenities, The Robinson.

Super lobby entrance.

Whimsical door knockers.

Bank seating in the residents' lounge.

Multi-layered art wall.

Work-from-home camper vans.

Courtyard space, with adult-sized slide connecting levels.

Damien Hirst-inspired taxi coffee machine being craned into place, The Robinson.

The taxi coffee machine in-situ in the residents' lounge.

Mad Hatter's Tea Party Garden area with BBQ and eating area.

Baby pink post room.

Striped post boxes with Dr Martens feet.

CHAPTER EIGHT – CASE STUDY 5 – WEMBLEY PARK 175

Madison, Lexington and Bowery

The design theme for Madison is more relaxed than Canada Gardens or The Robinson and signals northern-European inspired health, wellbeing and protection expressed through clean, simple design, with timeless modern influences and clutter-free living.

A sense of calm and precision is invoked throughout, starting in the super lobby. Large, circular ceiling lights deliver a bright, daylight feel that makes the space feel fresh. Golden post boxes provide a warm glow on the opposite side of the lobby. A gym and nursery are located beneath the building.

The residents' lounge sits above the super lobby. It is designed with a variety of functional spaces, connected throughout by a distinct herringbone pattern timber floor.

The breakout area that overlooks the lobby below is ideal for working privately, while also feeling connected to other residents. A backdrop of park views delivers a feeling of wellbeing and connection with nature. Within the space are areas of plush seating, a pool table, a coffee machine, a meeting room or work-from-home area and a TV room. Folding, sliding doors allow flexibility for opening up or closing the space as required.

At roof level an internal lounge in a deliberately oversized lift lobby has zones to work or relax, which lead out to the sky lounge, with views over the new Olympic Steps. The lounge gives access to the larger of the two roof terraces, which has multiple zones providing a range of activities including individual yoga routines and pop-up rooftop cinema events. Arched walkways provide the residents with strolling routes with a close-to-nature feel, with plants enveloping the arches. These tunnels of greenery support residents' inner wellbeing, delivering a sense of safety and enclosure in the heart of the Wembley Park. Children have their own dedicated roof terrace zone as well, with a play area next to one of the green tunnels, backed by a spectacular view of London.

Madison also has a smaller roof terrace with a very simple design, focused around open space, greenery and seating.

The development's podium garden provides another area for residents to connect with nature. Enclosed areas, divided by plants and greenery, provide places for residents to sit and relax. A pet lawn overlooks the stadium and a children's play area nearby is fitted with natural and plastic-free timber play equipment. An adjacent BBQ space is planned with seating that allows residents to be as private or communal as they feel. A distinctive circular lawn area provides for an inclusive sense of wellbeing and togetherness.

Children's play area.

Olympic steps, Madison gateway building.

View of Madison from Union Park.

CHAPTER EIGHT – CASE STUDY 5 – WEMBLEY PARK

Multi-use games area.

Green link tunnel.

The courtyard nursery with resident amenity gardens above.

178 THE RISE OF BUILD TO RENT IN THE UK

Aerial view of Madison, Lexington and Bowery looking towards Wembley Stadium.

Architectural fins and brick detail.

Podium amenities and balconies with directional privacy.

Communal residents' room.

Madison fronting onto the Olympic steps.

Seating in the entrance lobby.

Rooftop pergola.

CHAPTER EIGHT – CASE STUDY 5 – WEMBLEY PARK

CHAPTER NINE
Conclusions

One of our clients, a residential developer located close to our London studio, organises occasional breakfast presentations at their offices, where topical issues facing the sector are aired. A recent session involved one of the people who has appeared in this book, Hashi Mohamed. Hashi spoke about his experiences as a young refugee arriving in this country and about the growing challenges of equality and supply in UK housing today. Afterwards, we chatted for the first time and I told him I was in the middle of writing this book. He instantly remarked that "Build To Rent is a solution to a problem which shouldn't exist."

This thought-provoking observation may well succinctly summarise the UK housing sector as I have described it in Chapter One. It also partly explains the general acceptance of UK social housing providers of a new form of housing that is making such an impact in the UK, that it is part of the solution to a sector in crisis. Hashi's words codify his concerns about inequality and how safe, well-constructed homes should be a basic right for everyone in the country, which in turn would solve many of society's problems. Hashi's words also suggest, of course, that in an ideal social structure, BTR would not be required.

This book has sought to set out the reasons for the existence and huge potential that BTR has to raise the housing game in so many areas. The book also examines areas of potential concern. Fortunately, there is also no sign, thus far, of the baleful predatory practices that are prevalent in some parts of the American single-family scene, where the maximum is being squeezed from their assets by professional money-managing rental companies. This suggests that the rise of Build To Rent need not come at the increased social cost of wealth inequality. I recall, on a visit to the completed trio of projects of our Wembley Park scheme, seeing an animated conversation between children on a fifth floor balcony and their friends playing in the park at the base of the building. The children were clearly happy with their new homes, living within a block being managed by the Council and housing their tenants. This building contains affordable rental homes which would not exist without the surrounding BTR masterplan that it sits seamlessly within.

This is not to say that BTR funders and managers should lead the line on social conscience in UK housing. However, the nature of their long-term vision and their ultimate material interest in customer satisfaction means that they are effectively leading the line in any event. They are better placed than most to develop ESG

FACING PAGE The Robinson, Wembley Park, Wembley, London.

protocols, as suggested in Chapters Four and Five. The focus on environmental and social aspects of the residential sector will only increase in the years ahead. The sizzling European summer of 2023 will sharpen this focus.

In his book, *Upheaval*, Jared Diamond explains the importance of "social capital" and why its decline in the United States poses a threat to the wellbeing of that country. Social capital refers to connections amongst individuals, including face-to-face social networks and group activity and the trustworthiness that arises from them.

> *It's the trust, friendships, group affiliations, helping, and expectation of being helped built up by actively participating in and being a member of all sorts of groups, ranging from book clubs, bowling clubs, church groups, community organisations, and parent-teacher associations to political organisations, and societies, rotary clubs, town meetings, unions, veteran's associations, and others. Participation in such group activities fosters generalised reciprocity: i.e. doing things for and with other people, trusting them, and counting on them and on other members of the group to do things for you.*[1]

The rise of social media is antithetical to the basic form of communication between human beings that has naturally evolved over millennia. Perhaps the pioneering BTR operators are doing society a huge favour by encouraging inter-personal activity and investing in social capital within BTR developments without even knowing it. What can they achieve if they concentrate their power for good more directly?

NIMBYs might be viewed as a grouping for which social capital is anathema. This is the acronym for those who object to residential development in their locality, literally "not in my back yard". Ironically, many of them have benefitted from moving into new developments in the face of local objections, a benefit they now wish to block for others. They represent a considerable barrier to progress within the UK housing sector and more importantly the economy as a whole as they have become a major influence in the politics of the nation. This is because they include amongst their number not only local residents raising the drawbridge to further development, but also local councillors and Members of Parliament who represent the constituencies of those who refuse to be dispossessed of their idea of rural tranquillity. Such is their influence that pressure to build at scale is once again concentrated on an ever-diminishing quota of brownfield land or within dense urban centres, while multiple green chastity belts are to be defended at all costs.

Most BTR investors are not interested in the Green Belt. But the barrier this protection presents, taken together with environmental watchdogs, regional imbalances, restrictive planning policies and the specifics of the ageing UK demographic that have been touched upon within this book all combine to create a savannah-like plain of opportunity for newly arrived real estate speculators. But just as on the savannah, these speculators perform a necessary function in the natural cycle of things. This is not just because of the alternative form of housing supply that BTR represents. It is also because an increase in the number of rental properties would serve to halt rising rent levels through increased supply, even if there is a growing recognition that the rising BTR market may struggle to replace those properties being lost within the private rented sector. Government tax changes over the years, which have made small-scale private rental investment unattractive, suggest that the Government has got it wrong. There is much headroom for a private sector providing long-term homes to rent alongside a growing Build To Rent sector as long as it is not regulated and taxed out of existence. Tax incentives to restore market equilibrium beat rent control hands down in this regard.

Imagine for one moment if BTR had not taken off in the UK. Would the Government by now have stepped in with other solutions to the crisis? It is difficult to reason that this would have happened given how constrained the Conservative Government of recent years has become, caught in aspic by its own NIMBY constituents.

The beginnings of the UK housing crisis are described in Chapter One. The words "housing" and "crisis" have become inextricably linked and matters are not improving. There have been thirty years of decline since the early 1980s before BTR first appeared. That is a long time for a problem to fester. So, if we accept that BTR is a credible part of the solution, it is not the whole solution and other remedies must be found.

A huge and understated advantage of BTR is its ability to rapidly transform whole districts. We, as architects, have been amazed at the speed of construction that is possible in the absence of programmed sales cycles. What has happened on huge building sites at Wembley Park, at Coppermaker Square and at The Mercian is breathtaking in this regard.

The BTR part of the solution is pointing the way to better methods of building and better quality in housing design which will certainly benefit the UK housing sector and is a boon to UK architects. The movement is, of course, buffeted by the same economic headwinds that all housing providers face. With interest rates gradually ratcheting upwards in 2023 to combat inflation, the housing market has had its biggest annual decline since 2009. Construction costs and availability of labour are real problems which will remain with us for some time. These challenges are measured through a much longer field of view by BTR investors so despite the market challenges, many profilers see a bright future for the sector, although this presupposes that UK inflation is brought under control relatively soon. Not even BTR operators can happily invest when the cost versus value of a development, which includes the high cost of debt, is uncertain. Operators need investors and the economic turns of 2023 have slowed investment, particularly cross-border investment, which dipped significantly during the course of 2023.[2]

> *The major insurance companies that were investing in real estate as a bond surrogate are pausing and saying, real estate is good, but why would I invest in it at a 3 percent yield when I can buy good corporate credit at 2 percent?* [3]

A return to "normal" levels of inflation will help calm the jitters of industry leaders. Such is the nature of the housing crisis in the UK, demand will continue to vastly outstrip supply for years and more likely decades to come. Despite 14 interest rate rises in a row by the time this book was published, house prices have remained more or less stable, albeit with a reduction in real terms owing to inflation. Against this backdrop, however, private rental levels in London saw their largest jump in October 2023 since 2006, rising 6.8% year-on-year and 6.1% year-on-year outside London. This was attributed to rising mortgage costs pushing landlords out of the market.[4]

A return to "normal" levels of inflation, evidence of which was beginning to emerge by late 2023, will help calm the jitters of industry leaders. Such is the nature of the housing crisis in the UK, demand will continue to vastly outstrip supply for years and more likely decades to come.

Resilient job markets and the post-pandemic shift to remote working will continue to stoke demand for more living space. Unless there is a dramatic change to the UK planning system, newly constructed homes in both the sales and rental markets will remain restricted and will keep prices high.

The UK population will continue to increase through immigration, both illegal and planned, stoking demand further. Net migration was 606,000 in 2022, higher than any previous year.[5]

The population is also ageing. The options open to the majority of the UK's ageing population are without a doubt limited. The options are even more stark for those living in affordable housing. The vast majority of those heading into their later years will stay put in the house they have lived in for years, even when it can no longer provide for their needs. Eight years ago, the evergreen CEO of Legal & General, Nigel Wilson, set out a visionary ten-point plan to ease the housing crisis by empowering the last-time buyers that we encountered in Chapter Four to help unlock housing supply. This included integration of housing, planning, health and social care and expansion of equity release schemes.[6] Little, if anything, has happened in the intervening years but opportunity exists, potentially through changes in the tax regime, to locate older people in the heart of new and existing communities in both urban and rural locations, to acknowledge that they are in fact a huge contributor to society and care deeply about staying close to friends and services that are familiar. Inter-generational living in various forms of tenure can bring fantastic benefits to local communities. These holes in the market should not be lost on the BTR sector.

The rise of Build To Rent in the UK is not over. It represents only 2% of the private rented sector and around 0.3% of the entire residential sector.[7] We have witnessed what is possible and we have seen end results which exude quality and longevity. Despite the political and commercial headwinds that lasted from 2022 to 2024, potential investors and their economic advisors have no reason to doubt that the UK will continue to be one of the largest, transactional, transparent and sustainably aspirational of the world's property markets.

ACKNOWLEDGEMENTS

I have been assisted in this endeavour by a host of colleagues from both inside and outside our practice.

Starting with my colleagues, I have had invaluable support from Niamh Gill-Ryan, Christina Thornley, Joss Stott and the trio of Ross O'Brien, Lukasz Mlynarczyk and Alan Blacker, who have set the graphic tone for the publication. The idea of producing this book would not have emerged without the realisation of design creativity through to construction from the hand of Richard Harvey at Wembley Park, which has informed so much of what we have subsequently carried out in the BTR sector and beyond. I am indebted to the hands-on expertise of Craig Sheach and Jamie Chubb. Craig's articles for BTR News have helped form the philosophical foundation for Chapter Four. Similarly, Jamie's delivery experience at Wembley is the basis for Chapter Six, assisted by Mike Richardson and Piotr Michalski. Much of the technical detail of Chapter Five has been provided by Kartikeya Rajput and Cynthia Espinola. Jenny Buterchi has contributed to the section on Later Living.

I have been astounded by the good will and intellectual support I have received from external sources, many of whom I had never met until commencing research for this book. I have had valuable insight from Guy Slocombe at Hyde, with perspective from a housing association, Richard Beckinsale from Gowling WLG, with legal and financial input and from Ian Fletcher of the British Property Federation, who I met late in the day on this venture and I am grateful that I did. The book would be poorer without his contribution. Julian Tollast of Quintain, a valued client for many years, has supported the narrative around our Wembley Park projects and Pete Cooper also contributed with his insightful view on the importance of good stewardship. A few brief conversations with Hashi Mohamed have helped steer the moral tone of the book. Kieran Everett, Technical Director at the engineering practice WP3, has given valuable input on building systems. I also owe a debt of gratitude to two architects: Robert King of Glenn Howells Architects and Martin Haymes of Falconer Chester Hall Architects, who have supplied me with the information I needed to present The Mercian and The Lexington case studies in the book and who led on the design and delivery of these significant BTR schemes for their respective practices. The last acknowledgement goes to the Fossey Arora team, under the direction of Chotip Arora and Andrew Fossey, whose inspirational and inventive approach to the design of spaces within and outside the buildings at Wembley Park have brought such vitality and fun to this new neighbourhood.

I have referenced sources throughout the book. Much of the information forming the basis for Chapters Two and Three has comes from the journals *Property Week* and *Inside Housing* which have reported consistently on the emergence of the sector. Finally, although reference is made to large language model-based chatbots in Chapter Seven, they have not been used in the compilation of the words on these pages.

BIOGRAPHY

Brendan Kilpatrick jointly leads PRP's London studio. The architectural team specialises in the design and delivery of all forms of housing in the UK across both affordable and private tenures, including Build To Rent, from bespoke infill projects to large estate and urban regeneration masterplans. The studio also encompasses specialist, inter-disciplinary teams covering urban design, landscape architecture and sustainability, working collaboratively with the architectural teams and making PRP uniquely equipped to coordinate and deliver complex regeneration projects from inception to completion.

Brendan's expertise spans all forms of housing, with an emphasis on housing-led urban and estate regeneration schemes where mixed-tenure, mixed-density residential buildings and non-housing elements need to be integrated into sustainable neighbourhoods. His team has a reputation for both designing and delivering high-quality, cost-effective housing solutions which match client budgets whilst achieving the practice's high standards of design quality.

Brendan co-authored a recent book describing in detail best practice in the regeneration of existing UK housing estates and entitled *Estate Regeneration: Learning from the Past, Housing Communities of the Future*. Brendan has also written a non-architectural, part-biographical novel, *Elephant on Main Street*, which was published in 2019.

IMAGE CREDITS

Thanks to the following practices for giving us permission to use valuable drawings and background information for each of the case studies:

Falconer Chester Hall – Moda, The Lexington

Howells – The Mercian

We gratefully acknowledge the following individuals and organisations for giving permission to reproduce photographs and computer generated images. Every effort has been made to contact copyright holders, but if any errors have been made we would be happy to correct them in a later printing. PRP own copyright to all the other images and give permission to reproduce them in this document.

Fossey Arora: p. 108 (left).

Bathsystem: p. 108 (middle and right).

Richard Chivers: p. 71.

Tim Crocker: p. 62, p. 68.

Michael Cunningham: p. 47, p. 48.

Robert Greshoff: p. 9.

Fred Howarth: p. 125 (top right and bottom), p126 (top right), p. 128 (right).

Greg Holmes: p. 72, p. 122, p. 124, p. 125 (top left), p. 126 (top left), p. 128 (left), p. 129.

Infinite 3D: p. 4, p. 94, p. 114, p. 116 (all), p. 117 (all), p. 120 (all), p. 121.

Simon Kennedy: p. 33, p. 86, p. 97, p. 130, p. 135 (all), p. 136 (all), p. 137, p. 138 (all), p. 140, p. 141.

Andy Marshall: p. 80.

Quintain/Chris Winter: p. 42, p. 49, p. 64, p. 67, p. 93, p. 95, p. 96, p. 100, p. 112, p. 152, p. 155, p. 156 (all), p. 160, p. 162 (all), p. 163 (all), p. 165 (all).p. 166 (bottom right and left), p. 167, p. 168 (top and bottom right), p. 169 (all), p. 171, p. 172 (all) p. 173 (all), p. 174 (all), p. 175 (top and bottom right), p. 176, p. 177 (all), p. 178 (top), p. 179, p. 182

UNStudio: p. 30, p. 35, p. 142, p. 145, p. 146, p. 148 (all), p. 149, p. 150, p. 151.

REFERENCES

CHAPTER ONE

1. Kilpatrick, B. & Patel, M. (2021), *Estate Regeneration: Learning from the Past, Housing Communities of the Future.* 1st edn. London: Routledge, p. 3.
2. Cowley, J. (2018), *Reaching for Utopia Making Sense of an Age of Upheaval,* 1st edn. Cromer, UK: Salt Publishing, p.18.
3. Kilpatrick, B. & Patel, M. (2021), *Estate Regeneration: Learning from the Past, Housing Communities of the Future.* 1st edn. London: Routledge, p. 69.
4. Halligan, L. (2021), *Home Truths – The UK's Chronic Housing Shortage,* 1st edn. London: Biteback Publishing Ltd, p. xiii.
5. University of York (2008), *Independent Review of the Private Rented Sector,* York, UK: Joseph Rowntree Foundation.
6. Department for Levelling Up, Housing and Communities. (2022), *A Fairer Private Rented Sector.* Available at: https://www.gov.uk/government/publications/a-fairer-private-rented-sector.
7. Baxter-Clow, D., Elliott, J. & Earwaker, R. (2022), *Making a House a Home: Why Policy Must Focus on the Ownership and Distribution of Housing.* York, UK: Joseph Rowntree Foundation.
8. *Panorama: What's Gone Wrong with Our Housing?* (2023), BBC One Television, 23 March.
9. Local Government Association (2023), *Almost 60,000 Homes Sold Through Right to Buy Will Not Be Replaced By 2030,* Available at: https://www.local.gov.uk/about/news/.
10. Sentance, A. (2017), 'Solving the Housing Crisis Will Take More Than Building Homes', *The Daily Telegraph,* 11 February. Available at: https://www.telegraph.co.uk/business/2017/02/10/solvinghousing- crisis-will-take-building-homes/.
11. 'Britain Can't Build' (2022),*The Economist,* 3 September, p. 21.
12. 'Britain Can't Build' (2022),*The Economist,* 3 September, p. 21.
13. Royal Town Planning Institute (2023), *Interim State of the Profession 2023,* Available at: https://www.rtpi.org.uk/policy-and-research/interim-state-of-the-profession-2023.
14. 'Britain Can't Build' (2022),*The Economist,* 3 September, p. 21.
15. 'Opinion' (2023), *City AM* , 13 April.
16. 'House Party – How long can the global housing boom last?' (2022), *The Economist,* 8 January, Available at: https://www.economist.com/finance-and-economics/how-long-can-the-global-housing-boom-last/21807002.
17. Kilpatrick, B. & Patel, M. (2021), *Estate Regeneration: Learning from the Past, Housing Communities of the Future.* 1st edn. London: Routledge, p. 312.
18. 'Why is the UK Rental Market in Chaos?' (2022), *Sky News Television.* 13 October.
19. Bingley, L. (2022), 'Rent Increase Equates to Losing a Room Over the Past Two Years', *Property Week,* 26 August, p.18.
20. Wallace, T. (2023), 'Stop Pitting Home Ownership Against the Rental Market, We Need Both for Londoners', *City AM,* 20 April, p.19.
21. Knight, M. (2023), 'Irish Resi Shortage underpins solid Performance by I-RES', *Property Week,* 2 March, p.12.
22. Nerval, C. (2022), 'Government urged to act as report reveals eviction risk', *Property Week,* 8 December, p.17.
23. 'Why Aren't There Any Houses to Buy' (2023), *Time Magazine,* 27 March, p.16.
24. United States Senate Committee on Banking, Housing, and Urban Affairs (2021), *How Private Equity Landlords are changing the Housing Market,* Available at: https://www.banking.senate.gov/hearings/how-private-equity-landlords-are-changing-the-housing-market.
25. 'The Strange Case of Britain's Demise' (2022),*The Economist,* 12 December. Available at: https://www.economist.com/britain/2022/12/12/the-strange-case-of-britains-demise.
26. Preston, A. (2023), 'The Curse of Village Sprawl: Why Britain Builds the Wrong Houses in the Wrong Places', *The Daily Telegraph,* 3 June, p.22.
27. 'First World Problems – how the west fell out of love with economic growth' (2022), *The Economist,* 17 December, p.74.
28. 'Bagehot – The Dark Ages. Britons in their thirties are stuck in a Dark Age' (2023), *The Economist,* 7 January, p. 20.
29. Crisis (2022), *The Homelessness Monitor: Great Britain 2022,* Available at: https://www.crisis.org.uk/ending-homelessness/homelessness-knowledge-hub/homelessness-monitor/about/the-homelessness-monitor-great-britain-2022/.

CHAPTER TWO

1. 'The Future of Family Living' (2023), *The Economist,* 11 February, p.24, 67.
2. Evans Pritchard, A. (2012), 'America overcomes the debt crisis as Britain sinks deeper into the swamp,' *The Daily Telegraph,* 22 January. Available at: https://www.telegraph.co.uk/finance/comment/ambroseevans_pritchard/9031478/America-overcomes-the-debt-crisis-as-Britain-sinks-deeper-into-the-swamp.html.
3. 'Hot Property' (2022),*The Economist,* 24 September, p. 72.
4. Brown, C., 'Andy Burnham Interview: The Talk of the Town' (2022), *Building,* Issue 08, 11 August, p.18.

CHAPTER THREE

1. 'Build it and they Will Rent' (2021), *The Economist,* 28 August, p. 26.
2. Lane, T. (2023), 'Nine Elms: How the Chinese Redefined Development in London', *Building,* 7 January. Available at: https://www.building.co.uk/buildings/nine-elms-how-the-chinese-redefined-development-in-london/5121024.article.

3. 'Greystar chief offers vote of confidence in UK with hint of expansion' (2022), *Financial Times*, 7 June, p.10.
4. Housing Forum National Conference (2022), *Keynote Speech by Lucien Cook*, Savills, London, October 18.
5. Jones, A. (2023), 'Supply Dearth Needs Mixed Offer', *Property Week*, 3 March, p. 42.
6. 'The chancellor hopes more child care will get more parents working' (2023), *The Economist*, 18 March. Available at: https://www.economist.com/britain/2023/03/15/the-chancellor-hopes-more-child-care-will-get-more-parents-working.
7. 'Belfast BTR Funding Deal is "Largest Ever"' (2023), *Property Week*, 9 June, p.10.

CHAPTER FOUR

1. Till, J. (2023), 'Architecture Criticism Against the Climate Clock', *Architectural Review*, 6 April. Available at: https://www.architectural-review.com/essays/keynote/architecture-criticism-against-the-climate-clock
2. Diamond, J. (2006), 'Our Sickly Suburbs – We have the Cure. Where's the Courage,' *The Globe and Mail*, 5 August, p.A15.
3. HTA Design, Pollard Thomas Edwards, PRP, Proctor & Matthews Architects (2019), *Distinctively Local How to boost supply by creating beautiful homes and places*. Available at: https://www.distinctively-local.co.uk
4. Barnes, J. et al. *What is the Future of High-Rise housing? Examining the Long-term Social and Financial Impacts of Residential Towers*, PurePrint 2023.
5. 'Vertical Limits' (2023), *The Economist*, 15 April, p. 23.
6. Bfl Homes (2020), *Spotlight on Port Sunlight*, Available at: https://www.bflhomes.com/spotlight-on-port-sunlight- December 2020.
7. Neal, P., Hall, P., Lock, D., Mitchell, W., Duany, A., Taylor, D & Worpole, K., (2003), *Urban Villages and the Making of Communities*, 1st edn. London: Taylor & Francis.
8. Anon - *A Guide to Worsley, Historical & Topographical* (Eccles Advertiser) 1870 c/o Tyldesley, Bert, The Duke's Other Village: Roe Green Story, Bert Tyldesley 1993, p. 6.
9. Mohamed, H. (2020), *People Like Us*, Profile Books Ltd, p183.
10. Diamond, J.(2020), *Upheaval*, Penguin Books, p. 296.
11. Diamond, J.(2020), *Upheaval*, Penguin Books, p. 294.
12. Fukuyama, F. (2020), *The End of History and the Last Man*, Penguin Books.
13. Mather, V. & Rogers K. (2015), 'Behind the Yogi-isms: Those Said and Unsaid', *The New York Times*, 23 September. Available at: .https://www.nytimes.com/2015/09/24/sports/yogi-berra-yogi-isms-quotes-explored.html.
14. Jones Lang LaSalle/Dixon, M., 'Living in the developments of the Future', *UKREiiF Annual Event* 2023. Royal Armouries Leeds & Leeds Dock, 17 July.
15. 'Our Approach to Energy Prices shows We want Climate Policies Only if They're Free' (2023), *CityAM*, 14 June. Available at: https://www.cityam.com/our-approach-to-energy-prices-shows-we-want-climate-policies-only-if-theyre-free/.
16. McCloud, K. (2023), 'The flaw in the Future Homes Standard' *Grand Design Magazine*, 14 April. Available at: https://www.granddesignsmagazine.com/kevin-mccloud/future-homes-standard/.
17. 'Groaning' (2022), *The Economist,* 17 September, p.60.
18. 'Land Locked' (2022), *The Economist*, 30 July, p.56.
19. 'The Crack-up' (2022), *The Economist*, 22 October, p.66.
20. 'Deciphering the "Doom Loop"'(2023), *The Economist*, 27 May, p.35..
21. UK Health Security Agency (2022), *UKHSA and ONS release estimates of excess deaths during summer of 2022*. Available at: https://www.gov.uk/government/news/ukhsa-and-ons-release-estimates-of-excess-deaths-during-summer-of-2022.
22. Greater London Authority (2022), *Housing Design Standards LPG*. Available at: https://www.london.gov.uk/programmes-strategies/planning/implementing-london-plan/london-plan-guidance/housing-design-standards-lpg.
23. Rees, R. (2023), ' Why Are You Still Participating in a Race to the Bottom?' *Building*, 12 June, p. 38.
24. Kilpatrick, B. & Patel, M. (2021), *Estate Regeneration: Learning from the Past, Housing Communities of the Future*. 1st edn. London: Routledge, p. 232.
25. Savills (2023), *UK Build To Rent Market Update – Q1 2023*. London, UK: Savills. Available at: https://www.savills.co.uk/research_articles/229130/347183-0
26. Savills (2023), *Build-to-Rent – Q4 2023*. London, UK: Savills. Available at: https://bpf.org.uk/media/7086/build-to-rent-q4-2023-british-property-federation.pdf
27. Lambert Smith Hampton (2023), *UK Investment Transactions Build to rent stars amid subdued Q1*, London, UK: Lambert Smith Hampton. Available at: https://www.lsh.ie/
28. Department for Communities and Local Government (2012), *Review of the barriers to institutional investment in private rented homes*. London, UK: Her Majesty's Stationery Office.
29. Europe Real Estate (2013), *M&G Investments finances private and social residential development (UK)*. Amsterdam, NL: REP. Available at: https://europe-re.com/mg-investments-finances-private-and-social-residential-development-uk/41380
30. Patel, B. (2022), *Railpen to fund BTR development at Trocoll House Barking*. Available at: https://btrnews.co.uk/railpen-to-fund-btr-development-at-trocoll-house-barking/
31. Quintain (2016), *Quintain announces £800 million corporate development facility for Wembley Park*. London, UK: Quintain. Available at: https://www.quintain.co.uk/news-and-media/press-releases/2016/15-11-2016.
32. Quintain (2022), *Quintain finalises £277m financing deal with J.P.Morgan to deliver two new Build-to-Rent residential buildings at Wembley Park*. London, UK: Quintain. Available at: https://www.quintain.co.uk/news-and-media/press-releases/2022/jpmorgan-financing.
33. Patel, B. (2023), *Precede Capital provides £188m for JV to fund Moda's Great Charles Street*. Available at: https://btrnews.co.uk/precede-capital-provides-188m-for-jv-to-fund-modas-great-charles-street/.
34. Kilpatrick, B. & Patel, M. (2021), *Estate Regeneration: Learning from the Past, Housing Communities of the Future*. 1st edn. London: Routledge, p. 232.
35. Hashi, M. (2020), *People Like Us*. London: Profile Books Ltd. p. 183.

36 UKGBC (2023), *Health And Wellbeing In Homes*. Available at: https://www.ukgbc.org/ukgbc-work/health-wellbeing-homes/.

37 Office for National Statistics (2021), *Families and households in the UK 2020*. London, UK: Office for National Statistics. Available at: https://www.ons.gov.uk/peoplepopulationandcommunity/birthsdeathsandmarriages/families/bulletins/familiesandhouseholds/2020

38 House of Commons Communities and Local Government Committee, (2018), *Housing for Older People*. Available at: https://publications.parliament.uk/pa/cm201719/cmselect/cmcomloc/370/370.pdf

39 Lichfields (2019), *Solutions to an age old problem: Planning for an ageing population*. Available at: https://lichfields.uk/media/5104/solutions-to-an-age-old-problem_planning-for-an-ageing-population.pdf

40 ARCO (2017), 'Written Evidence Submitted by ARCO (the Associated Retirement Community Operators [HOP060]', Housing and Local Government Committee: http://data.parliament.uk/writtenevidence/committeeevidence.svc/evidwnceddocument/communikties-and-local-government-committee/housing-for-older-people/written/49430.pdf

41 Branson, A. (2023), UK Property market is Best Value in Europe, *Property Week*, 4 April, p.28.

42 ARCO (2017), 'Written Evidence Submitted by ARCO (the Associated Retirement Community Operators [HOP060]'. Available at: https://committees.parliament.uk/writtenevidence/79332/pdf/

43 'Wear and Care' (2022), *The Economist*, 3 December, p.25.

44 'Wear and Care' (2022), *The Economist*, 3 December, p.25.

45 Underwood, F., Curis, C., How, R., Kickson, K., Latha, P. (2021), *Older People's Care in Social Housing; A manifesto for change*. London, UK: Altair Consultancy and Advisory Services Ltd. Available at: https://altairltd.co.uk/2022/06/22/a-manifesto-for-change-older-peoples-care-in-social-housing/.

46 'Wear and Care' (2022), *The Economist*, 3 December, p.25.

47 Mayhew, L. (2022), T*he Mayhew Review: Future Proofing Retirement Living Easing the care and housing crises*. London, UK: International Longevity Centre UK. Available at: https://ilcuk.org.uk/mayhew-review/.

48 'A nation of Homebodies' (2021), *The Economist*, 5 August, p.41.

49 Knight Frank LLP (2022), *Seniors Housing Annual Review 2022/23*. London, UK: Knight Frank LLP.

50 Mayhew, L. (2022), T*he Mayhew Review: Future Proofing Retirement Living Easing the care and housing crises*. London, UK: International Longevity Centre UK. Available at: https://ilcuk.org.uk/mayhew-review/.

51 Office for National Statistics (2021), *Families and households in the UK 2020*. London, UK: Office for National Statistics. Available at: https://www.ons.gov.uk/peoplepopulationandcommunity/birthsdeathsandmarriages/families/bulletins/familiesandhouseholds/2020

CHAPTER FIVE

1. United Nations (N.D.), *For a Liveable Climate - Net-zero commitments must be backed by credible action*. Available at: https://www.un.org/en/climatechange/net-zero-coalition.

2. United Nations Environment Programme (N.D.), *Energy Efficiency for Buildings*. Available at: https://www.euenergycentre.org/images/unep%20info%20sheet%20-%20ee%20buildings.pdf.

3. United Nations Environment Programme (2021) *2021 Global status report for buildings and construction*. Available at: https://globalabc.org/resources/publications/2021-global-status-report-buildings-and-construction.

4. CBRE. (2017), *Sustainability - Simple steps to better homes*. UK: CBRE. Available at: https://www.cbreresidential.com/uk/sites/uk-residential/files/CBRE%20Green%20Homes%20Sustainability%20Report%20July%202017.pdf.

5. The Parliamentary Office of Science and Technology (2021), *Environmental housing standards*. Available at: https://post.parliament.uk/research-briefings/post-pn-0650/.

6. Department for Business, Energy and Industrial Strategy. (2022), *2020 UK Greenhouse Gas Emissions, Final Figures*. UK: Office for National Statistics. Available at: https://assets.publishing.service.gov.uk/government/uploads/system/uploads/attachment_data/file/1051408/2020-final-greenhouse-gas-emissions-statistical-release.pdf

7. Committee on Climate Change, Department of Energy and Climate Change, Office of National Statistics (2016), *The Fifth Carbon Budget: How every household can help reduce the UK's carbon footprint*. Available at: https://www.theccc.org.uk/wp-content/uploads/2016/07/5CB-Infographic-FINAL-.pdf.

8. Greater London Authority City Intelligence Unit (2023), *The State of London - Summary statistics about London's economy and society*. London: Greater London Authority. Available at: https://data.london.gov.uk/dataset/state-of-london.

9. Greater London Authority (2022), *London Energy and Greenhouse Gas Inventory (LEGGI)*. Available at: https://data.london.gov.uk/dataset/leggi.

10. Element Energy. (2022), *Analysis of a Net Zero 2030 Target for Greater London*. Cambridge: Element Energy Limited. Available at: https://www.london.gov.uk/sites/default/files/nz2030_element_energy_final.pdf.

11. Greater London Authority (2021), *The London Plan 2021*. London: Greater London Authority. Available at: https://www.london.gov.uk/programmes-strategies/planning/london-plan/new-london-plan/london-plan-2021.

12. Statista (2023), *Residential rental market in the UK - statistics & facts*. New York, US: Statista Research Department. Available at: https://www.statista.com/topics/6428/residential-rental-market-in-the-uk/#topicOverview.

13. Savills (2023), *UK Build To Rent Market Update – Q1 2023*. London, UK: Savills. Available at: https://www.savills.co.uk/research_articles/229130/347183-0.

14. Flaherty, M. (2023), Keeping it in the Family, *Property Week*, 14 April, p.25.

15. Department for Business, Energy and Industrial Strategy (2022), *2020 UK Greenhouse Gas Emissions, Final Figures*. UK: Office for National Statistics. Available at: https://assets.publishing.service.gov.uk/government/uploads/system/uploads/attachment_data/file/1051408/2020-final-greenhouse-gas-emissions-statistical-release.pdf.

16. RIBA (2021), *RIBA 2030 Climate Challenge: Version 2 (2021)*. London, UK: Royal Institute of British

17. Arup (2021), *Where do we stand?* Geneva, Switzerland: World Business Council for Sustainable Development. Available at: https://www.wbcsd.org/contentwbc/download/12446/185553/1. 109.
18. United Nations (N.D.), *For a Liveable Climate - Net-zero commitments must be backed by credible action.* Available at: https://www.un.org/en/climatechange/net-zero-coalition.
19. WSP (N.D.) (2023), *Net Zero Buildings.* Available at: https://www.wsp.com/en-gb/campaigns/net-zero-buildings.
20. Wyatt, S. (2020), *Steps to Net Zero: Step 1 - Passive Design Optimisation.* Available at: https://www.cundall.com/ideas/blog/steps-to-net-zero-step-1-passive-design-optimisation.
21. Net Zero Energy Buildings (N.D.), *Passive Design.* Available at: https://nzebnew.pivotaldesign.biz/knowledge-centre/passive-design/.
22. Carrington, D. (2023), 'UK's record hot 2022 made 160 times more likely by climate crisis', *The Guardian.* Available at: https://www.theguardian.com/environment/2023/jan/05/uk-average-annual-temperature-tops-10c-for-first-time.
23. UK Parliament (2018), *Heatwaves: adapting to climate change.* Available at: https://publications.parliament.uk/pa/cm201719/cmselect/cmenvaud/826/82603.htm.
24. Loughborough University (2021), *Over 4.6 million English homes experience summertime overheating, new study finds.* Available at: https://www.lboro.ac.uk/media-centre/press-releases/2021/july/over-4.6-million-homes-experience-overheating/.
25. Trimble MEP (2021), *Sustainability in MEP Design - What You Need to Know.* Available at: https://mep.trimble.com/en/resources/mep-blogs/sustainability-in-mep-design-what-you-need-to-know-3.
26. Greater London Authority (2022), *London Plan Guidance - Whole Life-Cycle Carbon Assessments.* London, UK: Greater London Authority. Available at: https://www.london.gov.uk/sites/default/files/lpg_-_wlca_guidance.pdf.
27. Statista (2022), *Public sector expenditure on waste management in the United Kingdom from 2009/10 to 2021/22.* Available at: https://www.statista.com/statistics/298889/united-kingdom-uk-public-sector-expenditure-fuel-waste-management/.
28. Lemmens, C., Luebkeman, C. (2016), *The Circular Economy in the Built Environment.* Available at: https://www.arup.com/-/media/arup/files/publications/c/arup_circulareconomy_builtenvironment.pdf.

CHAPTER SIX

1. Rogers, R. (1999), *The Urban Task Force, Towards an Urban Renaissance*, Abingdon-on-Thames, UK: Routledge.
2. PRP Architects (2007), *Place & Home – The Search for Better Housing, London*, UK: Black Dog Publishing, p.111.
3. Blanc, F., Scanlon K. & White, T. (2020), *Living in a Denser London – How Residents See Their Homes*, London, UK: LSE.
4. Kilpatrick, B. & Patel, M. (2021), *Estate Regeneration, Learning from the Past, Housing Communities of the Future.* 1st edn. London: Routledge, p. 142.
5. Kilpatrick, B. & Patel, M. (2021), *Estate Regeneration, Learning from the Past, Housing Communities of the Future.* 1st edn. London: Routledge, p. 232.
6. Lewisham Council (2014), *Lewisham Town Centre Local Plan Adoption Version.*
7. HTA, Levitt Bernstein, Pollard Thomas Edwards, PRP (2022), *Altered Estates 2*, p. 78 & 86.
8. HTA, Levitt Bernstein, Pollard Thomas Edwards, PRP (2022), *Altered Estates 2,* p. 47.

CHAPTER SEVEN

1. Keppler, N. (2022), *Robot Landlords are Buying up Houses.* New York, USA: Vice. Available at: https://www.vice.com/en/article/dy7eaw/robot-landlords-are-buying-up-h 28 November.
2. Fields, D. (2021), *Housing, Financialization, and its Economic Effects.* Bristol, UK: Housing Matter. Available at: https://soundcloud.com/housingmpodcast/housing-financialization-and-its-economic-effects/recommended.
3. 'Pixels in your eye' (2023), *The Economist*, 4 February, p. 72.
4. dezeen (2023), *Ten AI companies that architects and designers need to know.* Available at: https://www.dezeen.com/2023/08/03/ai-companies-architects-designers/?utm_medium=email&utm_campaign=Altopia%20newsletter&utm.
5. Tsigkari, M., (2023), *Building, Artificial Intelligence and The Future of Construction*, p.33.6.
6. Digging for Digits' (2023), *The Economist*, 19 August, p, 57.
7. Autodesk (2023), *Autodesk Forma: Cloud-based software for early-stage planning and design.* Available at: https://www.autodesk.com/products/forma/overview/.
8. Patel, B. (2022) *Innovative tech supports sustainable renting at Quintain.* Harrow, UK: BTR News. Available at: https://btrnews.co.uk/innovative-tech-supports-sustainable-renting-at-quintain/.

CHAPTER EIGHT

No references

CHAPTER NINE

1. Diamond, J. (2020), *Upheaval.* London, UK: Penguin Books p.351.
2. 'The Worst May Now Be Behind Us' (2023), *Property Week*, 28 March, p.20.
3. PWC (2023), *Emerging Trends in Real Estate Europe 2023 Report.* Available at: Emerging Trends in Real Estate Europe 2023 Report.pdf (pwc.com) Chapter 3.
4. City AM, London Rents See the Biggest Jump on Record Amid a Surge in Landlord Exodus, 16.11.2023.
5. 'A Failed Experiment' (2023), *The Economist*, 26 August, p.19.
6. Wilson, Nigel, (2015), 'Its not just first-time buyers who need help in today's housing market', *The Daily Telegraph*, 1 June, p.B2.
7. 13th Annual Resi Investment & Build To Rent Conference (2022), *Donnell, Richard*, London, UK, 29 November.

INDEX

Symbols / Numbers

3D printing 104
4 New York Plaza 23
25 Water Street 23
66 Rockwell 58, 89, 93
1946 Land Act 6
1961 Act 8
2020 London Plan 93

A

Abrdn plc 35
Aberfeldy New Village 62
acoustics 118
Adult Social Care 68
AEW 67
affordability 8, 15, 47, 61
affordable 8, 11, 15, 20, 21, 54, 60, 62, 67, 70, 94
affordable homes 153
affordable housing 153, 184
affordable rental homes 183
Artificial Intelligence (AI) 82, 103, 104
AIG 63
Allied London 58, 59
Ambrose Evans-Pritchard 29
amenity 13, 17
America 16, 19, 21, 40, 50, 53, 55
American 91
American Embassy 38
Andy Burnham 29
Aneurin Bevan 6
Apache Capital 64
apartments 128, 131
Approved Document M 131
architects 183
architecture 123, 158, 161
Architectural Review, The 43
Argent 37
Art Deco 116, 118
Arup 34, 84
Assured Shorthold Tenancies 25
Atlantic Crescent 160
Athletes Village 28
attendant mortgage costs 19
Attlee 6
Australia 67
Autodesk 106, 109
Autodesk Forma 104, 106
Average Daylight Factor 131

ADF 131
Awaab Ishak 40

B

Baby Boomers 17
Bank of England 13, 16
Barking & Dagenham 62
Barking Riverside 25
Barings Real Estate 32
Bartlett School of Architecture 91
Battersea Park 33
Battersea Power Station 38
Becontree Estate 5, 6
be:here 63
Belfast 41
Belgian Congo 47
Ben Page 20
Berkeley 102, 108
Berkeley Homes 108
Berlin 28, 55, 89
Big Apple 23
Bill Clinton 102
BIM 104, 105, 106, 107, 108, 109, 110, 115, 116, 117, 118, 119, 120
BIM4Housing 110
BIM360 109
BIM Level 2 136
Biodiversity Gain 163
Biodiversity Net Gain 96
Birchgrove 69
Birmingham 3, 27, 32, 34, 47, 61, 64, 95
Blackfriars Bridge 92
Blackstone 24
Bloomsbury 58, 59
BMS 85
Bob Faith 39
Bob Kerslake 36
Boris Johnson 34, 38, 39
Bournville 24, 46, 47
Bournville Village Trust 47
Boxpark 64
Bradford 18
Brendan Sarsfield 7
Brent Council 153
Brent Cross 37
Brexit 27, 43, 49, 50, 53
Bridges Fund Management 69
Bristol 32, 61
Britain 7, 9, 11, 13, 16, 20, 21, 24, 29, 45, 50
British Coal 26

British Isles 16
British Land 12
British Property Federation 40, 41
Broad Street 123, 124, 126
Brooklyn 29, 58, 89
brownfield land 14, 184
Brunswick Centre 58, 59
BTR i, 2, 3, 5, 7, 8, 9, 10, 12, 13, 16, 17, 20, 21, 23, 24, 26, 27, 28, 29, 31, 32, 33, 34, 35, 36, 37, 38, 39, 40, 41, 44, 45, 46, 47, 49, 51, 52, 54, 56, 57, 59, 60, 61, 62, 63, 64, 65, 66, 67, 69, 70, 71, 74, 76, 77, 79, 83, 84, 87, 88, 89, 90, 91, 93, 94, 95, 97, 99, 104, 105, 106, 107, 115, 118, 128, 131, 137, 143, 145, 146, 153, 161, 164, 183, 184, 185, 186
BTR development 131, 145, 184
BTR dwellings 131
BTR funders 183
BTR investors 184, 185
BTR market 184
BTR operators 184, 185
BTR sector 34, 35, 36, 37, 39, 40, 41
Budget 27, 36, 37
building 115, 116, 118, 120, 123, 128, 129
Building Emissions Benchmark 162
Building Regulations 37, 45, 51, 53, 55, 74, 75, 82, 162
Building Regulations Part L1A 150
Building Safety Act 55, 110
buildings emissions 74
build quality 124
Build To Rent i, 2, 3, 12, 24, 25, 27, 31, 34, 36, 45, 60, 89, 115, 123, 131, 153, 183, 186
Build To Rent model 123
Build To Rent sector 184

C

California 19, 55
Camden Council 58, 59
Canada 44, 49, 63, 66
Canada Gardens 153, 155, 156, 162, 163, 164, 176
Canada Pension Plan Investment Board 63
carbon emissions 51, 53, 65, 75, 79, 83, 84
carbon offset contributions 50
Cardiff 18
CBRE 73
Chancellor of the Exchequer 27
charity 9, 19
Chief Investment Officer 12
China 29, 53, 54, 96
Chinese Communist Party 54
Chobham Manor 28, 70, 71
CHP 141, 151
Churchill 8
CIBSE TM 52, 163

circularity 139, 150
circular economy 3, 84, 85, 139, 150
Citibank Tower 144
cities 123
Citra Living 35
City AM 16, 18
City Intelligence Unit 74
City of London 12
cladding 39, 46, 57, 134, 136
Clanmill Housing Association 41
Clarion 11, 12, 40, 104
Clapham Park 25
Clean Air Act 96
climate 43, 44, 51, 52, 55, 92, 99, 101
climate change 3, 15, 43, 51, 52, 55, 73, 74, 77, 83, 139
Coalition Government 35
COBie 110
Code for Sustainable Homes 77
Cold War 50
Co-living 41, 60, 91
Combined Heat and Power 150, 151
Committee on Climate Change 74
community 88, 89, 90, 91, 92, 94, 97, 101, 107
Community Infrastructure Levy 15
compulsory purchase 6
Computer Fluid Dynamics model 118
Confluence Place 143, 145
community kitchen 118
Congo 47
conservation areas 144
Conservative Government 8, 10, 13, 54, 185
Conservative Party 10, 39, 45
constituencies 192
construction 91, 95, 99, 103
construction industry 24, 27, 34, 54, 77
construction quality 58
construction sector 43, 50, 55
consultations 116
Coppermaker Club 137
Coppermaker Square 15, 60, 87, 90, 97, 99, 101, 106, 113, 130, 131, 134, 136, 185
Corporation of London 23
Coronavirus 34, 43
cost savings 129, 139, 150
Covid 16, 19, 34, 50, 53, 68, 101, 105
cross-subsidy 11
Council Tax 67, 68, 71
co-working 91
CO2 129, 151
Dagenham 5, 6
Dame Judith Hackitt 110
daylighting 118, 139
Deansgate 32
Decent Homes Standard 10
Delph 32
Delve 104

INDEX **195**

Denmark 5
Densification 89
density 88, 89, 92, 93
Department for Business, Energy and Industrial Strategy 74
Deptford 32
Derby 32
Design Guardian 131
design quality 15
design review panel 116
design team 115, 118, 131
detailed planning 15, 25
developer 87, 88, 92
Development Plans 68
devolved authority 21
Digital Twin integration 83
Discount Market Rent 94, 153
'Distinctively Local' 45
DLR station 143
docklands 13
Docklands Light Railway 131
downsize 71
Dr Desiree Fields 19, 24, 102, 103
dual flush WCs 150
Dublin 18, 19

E

East Berlin 94
East India Dock 62
East London 28, 33, 41, 62, 70
ecology 96
Edinburgh 25, 35
Elephant and Castle 34
Elephant Park 34
Elon Musk 108
embodied carbon 96, 116, 118, 141
energy 141, 151
energy centre 31
energy consumption 73, 79, 82, 83
energy crisis 39, 51
energy efficiency 52, 53, 77, 79, 84, 85
energy efficient technologies 120
energy hierarchy 75
Energy Performance Certificates 37
energy wastage 120
England 11, 13, 16, 21, 25, 39, 55, 67, 74, 79, 81
Enscape 107
Envac 162
environmental and social aspects 184
environmental impact 141
environmental performance 129
environmental strategy 82
Environmental Sustainability Aspects 118, 129, 138, 149, 162
Environmental watchdogs 13
EQT Real Estate 25

ESG 51, 118, 183
ESG Performance 118
ESG Protocols 183, 184
Essential Living 26
estate regeneration 7, 11
EUI 53
Europe 5, 11, 40, 43, 53, 54, 63, 101, 131, 164
European Court of Justice 16
European Union (EU) 27, 77
Evergrande 54
exo-amenities 91

F

factory assembled production 26
feedback 116
FIFA World Cup 44
Fifth Capital 62
financial crash 13, 17, 19, 24, 50
fire safety 43, 46, 55, 56, 57, 109, 110
first-time buyer 10, 13, 19, 69
Fizzy Living 25
'fleecehold' 45
flexible tenure 68
Fossey Arora 99, 153, 164, 170
fossil fuels 53, 74
Foster and Partners 104
Francis Fukuyama 50
Future Homes Standard 79

G

Garden City 5
Geoffrey Close Estate 92
George Cadbury 47
George Osborne 27
General Election 39
generation rent 17, 18
Germany 5, 20, 29
Get Living London 28, 34
GHA 131
GHG 73, 74, 79
GIC 39
GLA 11, 56, 74, 75, 78, 84, 87
Glasgow 18, 34
GlaxoSmithKline 33
Glen Howells Architects 131
Global Financial Crisis 10
global warming 73, 77
Goldman Sachs Asset Management 35
Google 104
Government tax 184
Government 184, 185
Grainger 26, 32
Grand Union Canal 33
GRC cladding 134
Great Charles Street 64
Greater London 11, 75, 78, 83, 84, 87

Greater London Authority 11
great housing programmes 8
Great Recession 16, 102
Green Belt 13, 14, 184
Green Deal 77
Greenford 27
Greenford Quay 33
Greengate 29
greenhouse gas 73, 75, 77, 79, 81
Grenfell 39, 43, 46, 51, 55, 56
Greystar 27, 33, 38, 39, 41, 104, 130, 131
GRIP 32
Guy Slocombe 12

H

Hackitt Review 55
Hammerson 59
Harlow 6
Harrison Street 64
Hashi Mohamed 50, 65, 183
health 118, 129, 176
health and safety 15, 56, 65
heat pumps 82
Help to Buy 10, 18
Henderson Park 38
heritage 115, 144
high-rise 13, 89
high density 24, 45, 82
high street 71, 91
Holland 5
homes 153, 160, 162, 164, 183, 184, 185
homes for rent 123
home ownership 10, 11, 13, 18, 20, 45, 46, 62, 70, 76
Home Secretary 38
Homes England 11, 25
Homes for Heroes programme 5
Hong Kong 45, 74
housebuilders 7, 15, 23, 34, 39, 40, 88, 108
Housing and Town Planning Act 5
housing association 7, 9, 11, 12, 25, 40, 44, 56, 62, 67, 68, 70, 92, 108
housing benefit 19
housing crisis 6, 10, 12, 13, 15, 27, 36, 54, 185, 186
Housing Data Coalition 103
housing design 183
housing design standards 56
housing estates 6
housing providers 61, 70
'Housing Regeneration' 91
housing sector 44, 50, 67
Housing Stimulus Package 36
housing supply 184, 186
Housing White Paper 31
Hull 18

HVAC 82
Hyde 12
Hyde Group 12
Hypar 104

I

Ian Fletcher 41
Iceland 77
Ilke Homes 108
immigration 186
India 96
industrial revolution 49
inequality 181
inflation 185
Inflation Reduction Act 53
Information Management 110
infrastructure 120, 123, 158
Innovate UK 53
insulation 120, 139
interest rates 16, 35, 39, 40, 53, 62, 185
inter-generational 65, 70, 71, 186
Inter-generational living 186
interior design 118, 136
international investment 18
Invesco Real Estate 37
investors 184, 185, 186
IoT 120
Ipsos 20
Ireland 3, 5, 18, 19, 21, 23
Irish Government 18
Irving Trust Company Bank 23
Islington 60
Italy 101

J

Jack Diamond 44
Japan 28, 50
Jared Diamond 184
Jason Cowley 6
JLL 51, 64
job markets 184
Job Retention Scheme 34
Joint Venture (JV) 12, 20, 25, 27, 34, 35, 37, 92
JP Morgan 64
JRF 9, 10

K

Ken Livingstone 38
Kennington 38
King 39
Kings Cross 37
King's Speech 39
KKR 35
Kyoto Protocol 77

L

Labour Government 88
Labour Party 10, 16
Lacuna Developments 41
Lambeth 92
Lanark 46, 48
land-banking 14, 16
Land Compensation Act 8
landscape 93, 96, 97
landlord licencing scheme 27
landlords 179, 183
land value 8, 16, 55, 58
LaSalle Investment Management 29
later living 9, 20, 60, 66, 67, 68, 69, 71
Lawrence Peter "Yogi" Berra 50
leaseholder 39, 46
leasehold laws 39
leasehold management corporation 46
Leatherhead 34
Leeds 32, 61
Legal & General 26, 27, 32, 41, 108, 153, 184
Lendlease 32
LETI 77
letting agency 27
Levelling Up 34, 39, 40
Lewisham 34, 35
Lewisham Gateway 25, 26, 34, 35
Lewisham Shopping Centre 144
'Lewisham Town Centre Mixed Use Briefing Document' 92
LGDL 143, 145
Liam Halligan 8
Lincolnshire 109
listed structure 115
Liverpool 3, 32, 35, 77, 93, 94
LLDC 131, 134
Lloyds Banking Group 35, 64
local councillors 184
local markets 19, 20
local plans 15
lockdown 17, 34, 53, 101, 105
London 6, 7, 8, 11, 12, 13, 16, 17, 18, 21, 23, 25, 26, 27, 28, 29, 31, 32, 33, 34, 35, 36, 37, 38, 39, 40, 41, 43, 44, 45, 52, 56, 58, 59, 61, 62, 63, 64, 66, 67, 69, 70, 71, 73, 74, 75, 76, 77, 78, 81, 83, 84, 87, 89, 90, 92, 93, 95, 96, 97, 99, 101, 103, 110, 113, 130, 131, 142, 143, 145, 151, 152, 156, 158, 164, 165, 170, 176, 177, 179
London Borough of Lewisham 34
London Designer Outlet 90
London Legacy Development Corporation 131
London Environment Strategy 74
London Olympics 28
London Plan 75, 78, 84, 85
London School of Economics (LSE) 89
London School of Economics and Political Science 89
Lone Star 27, 31, 63, 69
Lords Chamber 39
Lord Taylor of Goss Moor 45
Loughborough University 81
LVC 8
low-carbon 120, 141
low-density 24
low energy 120
low energy LED lamps 120

M

Macmillan 8
Madison 153, 160, 161, 176
Maidenhead 34
Manchester 13, 18, 26, 29, 32, 48, 61
Manhattan 23, 29, 58, 99
Margaret Thatcher 10, 45
Marks & Spencer 132
Martha Tsigkati 104
Mayhew Review 68, 69
Mayor of London 18, 27, 74
Mayor of Manchester 29
McCarthy Stone 69
mechanical cooling 82
Mechanical Ventilation and Heat Recovery 120
Mechanical Ventilation with Heat Recovery 139, 150
MVHR system 139
Members of Parliament 184
MEP 82, 83
Mersey 32
Merseyside 47, 48
M&G Secured Property Income Fund 62
Michael Gove 37, 38, 39
Microsoft Teams 102, 105
millennials 21
Milton Keynes 32
mixed-use 32, 56, 59, 61, 143
Moda Living 34, 35, 41, 64, 88, 99
modern methods of construction 23
modular construction 83, 84
Montague Review/Report 35, 36, 41, 62
Montfitchet Road 131, 135
mortgage costs 179
Mr Gove 39, 40
Mr Halligan 8
multi-family 3, 19, 20, 39, 41, 44, 58, 88
multi-generational 17, 70, 89
multi-tenure 12, 28
municipal power 21
Muse 34

N

National Health Service 7, 17, 20, 67, 68
National Insurance Act 7
National Planning Policy Framework 41
National Stadium 153, 155
Nationally Described Space Standards (NDSS) 97
natural daylight 156
natural lighting 156
Natural England 16
net carbon 104
net zero 55, 64, 73, 74, 75, 77, 79, 80, 85
Newcastle 18, 32
New Earswick 9
New Lanark 48
New Lodge 9
New York 23, 24, 58, 99, 95, 103
New Zealand 67
NFU Mutual 64
Nice 81
Nicosia 81
Nick Keppler 102
Nigel Wilson 184
NIMBYs 184
Nine Elms 38, 89
'no fault' evictions 39
noise pollution 163
North East Lands 65
Northern Ireland 21, 41
North London 37
North-West 25
Norway 77
not-for-profit 27, 40, 41
NOx 162
nutrient neutrality 16

O

Oculo 110
Older People's Task Force 69
Olympic Park 28, 29, 71, 131, 132
Olympic Stadium 132
Olympic Steps 153, 176
Olympic Velodrome 28
Olympic Way 89, 90, 153, 160
One Wall Street 23
OPEC 40, 50
Open Data 105
Openspace 110
operational costs 52
Outline Planning Consent 143
overheating 139, 149, 150, 152, 163
owner-occupiers 68

P

pandemic 16, 17, 19, 21, 23, 34, 35, 39, 40, 43, 44, 49, 55, 59, 65, 68, 88, 96, 101, 105
Paralympic Games 28
Paris Agreement 73, 79
Part O 55, 82
passive cooling 82
passive design 79, 80, 82
passive Electric Vehicle charging points 160
Passive Features 139, 149
passive solar heating 139, 149
passive ventilation 120
Paul Bridge 89
Paul Ormerod 52
Peabody 7
pension funds 64
People at the Heart of Care 68
Perimeter Way 160
Permitted Development Rights (PDR) 36, 37
Peter Apps 55
Peter Bishop 60, 91
Peter Cooper 58
PGGM 27
Pier Head 35
Placefirst 77
placemaking 88, 89, 91, 92
planning application 15, 36, 131
planning conditions 15
'Planning for the Communities of the Future' 88
planning permission 131
planning policy 43, 46
planning system 6, 13, 14, 16, 20, 71
Poland 102
Poplar HARCA 62
Portobello Square 92, 93
Port Sunlight 24, 46, 47, 48
PPC finish 134
PPC metal railings 136
PRCs 6
Pre-cast Reinforced Concrete 6
Precede Capital 64
President Biden 53
Prime Minister 34, 39
private developer 31
private equity 24, 27, 31, 35, 38
private rental 184, 185
private rental levels 179
private rented sector 3, 8, 9, 10, 32, 39, 44, 71, 182, 186
Private Rented Sector Task Force 36
private retirement living 68
private sale 94
private sector 15, 45, 184
property developer 26
property management company 26

property markets 184
prosperity-sharing 47
PRP 2, 3, 6, 7, 9, 11, 14, 17, 32, 34, 36, 38, 52, 55, 58, 60, 70, 92, 101, 104, 130, 131, 142, 143, 145, 152
PRS 3, 51
PRS REIT 41
PTAL rating 138
public sector 44
public transport 31, 45

Q

QA 162, 164
Qatar 44
QR codes 109, 162, 164
Quaggy 143, 145
quality 183, 184
quantitate easing 28
Queen Elizabeth Line 132
Queen Elizabeth Olympic Park 71, 131
Quintain 27, 31, 34, 49, 63, 64, 67, 69, 71, 93, 96, 110, 152, 153, 154, 155, 156, 158, 159, 160, 162, 163, 164, 165, 166, 167, 168, 169, 171, 172, 173, 174, 175, 176, 177, 178, 179

R

Railways Pension Scheme 62
Ravensbourne 143, 145
real estate 184, 185
real estate developer 27
recession 24, 54, 57
recycling 141, 162
Redhill 32
refugee 183
regeneration 87, 92, 93, 97
'Regeneration, Turning Threat into Opportunity' 89
regenerative design 73
regenerative masterplanning 82
regional developers 16
Registered Provider 21, 40, 53, 67, 69
regulation curse 15, 55, 55, 56, 57
REIT fund 32
Related 37
renewable energy 129
rent 184
rent control 184
rental market 25, 26, 27, 128, 186
rental properties 184
rental sector 3, 13, 27, 36, 37, 39
rental yield 32, 60, 61
rent controls 8, 18, 21
Renters Reform Bill 39
Reserved Matters Applications 145
residential building 131

Residential developers 56, 59, 60
Residential Property Developer Tax 38
residential sector 29, 55, 56, 59, 65, 73, 74, 77, 103, 184, 186
residents 118, 123, 128, 129, 138, 148, 150, 155, 156, 158, 160
Residents Amenity Hub 138
residual income stream 62
resource curse 55
Retirement Villages Group (RBG) 69, 70
RIBA 77, 78
RIBA 2030 Climate Challenge 77
Richard Rogers 88
Rightmove 18
Right to Buy 10, 11
River Mersey 93, 94
River Thames 13, 38, 92
Robert Owen 48
Robot Landlords are Buying Up Houses 102
Rochdale 40
Royal Borough of Kensington and Chelsea 92
Royal Town Planning Institution 15
RPDT 38
Rugby 35
Russia 40, 43

S

Sadiq Khan 27
sales sector 17, 19
Salford 48, 49
Saltaire 24, 46, 48
Sanctuary 108
San Francisco 55
Scotland 21, 25, 48, 67
Scottish Government 25
second homes 27
second staircases 56
Second World War 102
Section 106 15
service industry 20
shared risk procurement 20
Sheffield 32
Shelter 19
short-term holiday lets 18
short-term lets 41
Sigma Capital 25, 41
Signature Senior Lifestyle 69
Silicon Valley 55
single-family 44, 70, 88
Sir Hugh Beaver 96
Sir Oliver Letwin 40
Sisk 108, 109, 122, 152, 153, 163
skyscraper 123
Slate Yard 26
Smithfield 101
social capital 184

social care levy 67
social conscience 183
social housing 5, 7, 8, 10, 11, 12, 21, 40, 56, 67, 89
Social Housing Regulation Bill 40
social landlord 10, 25
social media 184
social rent 12, 21, 68, 97
social value 56
society 184, 186
solar gain 81, 116, 120
solar sources 129
Solomon Islands 47
South-East 13, 16, 26, 81
South London 25
sovereign wealth fund 25, 39
Spain 29, 101
Spinningfields 58
stamp duty 27, 69
Standard Life Aberdeen 35
St Andrew's Park 27
state benefits 20
State Opening of Parliament 39
Statista 75, 83
St Modwen 27, 28
St Stephens Church 144
St Stephens Square 145
Stockport 29
Stratford 28, 29, 33, 60, 70, 71, 87, 97, 99, 101, 103, 130, 131
Stratford Station 131
student accommodation 61, 94
student housing 27, 39, 41
Student Roost 39
suburb 17, 24, 34, 45, 92, 97
Sufra 163
Surrey 32
sustainable design 118
Sustainable Housing Finance Framework 64
sustainability 88, 92, 97, 118, 129, 138, 149, 162
sustainability requirements 120
sustainable residential neighbours 129
sustainability strategy 150
Swan 108
Sweden 5

T

tall buildings 46, 56
tech curse 55
tenants 8, 10, 11, 12, 19, 48, 183
tenure blind 94
Thames Valley Housing Association 25
Thames Water 160
The Addison Act 5
The Brooklyn Academy of Music 58
The Duke of Bridgewater 48
The Economist 13, 16, 20

The John Lewis Partnership 35
The Joseph Rowntree Foundation 9
The Lexington 93, 94, 99
The Mercian 95, 99, 183
The Ministry of Housing, Communities and Local Government 32
thermal insulation 139
The Robinson 98, 109, 113, 153, 158, 159, 163, 164, 170, 171, 176
The Shard 92
The Town and Country Planning Act 6, 7
Thomas Piketty 54, 57
three red lines 54
Timberyard 32
Titanic Quarter 41
Tokyo 92
Tories 8, 16
'Towards an Urban Renaissance' 88
Trimble 79, 82
Trocoll House 62
Troubadour Theatre 64
Trowers and Hamlins 56
Twinmotion 107

U

UCL 91
UK i, 2, 3, 23, 24, 25, 26, 27, 28, 29, 31, 32, 33, 34, 35, 38, 39, 40, 43, 44, 45, 46, 49, 50, 51, 53, 54, 55, 56, 59, 61, 64, 65, 66, 67, 68, 69, 71, 73, 74, 76, 77, 78, 81, 82, 87, 88, 89, 91, 95, 96, 101, 102, 104, 105, 108, 110, 115, 134, 145, 170, 181, 183, 184, 185, 186
UK architects 185
UK demographic 184
UK housing crisis 185
UK housing 183, 184, 185
UK housing sector 183, 184, 185
UK population 186
UK social housing 183
UK social housing providers 183
Ukraine 40, 43, 50, 53, 54, 74
Unibail-Rodamco-Westfield 33, 130, 131
Unilever 47
Union Park 31, 155, 158, 160, 164
United Nations 73, 77, 79
United Nations Energy Programme 73
United Nations Framework Convention on Climate Change 77
United States 2, 3, 5, 19, 23, 24, 27, 67, 102, 184
Unite Students 41
University of California 19, 102
University of York 9
UN Studio 34
Upheaval 184
urban 91, 92, 93, 94, 95, 96, 97
URW 130, 131

Urban & Civic 35
urban decay 88
urban design 88, 89, 90, 91, 92
Urban Greening Factor 93, 96, 163
Urban Heat Island Effect 81, 96
Urban Task Force 88
US 23, 24, 27, 37, 39, 50
US Senate 19
Utopi 120
U-values 120, 139, 149
Uxbridge 27, 28

V

Vauxhalll 13
viability 15, 51, 57, 63, 91, 92
Volumetric construction 108
VR 105, 107

W

Wales 21, 67
waste 124, 138, 139, 150, 162
water conservation 140
Waterloo Station 38
Watkins Jones 27, 41
Welcome Trust 35
welfare state 6, 20
wellbeing 10, 40, 46, 47, 49, 50, 59, 60, 65, 69, 70, 72, 93, 97, 118, 128, 129, 139, 149, 176, 184
wellness 17, 65
wellness score 120
wellness spa 131, 134, 137, 141
Wells Fargo 63
Welsh Streets 77
Wembley Arena 89
Wembley Opportunity Area 158
Wembley Park 23, 27, 31, 34, 3, 49, 63, 66, 69, 89, 90, 93, 94, 95, 96, 98, 99, 101, 106, 108, 109, 110, 113, 131, 152, 153, 155, 160, 162, 163, 164, 170, 176, 181, 185
Wembley Stadium 31, 34, 89, 131, 153, 160, 179
Western Europe 92
Westfield 33
Westfield Avenue 131, 135
Westfield Shopping Centre 131, 132
Westfield Stratford City 131
West Ham United FC 132
West London 27, 33
White City 33
Whole Life Carbon Network 77
Whole Life-Cycle Carbon Assessment 75
William Hesketh Lever 46
Willmott Dixon 62
wind tunnel studies 116

Wirral 47
WLC 83
work remotely 34
work from home 17, 18, 34, 44, 65, 102
World Health Organisation 65
Worsley 48
Wroclaw 102
WSP 79

X

Xi Jinping 54

Y

York 9, 10, 32, 41
York Street 41
young professionals 9, 41

Z

Zoom 102, 105